The Company
of the Future

Markets, Tools, and Strategies

Springer-Verlag Berlin Heidelberg GmbH

Hans G. Danielmeyer
Yasutsugu Takeda
Editors

The Company
of the Future

Markets, Tools, and Strategies

With 64 Figures
and 23 Tables

 Springer

Prof. Dr. Hans G. Danielmeyer
Meisenstr. 4
D-85521 Ottobrunn
Germany

Dr. Yasutsugu Takeda
Hitachi Ltd.
5-1, 1-chome,
Maru-no-uchi, Chioda-ku
Tokyo 100-8220
Japan

Library of Congress Cataloging-in-Publication Data
Die Deutsche Bibliothek – CIP-Einheitsaufnahme
The company of the future: markets, tools, and strategies / Hans G. Danielmeyer; Yasutsugu Takeda ed. – Berlin; Heidelberg; New York; Barce-
lona; Hong Kong; London; Milan; Paris; Singapore; Tokyo: Springer,
1999

   ISBN 978-3-642-64298-2   ISBN 978-3-642-60192-7 (eBook)
   DOI 10.1007/978-3-642-60192-7

© Springer-Verlag berlin Heidelberg 1999
Originally published by Springer-Verlag Berlin . Heidelberg in 1999
Softcover reprint of the hardcover 1st edition 1999

Hardcover-Design: Erich Kirchner, Heidelberg

SPIN 10728838   42/2202-5 4 3 2 1 0 – Printed on acid-free paper

Preface

This is a challenging book on corporate management in the 21st century. It is based on the experience of senior executives in electronics companies and on that of university professors familiar with industry. It is evident that one of the most valuable outcomes of the exchange of views from which the book is derived was the emergence of mutual understanding across quite different cultural backgrounds. This was stimulated by and built upon a working relationship between the present two editors, which started in the middle of their careers and developed over a period of 25 years into a special friendship. All the participants came to appreciate the spectrum of management concepts practiced in the companies represented, and they gradually learned to distinguish between the academic requirement to understand and the business requirement to improve economic quality.

After a series of discussion meetings and several intermediate reports to MITI and the EU Commission, the chapter authors wrote six primary papers. In the case of the academic writers there were considerable contributions by MBA and doctoral students. I have had the privilege of compressing this material into the shorter manuscript for this book, designed to be read by busy people, and in so-doing converted its content into more conventional English. This was done in liaison with the authors and their colleagues and in all cases in close co-operation with Hans G. Danielmeyer, the principal enthusiast in promoting the project and the publication of this book. From a basis of many years of industrial research management experience in both 'upstream' research areas [1] within companies and collaborative projects between industry and universities, I can thoroughly recommend this handbook to readers from a wide spectrum of academic disciplines and industries.

In the first chapter a general reference frame for innovation and management processes is developed. It starts with a new, conceptually reliable model on economic growth, pointing out how closely long term corporate growth is connected to the real growth per capita of every country in which the company is operating. The generation gap is shown to be the dominant parameter for innovation, capital stock, and economic growth. Individual differences can be accounted for by a scaling factor and a time shift. The model explains the structural development of the gross domestic product and of the capital stock per capita from 1850 to the present time, quantitatively in closed form, as well as the consolidation pressure and employment problems following periods of strong growth. "Relevant knowledge" is identified as the normative force behind social and corporate development. The model is used to derive and recommend a number of effective management tools. The central tool is the Value Added Diagram. It promotes more effective integration of well established concepts from sales, production, R&D, and corporate strategy, allows to generate the production function of R&D, and is applicable at any level with any desired resolution. The tools are sufficiently general and robust to be adaptable to many types of businesses.

The second chapter reports on rules identified for the allocation of R&D resources. The elasticity concept is applied to the ratio between research and development. Extensive work with many companies shows that this ratio clearly correlates positively with business success, but negatively with the interest rate on capital. The use of project- based research funding is recommended, as well as a balanced project portfolio. Continuous investment in research is seen to increase the competitiveness of a company's performance and supports a broad range of activities which will contribute to future success. The choice of research projects depends on the time to market the product. Interviews within European and Japanese companies revealed differences in the handling of relevant knowledge which are grouped into three clusters: 'hands on transferers', 'hermits', and 'active distributors'. Industrial research must be integrated with the scientific community as a whole, and structured co-operation between industry and academia is an increasingly important part of the strategy for an industrial company.

In the third chapter the characteristics of a Systems Company are described. It is shown that the strategic behavior can be optimized by considering the quality of a company's technology, the configuration of the market, and the nature of the contracts with component producers. Technological strategies must be established for appropriate 'make or buy' decisions. Total control of technology may not be the most desirable option, and the degree to which this can be achieved in practice by good management is discussed.

Chapter IV considers the commercial, technological, and social missions for the Company of the Future. The author's dual position as corporate CTO and CEO of two business units lead to new insights into the optimum balance between profit, depreciation, and R&D expenditure, the sum of which equals the 'Fund for Future Growth'. This additional index and its relation to sales have been formally introduced to stimulate innovation in

Japan. Taking an actual example of business planning, the restrictions are worked out which result from budget limitations and product cycle requirements for optimizing an innovative product portfolio. Global partnerships are propagated as an important part of company management. In this regard a clear definition of a company's business strategy and its relative level of competence in all business functions are necessary for success. Important company assets include the capabilities of employees and its bank of intellectual property.

The fifth chapter analyses the cultural differences in business practices between Japan and the United States, the necessary adjustments to the industrial development levels of the countries of operation, and the competition between governments for attracting industry and securing employment. In recognition of the change in emphasis from hard to soft assets a capitalization method for R&D is proposed which is initially neutral for business and internal revenue services, but would immediately improve performance and rectify the shareholder value. It is based on the 'competence product' which places due value on the lifetime of relevant knowledge in R&D. A strong case is made for endogenous company growth rather than growth by acquisition.

In Chapter VI the accounting methods used to date for defining R&D budget allocations are compared with a new approach. The latter is based on target costs. Two extensions take into account the objectives of the company and the inter-relationships between R&D and other operations. The use of flexible methods is exemplified by their recent application in chemical, pharmaceutical and automotive industries.

Consequently, the book sets out to provide a better basis for research management in the next century, bearing in mind that research and its results can be optimized only by sound planning. The book as a whole indicates that by identifying the wider role possessed by each function within an organization, and quantifying this, a better basis for assigning the most appropriate distribution of funding can be found.

It is clear that the insights generated herein are applicable to forthcoming industrial practices in many business sectors, and that this text is in effect a practical guide for managers, particularly for those involved with the effectiveness of research. The worldwide availability of information means that it is increasingly important to generate and keep proprietary knowledge in-house. 'In-house' itself means an internal international network for the many companies which now operate on a global scale. The creation of multicomponent imaginative teams is recommended, centred around creative employees who provide original ideas and leadership based on enthusiasm and diligence, managed in a perceptive manner, bearing in mind all the many variables present in the advanced information technology world of the 21st century. The valuable knowledge retained by employees in this regard contrasts with the relatively new trend for employees to have a series of employers during their active life. Thus, on the one hand worldwide communication networks make a vast proportion of currently generated information readily available to everyone, but on the other it is vital for companies to patent and to cherish the tacit knowledge of employees.

The importance of the university-industry interface in the generation and identification of ideas is emphasized, and the growing realization that this is so by people in both of these spheres and by governments and their agencies is welcome [1]. To some extent the collaboration between universities and industry has been asymmetric. Due to their training periods at university, lifelong education, generation of ideas for new products and processes, and collaboration in project work, initiatives for secondment of industrial personnel to university takes place to a significantly greater extent than for the secondment of academics to industry. The merits of encouraging more movement in both directions to the benefit of teaching and research will become apparent from the contents of these pages.

It was interesting to observe that many additional ideas and insights of the authors spun off only in the compression phase. Obviously there was a second round of thinking after the formal project was finished, stimulated by digesting whatever the other team members had synthesized for their first draft description of the Company of the Future. A lot of unexpected added value became apparent during this iterative process, perhaps partly promoted by my questions.

Created by innovative people with a feeling for future management tools, this book has no sensational ambitions, but just because of this it does full justice to the title. It will have an obvious attraction for industrialists; but I would suggest that academics with an interest in the application of their research to the benefit of society, and to industry in particular, will find it stimulating as well.

David T Thompson
Reading, UK

Reference

E Konecny, C P Quinn, K Sachs and D T Thompson, 'Universities and Industrial Research', The Royal Society of Chemistry, Cambridge, UK, 1995. 'Upstream research', which is similar to the 'North Star' research (see Chapter IV), is defined as basic research with an industrial orientation, and may be conducted either in-house in industry or by a university team without association to a specific company.

About this Book, its Genesis, and Acknowledgements

This book results from the collaboration between four R&D executives of large companies and three university professors of management in a research project designed to study the integration of industrial management concepts. The idea for this project stemmed from a meeting between three of the authors in 1991 under the auspices of the first Portland International Conference on Management of Engineering and Technology (PICMET).

At the turn of the millennium we are experiencing the combined challenges of open world markets, huge technology- and capital-transfer between mature and developing countries, transitions from mature industrial to service societies, and massive consolidation of enterprise in general. These external challenges divert top management's attention away from the internal challenges of corporate management. The emphasis on (and often reduction to) financial issues and internal cost-saving drives signal this diversion.

The authors of this book have a deep conviction that the real asset of a company has been proven to be, and will always be, its internal strength. This is the basis for innovation, competitiveness, growth, stable profit, and shareholder value, as an integrated sequence. To build and maintain internal strength is a long term challenge which is in competition with the achievement of short term financial goals. A quarterly earnings report is a tool which can be used to quickly discover profitability problems but these will have arisen as the a result of a long chain of decisions and business processes. A typical characteristic of all financial management tools is that they usually reveal problems too late to apply an effective cure.

Our experience had convinced us that the Company of the Future will need new management tools which will essentially fulfil the following four requirements. The first three are to redirect the attention of management to the internal challenges within the company, to devise methods which reveal problems well before final financial data are available, and to integrate basic management concepts from all the business functions, *ie* marketing, R&D, production, services, finance, and strategy. The fourth requirement is that the tools should be simple enough to be implemented by busy people who will have their own well established tools, but they must be sufficiently sophisticated to meet the challenges of the future.

We knew that a traditional research project into the practices of existing businesses would not suffice, and we did not wish to gather together a collection of fashionable recipes. As one of us noted, we needed to do some 'pre-search' work with respect to definition of a virtual, ideal company. Then the core work would be done by meeting in various locations in Japan and Europe in order to propose and define new tools, compare them with those already existing, and discuss their relative merits. The first meeting took place in the Japanese-German Center in Berlin with subsequent sessions in Brussels, Munich, Osaka, Rome, Tokyo and Venice.

This work has been made possible by the support of DGIIIF, the ESPRIT directorate of the European Commission's industrial commissariat. DGIIIF financed the initial phase of the project in which we set up the core team (which included the authors of this book) and the project plan with the schedule for the meetings. Then it financed under ESPRIT Project No. 9803 (COF) the project's academic staff and travel expenses, the project reviews, and finally the editing into natural English. We thank in particular Dr G Metakides of the IST programme in DGXIII, and his staff, especially Dr R Zobel and F Reimann-Pijls.

With regard to the participation from Japan, we are grateful for the support received from the Ministry of International Trade and Industry (MITI) and in particular to H Inaba, H Miyama, N Myake and M Yoshikai. We also thank T Sumigama of the Japan Research Industry Association (JRIA) and the Japanese Techno-Economics Society (JATES) for support. The European Industrial Research Management Association (EIRMA) was informed about the goals of the project at its 1996 annual meeting. The first results of our work were reported to the second PICMET in 1997 by three of our authors and Mrs Zobel.

The collaboration with business management professors was not only vital for the effectiveness of our discussions, it was essential in order to enable our findings to be included in textbooks designed for MBAs. We acknowledge significant contributions by their young research teams: at the University of Mannheim, M Hollax, R Schrank and K Schug who managed the reporting to the European Commission and launched their own spin-off consultancy company 'm^{2}c', partly as a result of this project; at the University of Rome-CEIS, V Atella, L Becchetti, F Bellini, A Bonaccorsi, M Cicculelli and S Tani; and at the University of Kiel, J Bardenhewer and D Jensen.

We personally thank Dr Y Kuwahara and Professor T Martinetz for their creativity in managing the meetings and for fitting them into our busy schedules, Dr D. Höfner of Siemens AG for his participation and particularly for efficiently supervising the entire European financial account, and Dr A Felder of Siemens KK Tokyo for making effective the continuous linkage between Hitachi Ltd and Siemens AG. Professor E Konecny of the Medical University of Lübeck, past Research and Development Director of Dräger, and Board Member of EIRMA, reviewed all the chapter manuscripts at an early stage; and we are very grateful for his professional comments and recommendations - they promoted an intensive selection and streamlining process. We were then fortunate to find in Dr D Thompson a natural English speaker who himself is an experienced writer in our field (see reference 1 in the Preface, 2 in Chapter II and 4 in Chapter IV) - he managed to combine streamlining of the editing process with improvement of the English, and we are grateful for his writing of the Preface.

We hope that our new tools and recommendations will help our readers to better meet the internal challenges of managing R&D intensive companies. The reader must decide which of these tools will be most appropriate for his/her own company in relation to its particular needs and challenges. The real achievement will lie in the manner in which a tool or recommendation is implemented and adapted to the company's requirements. We have therefore not gone into too much detail, nor do we claim that our set of tools is complete; but we do believe that our set is internally consistent and free of unnecessary overlap. We wish that some of our new tools had been available in the middle of our careers; but we then may have lacked the experience to identify what was missing and the power to implement them. It takes time to develop the most appropriate tools, and they are an important part of the corporate culture.

Hans G Danielmeyer
Berlin

Yasutsugu Takeda
Tokyo

Contents

Chapter 2 A
Research in the Company of the Future
Klaus Brockhoff...49

Chapter 5
Global Strategies and the Role of Research

Chapter 6
Accountability of Technology

Chapter 1
General Framework and Concepts

Hans G. Danielmeyer and *Angelo Airaghi*

This chapter delivers a general reference frame for innovation and management processes. The first four sections deal with external challenges. A new theoretical framework is developed for international economics and corporate growth, separating long term structural growth from short term fluctuations. It introduces a small set of fundamental constants, formulates conservation laws for economic and corporate development, and derives basic growth processes for start up, catch up, and pioneer countries and companies. Save miracles and disasters, they allow to predict the next generation's market volumes for investment and consumer goods. The nature and cause of employment problems, the transition from the industrial to the service society, and the closing gap between Asia-Oceania and Europe-North America are explained quantitatively. A general strategy concept concludes this part.

The two centre Sections produce an effective production function for R&D and propose the Value Added Diagram as a strategic tool to integrate financial control, sales, purchasing, R&D, and production. It can be used at any level and with any granularity by all parts of the business to improve performance. The importance of key components for leadership and innovation is stressed. A continuous accounting system for planning and production of components is proposed which is based on the framework developed for structural growth.

The last four Sections concentrate on internal management challenges including creativity, the role of R&D, internal communication in times of change, and integration of management concepts. Special attention is given to the change from hard to soft assets for the company of the future.

---

1 Introduction

In this chapter we describe an integrated view of industrial management using advanced practical concepts and tools for setting up and maintaining an innovative and profitable business.

In order to be practical, concepts and tools must be simple enough to be understood and followed by all employees. In general, management and employees have plenty of experience with their own well established concepts and methods, and little time to go out of their way to learn how to use others.

On the other hand, the concepts and tools must not be over simplified. Our world has changed dramatically. The largest increase in complexity has occurred in financial management. Although this is still based on the four simplest mathematical operations with quantities of zero dimension, computers have facilitated the running of complex financial models. Financial complexities often require more attention from boards of directors than was the case with earlier complexities of science, technology, and production.

What matters is the total overall integrated effect of the whole set of concepts and tools used by the company. No single business function must be allowed to dominate in this set, nor in the complexity of its concepts. We need harmonised, balanced sets of principles, concepts, rules and tools. Figure 1.1 gives an overview of the set covered in this chapter. It can be considered as the base set of tools and concepts for the innovative, global production company. The numbers correspond to the sections of this chapter.

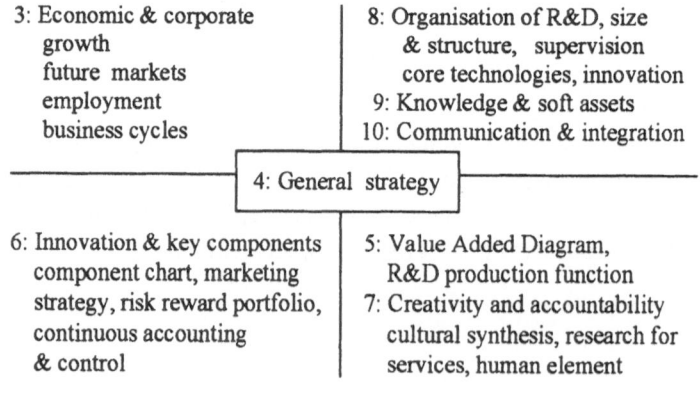

Fig. 1.1. Strategic concepts for the Company of the Future.

2 The Development Phases of Industry

Most of our fundamental financial concepts are derived from what was practiced in medieval banks and trading empires like that of the Medici family. The Italian roots of the banking system are still present in the words used by the financial world.

Production concepts were developed during the late eighteenth century's rise of UK's manufacturing industry. Adam Smith's 1776 book [1] on the origin of wealth (division of labour, accumulation of capital, technical progress, legal framework, and perfect competition) is still unparalleled in its scope and importance. But even Smith would not have predicted two orders of magnitude improvement in productivity during the following 200 years, with all the progress from the most primitive work conditions he was familiar with to the luxurious ergonomic work places of chip designers.

While mechanical and chemical technologies were quite well developed at an early stage, electrical technologies developed only after the middle of the 19th century. We can divide European industrial development to date into four phases:

The *first phase* took place from around 1850 through to 1900 and can still be regarded as a period of craftsmanship (see Figure 1.2). For example Werner von Siemens started his business in 1847 in collaboration with the Berlin University mechanic Halske, and the first automobile manufacturers were also craftsmen. This was 100 years after Boulton and Watt, also a businessman and a fine mechanic, founded their company for the manufacture of steam engines which marked the beginning of the industrial society.

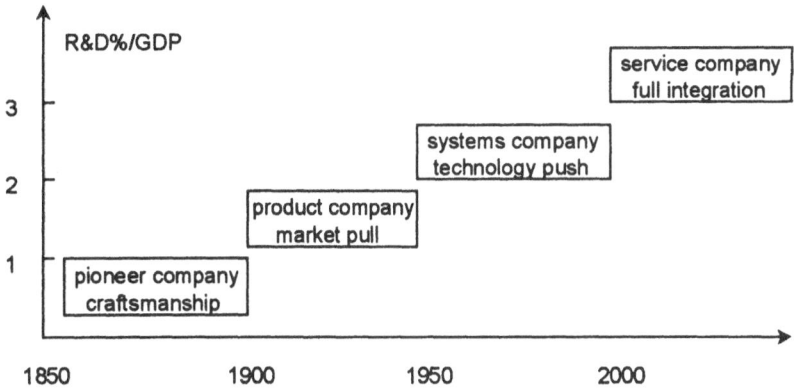

Fig. 1.2. The four development phases of electrical engineering and electronics businesses.

The *second phase* (1900 - 1950) was characterised by a strong demand for well engineered technical products. We can call this the market pull period. Mass production was required. The first production line was built for the Ford Model T. Automation began, stimulated by the demand during and after both world wars. Enormous improvements in manufacturing equipment stimulated research into the man/machine interface. The feedback into better designs raised the productivity level still further.

Unexpected breakthroughs in physics during and immediately following the second world war gave rise to the *third phase*, the technology push period, from 1950 until 1990. It culminated in micro-and optoelectronics allowing the operation of systems of nearly unlimited complexity with fingertip or voice controlled software. The industrialised countries owe most of their wealth and superiority to this period. Big science parks were established during and after the war. The Sputnik shock enhanced the East-West technology race, symbolised by the Route 128 phenomenon, first exemplified by the formation of a belt of high technology companies situated some 50 miles around Boston in the USA. Most large companies decided to build big central laboratories in secluded, beautiful park areas. University research boomed as never before.

As a result of the overwhelming influence of science and technology, the other business functions finance, production, sales, and services felt neglected, and often this was true. This is one reason for the problems experienced by many high technology companies towards the end of the technology push period.

Another reason was the rapid rise of R&D. Financial and production management concepts and tools had had time to evolve through the centuries. Their state of the art was mostly in equilibrium with the nature of the demands from education and business. The demand for R&D rose so fast that related management concepts and proper education were way behind the state of the art required. When universities began to teach R&D management it was already too late. The necessary integration of R&D with former management concepts did not even start until the technology push period was over.

The technology push period came rapidly to an end when the speed of innovation in microelectronics, optoelectronics and software reconverted systems businesses into product businesses. Simultaneously, the East/West conflict ended. With it vanished the umbrella for long term R&D. The neocapitalism of industrialising Asian countries forced mature societies into a violent cost reduction drive. The pendulum swung back very quickly to the dominance of financial management concepts which favour short term return on investment (ROI) decision rules.

At the turn of the millenium the industrial society finds itself in the transition to a *fourth phase* in which the Company of the Future will have to operate. We cannot know for sure where this phase will end. But sufficient evidence is available to warrant the following projections.

3 World Economics and Corporate Growth

A company's investments in a particular country are mainly based on expectations about the development of the country's economy and of the whole company. Growth will follow investment if the expectations materialise. Short-term predictions are usually based on the assumption of steady growth rates, at least under the surface of business cycles. This section deals with long term economic development of companies and economies, including the start up phase and maturity.

It will be shown that the industrial society obeys for the largest part of its development a well defined, natural growth law which scales for individual economies and companies, provided one discards the textbook case of exponential growth and catastrophic events. The mathematical forms may appear difficult for a reader not familiar with calculus, but the text is understandable without it.

The long-term developments of companies and economies consist always of the same three processes (see Fig. 1.3): The start up process (in most cases with the help of foreign capital), the endogeneous catching up process to compete with the best, and the pioneer process to lead. It will be shown that each process has a regular growth law, and that the set of management tools for corrective action depends very much on the position of a country or a company along the growth laws. A generally valid policy for dealing with economic growth problems does not exist.

The existence of three regular growth processes defines two critical points in the development of companies and countries. The first refers to the transition from foreign capital dominated to endogeneous growth, and the second to the transition from endogeneous to pioneer growth. Generally these points call for profound structural, social, political, and managerial changes, and there the victims of growth pile up.

For a deeper understanding of the intricate connections between innovation, economic growth, investment, global development, employment, and future markets this section starts with a new conceptual framework. It helps to gain confidence in the following insights and predictions.

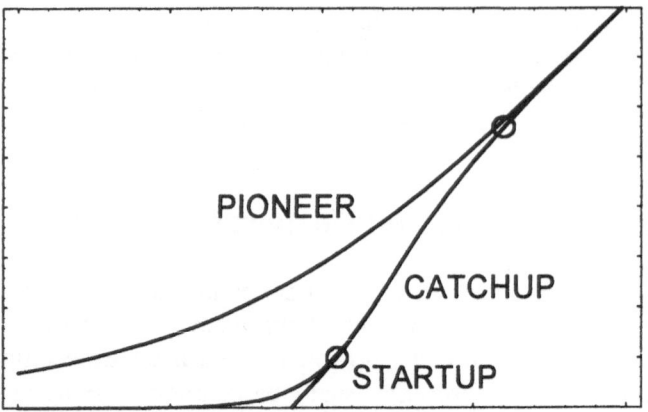

Fig. 1.3. The three regular growth processes with two critical transitions in the development of companies and economies.

3.1 Conceptual Background for the Three Basic Growth Processes

The expressions "growth" or "growth rate" usually imply the textbook case of exponential growth

$$a = a_o \, e^{\alpha \cdot t} \tag{1.1}$$

where the time t is usually measured in years. The unique, very convenient (but, as will be seen, when getting used to it very dangerous) property of this function is, that for a constant growth rate α all derivatives with respect to time yield the same function. E. g., capital stock and its annual increase always differ only by a constant factor. Thus, the annual increase in turnover or gross domestic product (GDP) is

$$\dot{a} = \alpha \, a \tag{1.2}$$

This means that the annual increase is at any time proportional to the level achieved up to that time, and that nothing limits this proportionality.

However, in our world everything is limited. Economists and accountants acknowledge this every time they readjust the growth rate to fit a given time period. This practice introduces unreal steps in real economic functions, prevents to recognize that investment and output do generally not follow the same function in time, and fails notoriously to distinguish between a fundamental process and higher order disturbances. A fundamental process governs long term structural (social, technological) development. Higher order disturbances mean short-term fluctuations. Since a mix of processes cannot be the result of any basic law, predictions based on the exponential function and associated practices cannot be relied on. The company and the economy of the future deserve a better concept.

3.1.1 The Pioneer Process

This well-known basic growth process is fundamental to the growth processes in nature, where a limit always exists. Using the notation Δa for this limit implies an evolutionary step, e. g. from an agricultural to a knowledge society, or from a newcomer to a respected competitor. The annual increase is now proportional to the product of the level endogeneously achieved and to the difference (the gap) remaining between the achieved level and the limit:

$$\dot{a} = \alpha\ a(1 - a/\Delta a) \tag{1.3}$$

In economics the term in brackets is known as "Ricardo factor" which explains diminishing returns on investment. It always dominates when a company, an economic sector, or the whole economy reaches a ceiling of its market or its competence.

There is one (and only one) case where (1.3) reduces to (1.2), and this requires that Δa is infinitely large. Thus, (1.3) is the general case, including (1.2) as an unlikely special case.

The integral of (1.3), called the "S-curve", is

$$a = \frac{\Delta a}{1 + e^{\alpha(T-t)}} \tag{1.4}$$

It is symmetric to the time $t = T$ where $a = \Delta a/2$. It also has the property that the period in time for the bulk of growth (76%), given by the slope at T,

$$\Delta t = 4/\alpha, \tag{1.5}$$

is independent of the height of the step. This independence of the two dimensions makes sense since the speed of change is subject to internal (generic) powers while start, end, and volume of change is subject to external (competitive) powers. This is the basic operating principle of life. The economy is life, in contrast to artificial constructs like the stock market. (As a final disqualification: The exponential function lacks this feature of independence.)

The seemingly small change that the exponential function is now in the denominator has profound consequences for understanding and controlling economic and corporate growth. The most important consequence is that the level achieved (turnover, GDP), the annual increase (new investment, growth of turnover or GDP), and the growth rate $\dot{a}/a$ are no longer proportional to each other. If the level grows like an S-curve, the annual progress grows like a bell shaped curve, and the growth rate decreases like an inverted S-curve. The momentary ratios between these quantities are always well defined in closed form, but depend very much on the maturity position of the company or economy. There is no way to cut this closed set of relations because annual progress is defined as derivative with respect to time of the level, and the growth rate is defined as the ratio of annual progress divided by the achieved level. It will be shown that these inevitable consequences include on a global scale the ongoing consolidation of industry, structural (non-equilibrium) unemployment, and ultimately the social change to the service society, irrespective of limits to global resources.

The S-curve (1.4) will be identified with the pioneer process.

3.1.2 The Catch Up Process and the Dynamic Capital Coefficient

In reality we live in a world with ongoing evolution, where new species, companies or economies always enter, grow, and compete. We need therefore an extension to the case of several players and an evolving upper limit $a(t)$ representing the moving state of the art. This extension has been introduced in Reference 2 in a new framework where the capital stock per capita (investment per employee, respectively) represents the instituted knowledge, and the GDP per capita (added value per employee, respectively) the procedural knowledge. This reflects the close relationship always existing between output and infrastructure. It is important to work on a per capita or per employee basis when quality, well-being, or competitiveness is concerned as opposed to gross figures like quantity, turnover, or the wealth of nations.

Social development is a process of increasing order implying increasing relevant knowledge. If total human knowledge grows exponentially with time, the relevant knowledge in this framework grows linearly with time. The same logarithmic relation exists between information content and data flow, sensory perception and sensory signal strength, and between a system's entropy and the probability of its states of nature. Applied to economics, it turns out that the perceived gap in relevant knowledge (see below Eq. 1.14) is the natural driver of economic growth. The larger the gap, the higher the growth potential. The generic skill of the company (or the society) to close the gap effectively determines the speed of growth. It can be much higher than the speed of the pioneer process since catching up systems can copy, avoiding the mistakes of the pioneer.

This framework results in the following equation for the output y:

$$\dot{y} = \beta \; y\big[1 - (1 - \dot{a}/a\beta)y/a\big] \qquad (1.6)$$

The Ricardi-factor is now modified so that the growth rate $\dot{y}/y$ goes not to zero when the achieved level y reaches the pioneer's level $a(t)$ but merges with the pioneer's growth rate $\dot{a}/a$.

In spite of its complex appearance, (1.6) has a very simple solution valid for any $a(t)$:

$$1/y = 1/a + 1/\varepsilon \; e^{\beta \cdot t} \qquad (1.7)$$

The integration constant ε has the character of a shift τ between the catching up process $y(t)$ and the state of the art $a(t)$. Obviously, this system of processes has the very useful property that individual processes can be sequenced or interlocked continuously under any output $a(t)$. In section 6.3 this property will be used for continuous production planning and accounting under the roof of a desirable total turnover function. Here we use it to sequence the catch up entity with the pioneer. This just requires inserting (1.4) into (1.7). Resolved for the output (the GDP per capita, or the turnover per employee) the result for the catch up process is

$$y = \frac{\Delta a}{1 + e^{\alpha(T-t)} + e^{\beta(\tau-t)}} \qquad (1.8)$$

The former symmetry is lost (see Fig. 1.3), and the whole process consists of three consecutive phases: The initial phase with exponential growth and growth rate β; a long phase of nearly linear growth around $t = \tau$ resulting from compensation of the state of the art growth by the modified Ricardo factor; and a consolidation phase when the growth rate decreases to the pioneer's α. It will be shown that the latter is an additional, inadvertent cause of corporate mergers and sudden unemployment after long periods of strong growth.

Eq. 1.8 models the typical long-term evolution of companies and economies. Negative growth usually happens catastrophically. However, in case a company should prefer an orderly, possibly profitable retreat of a subsidiary to a lousy sale, it can now do so in a controlled way. Eq. 1.8 allows to model smooth transitions and works for any signs of α and β.

Endogeneous growth means that the capital stock is financed from real time saving. For an economy, saving is the difference between the GDP and consumption c per capita, for a company it is the difference between turnover and total cost of sales (including profit and taxes, excluding investment) per employee. Therefore, the output (1.8) is also given by

$$y \equiv (\gamma/\mu)k = \gamma \cdot k + \dot{k} + c \qquad (1.9)$$

The ratio in brackets is the productivity of capital. Its inverse μ/γ is the conventional capital coefficient. In the textbook case where y and k grow exponentially, the capital coefficient is considered a product specific constant, readjusted with the growth rate as required. For non-exponential growth laws it is essential to distinguish between the annual net increase $\dot{k}$ of capital stock, increasing the productivity, and the annual maintenance $\gamma \cdot k$ of capital stock, because their time dependence will not be the same. γ is the physical (not fiscal) decay rate of capital stock. It ranges from 0.02 per year for buildings to 0.2 per year for research and leading edge equipment. It is a product specific constant, even for social averages like the capital stock of mankind, as will be seen.

$\mu(t)$ will be called the dynamic capital coefficient. It is the fraction of the GDP needed at any time to maintain the level of capital stock. From the left hand part of (1.9) one gets $\dot{k}/k = \dot{\mu}/\mu + \dot{y}/y$. Inserted into the right hand part of (1.9) yields a fundamental relation between the growth rate of an economy or a company and the capital coefficient:

$$\mu/\gamma = \frac{1 - c/y - \dot{\mu}/\gamma}{\gamma + \dot{y}/y} \qquad (1.10)$$

It is proportional to the capitalization level $1 - c/y$ which is nearly constant for a product or for an industrial society, and inversely proportional to the sum of the capital decay rate and the growth rate. The growth rate $\dot{y}/y$ is given by (1.6) with (1.9). Except for unlikely conditions $\dot{\mu}/\gamma$ can be neglected compared to $1 - c/y$. Since initially $\dot{y}/y = \beta$, (1.10) yields $1 - c/y = \mu_o/(1 + \beta/\gamma)$ where μ_o is the initial dynamic capital coefficient of the industrial society. Checking this formula with the economies of Fig. 1 yields $\mu_o = 0.07$ for all of them. Clearly, μ_o is simultaneously the final dynamic capital coefficient of the agricultural society (thereafter see Fig. 1.5). With this result one gets finally

$$\mu = \mu_o \frac{1 + \beta/\gamma}{1 + \dot{y}/y\gamma} \tag{1.11}$$

Conceptually (1.6) and (1.11) formulate two fundamental economic conservation laws: An economic entity cannot sustain growth beyond the level backed by the state of the art, and the generated infrastructure must be maintained. As a result, the entire evolution of $y(t), \dot{y}/y, k(t), \dot{k}$, and $c(t)$ can be given in closed form by (1.8) - (1.11) with only six long term parameters $\Delta a, \alpha, T, \gamma, \beta$, and τ. The first four are external constants known from the market or the pioneer, the last two are internal.

3.1.3 The Start Up Process and the Lower Critical Point

As indicated in Fig. 1.3, the initial phase of the catch up process can be shortened with the use of foreign capital. The cost is interest and pay back at a later period, but then the economy or the company can hopefully afford it more easily because of a stronger position. As any upper limit is far away, and the endogeneous level is still too small to impress its internal dynamics, the output y just follows the invested capital stock according to the left hand part of (1.9).

The point is, that this is the only law. The stabilizing feedback loop of the right hand part is not yet functioning. If the foreign capital share dominates, the start up is at the mercy of investor's opinion, which may change erratically. The start up process is therefore in principle unstable.

Since the two growth laws (1.8) and (1.9, left hand side) are known, the transition related to the first critical point in Fig. 1.3 can be modeled in closed form as well. It is inevitable to define at first a transition period in which the share of the external investment is gradually decreased and replaced by capital obtained endogeneously. During the transition the replacement of external capital, the output, the investment and their derivatives with respect to time are required to be continuous functions, since jumps destabilize the transition.

The number of victims peaks here because these requirements are very difficult to fulfil simultaneously. However, the problem can be solved in full generality with products of the desired output function and trigonometric functions. The general result takes too much space to be given here. For a start up company a graphic representation will do in most cases. For a start up economy formal transition planning is indispensable. This must include a balanced distribution of capital stock for a society in equilibrium. Foreign capital is not primarily interested in such a balanced distribution. Since the pioneer's productivity is copied with every invested dollar, wealth is created, but employment drops. In comparison with earlier transition planning, the future requires a much higher weight of education, information, and communication in the national budgets. In view of this change, the company of the future will either extend its scope to include more services, or it must form consortia with other companies.

3.2 The Consumer Markets of the Company of the Future

Figure 1.4, taken from Ref. 2, proves that the conceptual background developed in the preceding section describes the economic development of the industrial society much better than any earlier theory.
The upper curve is a fit of the pioneer process (1.4) to the evolution of the real GDP per capita of the leading industrial nations UK and US from 1850 to 1995. The UK lead the industrial world from 1750 until commonwealth problems quenched its performance. A best fit of the parameters yields

$$\Delta a = \$75,000 \text{ per capita p. a.,} \ \alpha = 0.016 \text{ p. a., and } T = 2040. (1.12)$$

Within the accuracy of national economic data a slightly different set of parameters could be fitted, but this will not change the following predictions for the next generation.

The UK-US pioneer curve includes all innovations of man to date and all innovations to come with the same impact. Unless we assume that there will be a miracle or a disaster, in which case we quit planning, predictions based on this pioneer curve are on safe ground. This means that any economy trying to cross the pioneer curve can only sustain this excursion with innovations which have a larger impact than all innovations have had to date. Otherwise (1.6) predicts a return to the pioneer curve with possibly negative growth rates. (See next section's discussion of the German and Japanese economic problems).

That the initial growth rate of the pioneer process is so small is not surprising. The best of technical innovations like ease of work or food production does not even appear in economic data. Taking Albert Einstein's word seriously that a new idea does not carry through because of its intrinsic strengths, but because its enemies die out, leads to

$$\alpha \equiv 1/2g = 0.02 \text{ p. a.} \tag{1.13}$$

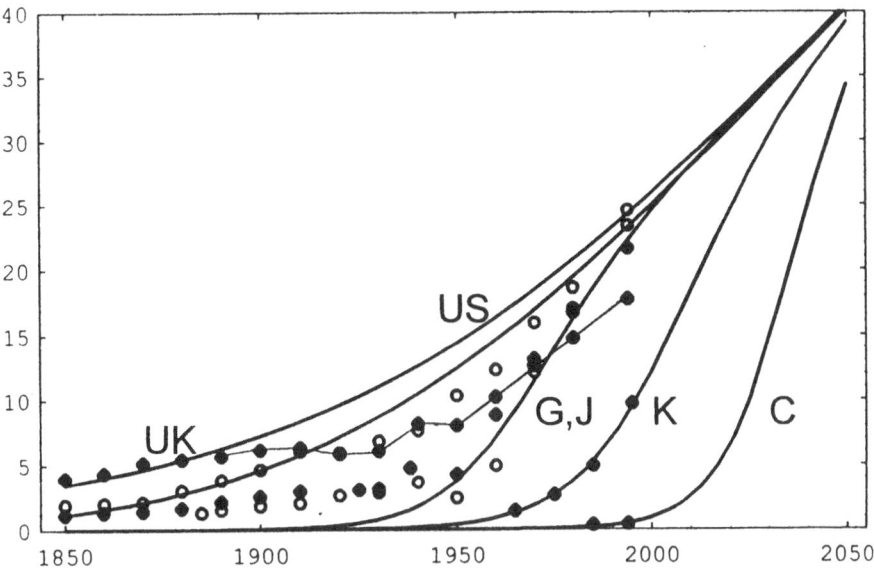

Fig. 1.4. The GDP per capita for the UK, US, Germany, Japan, Korea and China according to Ref. 2 in real $1000 at exchange rates of 1990.

where g is the generation gap of 25 years. (Great inventions are made with g, peers die out with $3g$, and the two world wars make up for the difference to the actual value of 1.12). The truth behind Einstein's word is that innovation is a diffusion process. Product and technological innovations alternate with process and organizational innovations, well established technologies and organizations fight back, and many expensive and time consuming mistakes are made.

Since the pace of discoveries is unpredictable, α cannot be derived from first principles. All what can be done is to link it with dependent processes. It is a characteristic of diffusion, that some stress and vacancies are necessary, equality and perfect order prevent it. This applies to corporate innovation as well. Hence the familiar and necessary friction between R&D departments and their customers. On the national stage the US can obviously maintain their pioneer position with a remarkable level of immigration and internal social looseness.

The trajectories for the US, Germany with Japan, Korea, and China are best fits of the catch up process (1.8) with the following parameters:

Table 1.1. Parameters for the catch up processes shown in Figure 1.4

Country	US	Germany	Japan	Korea	China
Time shift τ	1945	1975	1980	2005	2040
Initial growth rate β	0.04	0.09	0.11	0.08	0.11
Starting year	1865	1945	1945	1953	1980
Skill parameter s	0.20	0.31	0.44	0.24	0.38

At the beginning the US were catching up with the UK, now the US are the pioneer.

The starting year of the catch up process was in every case the end of a traumatic experience: The civil war in the US, the second world war, the Korean war, and the cultural revolution in China. Their infrastructure was partially destroyed, but not the talents of the people, united with government in their only goal to rebuild their economy with the state of the art infrastructure. The transfer of relevant knowledge from the pioneers was nearly free of charge. Then it can be expected that the larger the gap in relevant knowledge, the faster the initial growth rate, depending only on the country's skill to use the gap effectively in the spirit of the industrial society. Putting this simple logic into formal shape yields

$$\beta = \hat{\beta}(1 - e^{-s \cdot \ln(a_o / y_o)}) \tag{1.14}$$

where s is the skill parameter, a_o the pioneer's GDP per capita (1.4) at the starting year, y_o any low level normalizing GDP, and $\ln(a_o / y_o)$ the initial gap in relevant knowledge.

For large gaps there must exist a limiting growth rate. Considering characteristic social time spans for (1.5), and the actual range of growth rates, only the generation gap can be considered for determining a fundamental limit:

$$\hat{\beta} \equiv 4 / g = 0.16 \text{ p.a.} \tag{1.15}$$

This limiting growth rate corresponds to the case where the relevant knowledge of the next generation is totally new, so that the teachings of the parent generation are nearly irrelevant. Under such conditions the society and its economy must break down. It is possible to exceed the limiting growth rate in limited regions when there is a much larger, culturally intact reservoir for employees to be recruited from and returned to after their job or working period. This would not change the overall growth rate, but would cause interregional and social stress. Parallel thinking applies to enterprise. Family businesses know the generation problem very well.

The skill parameters of Table 1.1 follow from (1.14) with (1.15), (1.4), and $y_o = \$1000$. Any low level normalizing GDP could be used, it only changes the scale. The skill parameter is culture specific, includes all relevant contributions from education through organization, and is therefore a long term constant for an economy and for a company. This is the basis for the stability of economic growth. The relevant knowledge gap is the driver, and innovation is the agent.

The application to the consumer markets of the company of the future is as follows: The GDP per capita of the country is plotted into Fig. 1.4. This gives already a first impression of the future development of the country relative to the best possible development. Then the curve is analyzed with (1.8) and (1.14) to determine $\beta, \tau,$ and s. When these parameters are well defined, (1.8) is a good long-term prediction of future growth, and investments can be made accordingly. The risk of investments increases with problems to fit these parameters.

The next step is to consider the company's market in relation to the GDP development of the country. The normative forces of the industrial society are strong. It can be expected that during the essential development phase $4/\beta$ the consumer market shares converge from the present position to the share they have in the G7 countries. This fixes the likely growth trajectory of the company's market in the country. The result is multiplied with the future population. A final decision includes the risk assessment of the first step, and the knowledge about local competition. It is also advisable not to underestimate the logistics costs for materials and management. They can turn profits expected from cheap local labor into losses.

3.3 The Investment Goods Market of the Company of the Future

Here applies essentially the same procedure as for the consumer markets, except that the capital coefficient changes the time dependence. Neglecting the time derivative of the dynamic capital coefficient as in (1.11) one gets from (1.9) and (1.11)

$$k = \mu_o \frac{1 + \beta/\gamma}{\gamma + \dot{y}/y} y \qquad (1.16)$$

where $\dot{y}/y$ and y are given by (1.6) and (1.8), respectively. The bracket modifying the Ricardo factor in (1.6) is not negligible. The total annual volume of the capital goods market per capita is then given by

$$\dot{w} = \gamma \cdot k + \dot{k} \qquad (1.17)$$

which is the sum of the maintenance or replacement market of existing capital stock, and of the generation of new capital stock. Multiplied with the population, (1.17) predicts the total market volume. A company's share is then determined in analogy to the consumer goods market.

The capital stock analysis of the countries of Table 1.1 yields always a physical decay rate around 0.04 p.a., which fits even agricultural societies. Since this cannot be an accidental coincidence, the spirit of this section suggests and postulates the identity

$$\gamma \equiv 1/g = 0.04 \text{ p.a.} \tag{1.18}$$

In fact, it appears very natural that mankind arranges the effective lifetime of capital stock to last just about one generation gap. It appears here for the third time in basic rate determining capacity (see Eqs. 1.13 and 1.15). Thus, the generation gap is the most important "economic constant", not just a biologic parameter.

3.4 Employment and the Upper Critical Point

Figure 1.5 shows the industrial and agricultural employment in Germany which would result from (1.8) and (1.16) with the parameters given in (1.12) and Table 1.1, without reverting to any employment data. Only three assumptions were made: The labor productivity grows proportional to the capital stock per capita, and the final shares of agricultural and industrial production is 4 and 15 per cent, respectively. Before 1945 the agricultural employment is overestimated and the industrial employment underestimated, because there was of course an unsteady, slow growth precursor before the second world war (see Figure 1.4) neglected by the catch up process. After 1945 the actual employment data fit quite well. The peak of industrial employment was at 55% in 1955. It remained high in East Germany with relatively low productivity.

Because of the strong growth of the catch up process before half level time τ the service sector could absorb the productivity redundancies of 3% p.a. seen in the sum curve. Unemployment remained at a very low level. In 1980 the net fixed capital formation started to decline, as the unavoidable consequence of the dynamics of the catch up process. The ratio $\dot{k}/y = (\mu/\gamma)(\dot{\mu}/\mu + \dot{y}/y)$, shown as the lowest curve, stays nearly constant up to $t = \tau$. Thereafter it drops by $(1 - c/y)/(1 + \gamma/\beta) = 0.12$. This additional, dynamic drop of demand for work could no longer be compensated by the service sector, because Germany was approaching the small growth potential of the pioneer process. This is quantitatively the explanation for Germany's unemployment after 1990.

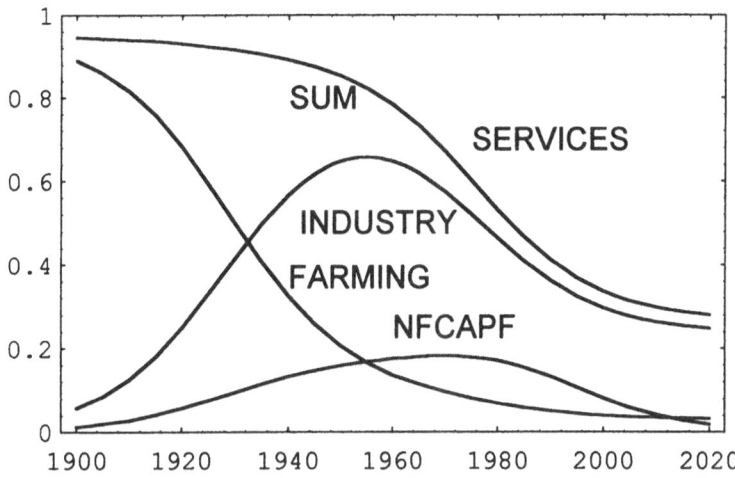

Fig. 1.5. Employment in Germany as derived from the catch up process, valid after 1945. The real drop of 3% per year after 1960, due to productivity gain, could be nearly compensated by the service sector because of strong growth. The sudden, additional drop of 12% total in new fixed capital formation (lowest curve), due to the dynamics of the catch up process, could not be compensated, causing rapid rise of unemployment.

This dynamic effect can only occur for $\beta \geq \alpha + \gamma = 0.06$ p.a., but then it must. The safe way to ease employment and other problems of the upper critical point is to deliberately slow down the growth rate already before $t = \tau$.

Another major problem is the generation of excess capital. The GDP is still increasing and with it the supply of capital, but for the generation living after $t = \tau$ the demand for capital stock is dynamically decreasing. There were times where ailing sectors of the economy were considerably subsidized, delaying timely action. Finally Germany was lucky that unification opened a perfect sink for excess capital, matched in volume and just in time. Since former East Germany had financed $\dot{k}$ by not maintaining its capital stock ($\gamma \cdot k$ in Eq.1.9) for more than a generation gap, the necessary capital transfer is just k. According to (1.9) this means to transfer \$98,000 per capita or \$88 Billion p.a. for over 20 years. The rate transferred in the first 10 years comes by chance quite close to this calculated transfer rate. But just because of the structural change this transfer could not stimulate industry as originally hoped, and the unemployment level soared. The right policy must stimulate service enterprises.

Japan was not as lucky with its upper critical point. Lacking a better sink for capital, the government tried to subsidize the growth rate by huge capital injections, pushing the country beyond the pioneer's GDP (Fig. 1.4, top point). But, by virtue of the first conservation law formulated at the end of 3.1.2, neither stimulation of demand nor of supply can sustain a GDP above the pioneer curve. Within the paradigms of the industrial society an economy can generally only perform worse, but not better than its catch up process predicts. In this case the result of using bygone tools was that the economy is charged for a long time with maintenance costs for idle capital stock. The right policy is to leave old paradigms, to open the society, to push for the extraordinary discovery, and to stimulate private services. The prospects are good since Japan still has the highest skill parameter of all countries.

The pioneer model of the US does not apply directly. Since its initial growth rate of 0.04 p. a. is smaller than $\gamma + \alpha$, the US have not and will never have the dynamic problems of Germany, Japan, and later catch up economies. A drop in $\dot{k}/y$ is for the US theoretically impossible. A plot or a calculation of the productivity redundancy performed in the same manner as done with Germany yields for the US a very steady level of 1% p. a. for the last two generations. This means that on a per capita basis Germany and Japan could so far cope with three times the pressure on their employment and educational systems. In the simplest possible approximation one would expect from the initial growth rates a factor of 2.5.

3.5 Outlook

In view of this economic analysis Germany and Japan must be congratulated, not criticized, in comparison with the US. Their temporary problems were caused by an extremely successful catch up process with memory and inertia, which has reached its goal. But industrial labor continues to decline as the productivity grows faster than the demand for industrial goods, familiar from the fate of agriculture. The elasticity of labor versus capital continues to decline as well, it is nearly zero for advanced equipment. There will be no return to catch up growth rates.

During the bulk part of the catch up process the creativity of leadership was not really challenged. Now it is. Structural changes cannot be mastered with tools for short-term fluctuations. The framework presented in this Section makes this very clear. It is a structural theory, separating short-term economic activity from long term structural change. The German language has two separate nouns for this, 'Konjunktur' and 'Struktur'. English, the language of economics, does not.

A theory of short-term fluctuations must respect the long-term structural changes presented here. The opposite order is not possible since fluctuations are pertubations of the basic growth laws, not vice versa. First indications of a pertubation theory [3] are that the circular frequency of the fundamental economic cycle equals the geometric mean of the consumption rate and the withdrawal rate from the whole value added chain of the economy or of the business, respectively. Since the volume of the value added chain continuously increases during structural growth, economic and business cycle frequencies decrease towards maturity.

The damping 'constant' of oscillations appears to be the arithmetic mean of that withdrawal rate and the growth rate, but the latter enters with its sign reversed. This means for a young, rapidly growing society that it can experience nearly undamped oscillations of 5 to 10 year's cycle time, and for a mature society that oscillations are strongly damped and long term, i. e., barely observable. Such behavior is not uncommon for countries and companies. It is also in line with intuitive thinking where one would expect small inertia and small friction in young systems, and the opposite in mature systems. These features are synchronized and can be very strong if the development of a company coincides with the economic development of its home base. They are less prominent of course if the company's business is fairly independent or spread out over different regions. In this sense it pays to distribute activities, but to be present wherever and just before good growth conditions appear.

To day's pioneer societies are service societies. Services create wellbeing, but the wealth generated by industry and its innovation is a prerequisite. As Adam Smith wrote, services are consumed instantly. The value added chain is short, accumulation of capital is not comparable to industry. Therefore, the service society is not a simple extension of the industrial society. With respect to capital and well-being it will reverse priorities. As the legal framework was decisive for the start of the industrial society, it will also have to play an important role for the service society. One of the major tasks is how to improve the standing and quality standards of services. Pure manufacturing businesses will find it increasingly difficult to operate in service dominated environments.

While the G7 and associated economies will make this transformation, the company of the future will see its traditional industrial markets grow to seven times their present volume within the next two generations in Asia-Oceania. This follows from (1.8) and (1.9) in spite of all problems associated with the lower critical point (see 3.1.3), just from the skill and the magnitude of the population. The major problem will not be the world's resources, innovation will ease this problem. The major problem will be unemployment and, as a consequence, political instability. There are large individual differences within this huge region. Quantitatively they can be taken into account as described at the end of section 3.2.

Needed are mainly existing products, not entirely new ones. Most companies have seen this as an opportunity to combine advantages resulting from regionalising their production, leaving R&D near their headquarters. Competitive progress requires however intense feedback between product and process innovations. By experience, an order of magnitude in volume must lead to an economy of scale improvement in price by at least a factor of 2. In the spirit of this section's framework, economy of scale improvements are a phenomenon of order. We might expect therefore about $ln10 = 2.3$ (save a product specific factor near 1) for the price improvement. In any case the feedback between product and process innovation must be well organized, not only by the use of information technology, and the same is true for the logistics of supply. The International Intelligent Manufacturing Systems Program, set up by Japan, Europe, the US, Canada, Australia and Korea, is just beginning to address such order of magnitude issues (see Footnote 1 in Chapter 5).

The structural gap between the transformation and the industrializing societies is a great challenge and opportunity for capital, companies, and governments, but also for social thought. The gap will close within the next two generations, and the world's population will stabilize.

4   General Strategy, Relevant Knowledge, and Corporate Structure

The difference between strategy and tactics was worked out by von Clausewitz, the German general and philosopher (1780-1831), in his unfinished book 'Vom Kriege' (On War) [4]. The American Management Association recommended it once as the best book on management of all times. The general wrote that you should make your strategy known to your troops, to the nation, and to your enemy, for its purpose is to avoid the war, and to win without any losses. Only when your strategy fails you must resort to tactics. These you must hide even from your own troops to deceive the enemy, to save resources, and to win or lose the war with least losses overall.

If we apply these thoughts within the business world, we can say that strategy should be to defy competition. Only when this fails we must employ tactics to beat competition. Strategic superiority is an asset, tactical remedies are a liability. It pays therefore to discriminate clearly between tactics and strategy along the lines of von Clausewitz. Needless to say that innovation and successful R&D in all business functions are strategic assets par excellence.

Consultants can be very helpful for advice on tactical problems. They must achieve short term improvements. They know that there is no universal strategy. Each company must have its own, adaptable and resistant one. It is nearly impossible to put a new strategy on an existing organisation, because strategy's ultimate purpose is to orient the selection of relevant knowledge. In the thinking of the preceding Sectionthe relevant knowledge selected by the company constitutes its organisational order and competence.

A new order must be built like a house, bottom up in an orderly way against gravity. Education is needed to achieve the required change of attitudes and methods, and this takes time. In contrast, the destruction of an existing order can be achieved top down and very fast. It does not defy gravity nor does it require education and methodical change. In the most fundamental way this asymmetry is embedded in the famous second law of thermodynamics. In simple terms it states that it is impossible to change the order of a system and maintain its internal states and their level of operation. The attempt to convert the former Soviet Union by decree to a capitalistic country is the most prominent proof of this impossibility. Order is life, and life cannot be bought.

The overriding task of a real corporate merger is to combine the relevant knowledge of the partners into one common set. This may be easy for businesses with simple value added structures and/or a high degree of automation. Typical examples are retail stores, service enterprises, even banks, hospitals, and manufacturers of cars and components. Long and complex added value chains require more complex relevant knowledge structures and more complex hierarchies, which is another inevitable embodiment of said famous law. Mergers between companies with complex value added structures are therefore very risky and rare. They can only work if the relevant knowledge sets are already very similar, which normally excludes mergers across language barriers.

In most cases the answer to 'what is your strategy?' will be a set of business goals, sometimes supplemented with a doctrine on implementation. There was a time when the doctrine was reduced to buzz words like 'aggressive', 'lean', 'shareholder value', 'customer orientated', *etc.* which are often conflicting when activated. Their simultaneous use reveals that there was not enough time spent on the advancement of the company's strategy. Leaders must take that time, that is their mission. If strategy is to orient the selection of relevant knowledge, it cannot be confined to a set of goals. Strategy is a process containing the four elements shown in Figure 1.6:

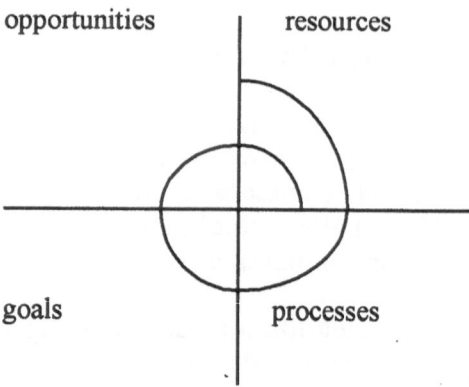

Fig. 1.6. The four elements of strategy.

This strategy is applicable to any living entity, *eg* in a person, a firm, or a country. The best practical examples are found in competitive sports. The process may be used as follows, and this chapter is organized in this way (see Figure 1.1):

Element 1: Start with an *unbiased assessment of your resources, ie* your strategic infrastructure: Human resources, plant and equipment, soft assets (see Section 9 below). Identify strengths and weaknesses compared to your competitors. Identify *via* this assessment the core assets and core deficiencies. Highlight for each asset the effort needed to maintain its level and the effort needed to extend or to change it. Many more competitions, businesses, armies and even countries have been lost due to neglected maintenance than due to insufficient combat strength. The latter gets all the attention; but even in periods of rapid growth at least half of the investment must still be assigned to maintenance. This applies to all assets, and especially to human resources. The value of people appreciates, that of capital stock depreciates.

Element 2: Continue with an *objective assessment of your opportunities*. Distinguish between those already taken and the new ones available. The key to vitality is the new opportunities available in the market, in the state of the art, and in the deployment of resources. Identify the most attractive opportunities regardless of resources currently available. What is attractive cannot be restricted to commercial aspects such as established demand, market share, and profit. These may be sufficient for mature product lines, but attractiveness should also mean entrepreneurial satisfaction, personal identification with the task behind the opportunity, and the challenge involved (see Section 6 below, on innovation). Finally, rank the opportunities with a list of criteria regardless of whether they have already been taken up or they are new ones.

Element 3: *Decide on the goals* using an objective comparison of your resources and your opportunities. Take stock of traditional decisions in the light of new opportunities and see how your resources could be developed. Do not forget the opportunities you have considered previously but have not as yet been developed. Your whole strategy may be determined by those you have not taken, because there are usually stronger reasons behind a no than behind a yes. Benchmarking against your own decisions may be more instructive than against competition. At the top, you cannot improve by comparison with others.

There are formal decision rules which depend on three possible states of nature, *ie* certainty, risk, and innocence. In real life these are not very helpful. Tacit knowledge is fortunately tacit. Decision formulae are normally too trivial compared with the complexities of real life. It is therefore essential to obtain the opinion of the innovative entrepreneur or, in large firms, of those few people in services, sales, production, and research with a proven innovative record. Their views should be especially cherished.

Element 4: When the goals are selected for attractiveness and best match between resources and opportunities, the processes (ways and means) for reaching the goals usually exist and are clear. Nevertheless, it is important to *monitor every process used in each operation*. It is not sufficient to assume that operations will automatically innovate with respect to various products, suppliers, or customers. Research, production, sales, services and administration all need to practice continuous innovation as well as the management. A good practice for the Company of the Future is to establish a fund for innovation in operations equivalent to the funds established for investment, training, and research. Another purpose for the operations supported by this fund is to keep explicit records of mistakes and successes, in order to establish the learning curves of each unit. For one of the most serious consequences of the increasing mobility of employees, the early retirement of professionals, and the global distribution of manufacturing is the loss of experience, and especially of knowledge about mistakes made in the past.

Customer relations, production technologies and the laws of nature cannot be sliced or broken down into projects or product generations. Discontinuities in the learning curve are very expensive compared with the possible profit derived from one generation of a product - they may even lead to the loss of the whole product line. To adapt a quotation from Albert Einstein on the simplicity of good theories: "Keep operations as lean as possible but not leaner".

In summary, a strategy is the set for *resources, opportunities, goals and processes* put together for achievement of success. This set focuses the selection of relevant knowledge by every employee. In the implementation of the strategy, its granularity depends on the size of the company and each hierarchical level. The set must be homogeneous enough for the working level to be able to recognise the board level's strategy and *vice versa*. The strategy must be periodically updated. Part of this can be synchronised with quarterly reports or the business year. Top updates are of course synchronised with the natural pace of activities, *eg* the olympic games in sports, or the product generation's period in business.

A successful strategy leads to availability of better resources, to the acceptance of more challenging opportunities, more rewarding goals, and improved processes. The expected improvements should be recorded for every element and for every line of business.

Whenever an improvement does not materialise, the whole business line must be reviewed, not only a particular element of the operation. Finally, it helps to set up for each business a check list, as detailed as is necessary to ensure that the strategy will be implemented.

5 The Production Function of R&D

The purpose of an enterprise is to generate added value for all the people in the network of customers, shareholders and employees. Profit is a consequence of added value, and not *vice versa*. The distribution of profit must be fair and have a socially acceptable relationship to the added value achieved.

For the Company of the Future added value will be optimised on a global scale. We avoid the use of the word 'maximised', because the globe is a finite base of operations, and not freely expandable (see Section 3). SMEs can be successful in a global network if they excel in a specific competence or link up with global players.

To optimise the added value requires a knowledge of the entire value-added chain for each product and system. We have often paid high consulting fees and gone to great pains with productivity programmes without realising the strategic importance and efficiency reserves hidden in the whole added-value chain. To make them visible makes all the difference in a well managed enterprise.

5.1 The Value-Added Diagram

The Value-Added Diagram in Figure 1.7 provides an introduction into the general concept:

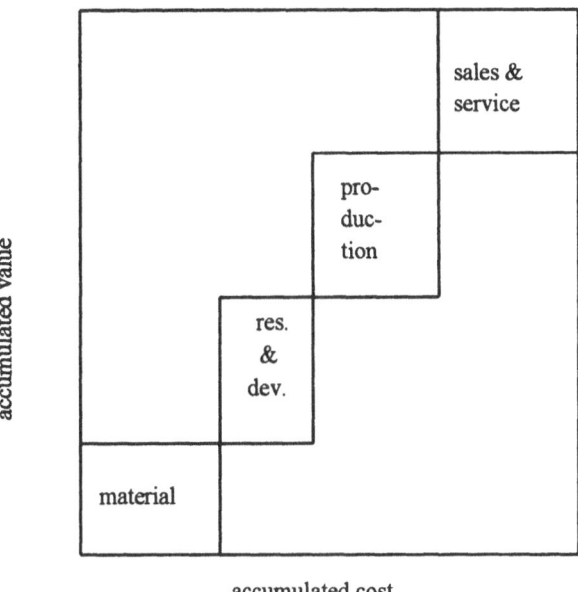

Fig. 1.7. The Value-Added Diagram.

Each contribution to the product is represented by a box with its cost as the base and its value added as its height. Thus, if cost equals value added, the box is a square, and profit is zero. The effectiveness of a contribution, a business function, or a business unit's performance can be seen immediately.

The sum of all the boxes yields the total cost and total value (price) of the product or system. If there are uncertainties with respect to the cost or value added of any part of the value-added chain, such as in the assignment of an overhead, the company cannot optimise its performance. It is of great importance to all the contributors that accounting deficiencies in particular units or parts of the value-added chain are eliminated before it is decided to measure the performance of any of them.

Purchases (materials) should be included since they can be traded against endogenous value added. The reduction of value added is not always a virtue; it makes sense only if endogeneous work is irreversibly less efficient than outsourced work. In most cases efficiency problems are often distributed throughout the entire value-added chain, and may not be attributable to a particular endogeneous function. This means that before any decision for outsourcing is made, the *whole value-added chain* must be considered and optimised. The final alternative is to phase out the product line in order to create room for new opportunities. Often this kind of action is taken too late, and only after heavy losses have been experienced by the employees and the shareholders.

It should be noted that the value of materials or products in stock depreciates. The purchase box is therefore a general loser in the value-added chart. 'Just in time' delivery just shifts the burden to suppliers and society. In addition, any charges of administration costs to material adds less to the added value than it costs. The same applies to other parts of the chain, except if one can claim to have a competitive edge in administration. In that case, administration would certainly deserve its own box in the Value-Added Diagram.

We note that an important feature of the Value-Added Diagram is its fractal character: Its granularity can be adapted to any level of aggregation. It can be used throughout the company, from board level to the shop floor, from systems to components, and for all corporate functions. All sub-diagrams are additive, in both dimensions. Furthermore, the Value-Added Diagram allows self-assessment and control using one and the same document. Learning curves are easy to generate using sequence charts for the same product/system/business unit. Natural updating periods are defined by the business reporting period and the product generation period. Finally, the Value-Added Diagram is very easily computerised.

5.2 The Production Function of R&D

The most difficult task for the diagram may be the assignment of the value added by R&D. The cost is comparatively easy, since cost accounting in R&D should in any case be broken down to the product level, but the value added is usually not known. At best, R&D departments charge only their cost to their customers. They do not have the privilege of a market price for their services. According to a study by J. A. Klein *et al* [5], the most valuable output of central R&D departments may be their advice, not any direct contribution to a product.

In Section 6 we will see that the major contributions from divisional R&D are those for the key components which determine the performance of products and systems. Consequently, they also provide a basis for assessing the value-added. Each key component should therefore have its own box as indicated in Figure 1.8.

There are two solutions to the question of value added by R&D: An easy one which tells us something, and a refined one which is a spin-off of the Value-Added Diagram and tells us a lot. The easy one is to split the total R&D cost per business unit into its key component contributions in proportion to the value added by the key component. Here we assume that the value added reflects the complexity of the key component and is therefore a better measure for the R&D value than the R&D cost. If there is a considerable advisory content in R&D, that should be given its own box and subtracted before the splitting takes place. The assignment of overhead must be fair.

The refined one makes full use of the Value-Added Diagram. If the product is sold in the market, its accumulated value is equal to its price. The value added for R&D is then given by

$$VA\ (R\&D) = \text{Sales Price} - VA(\text{Sales and Service}) \\ - VA(\text{Production}) - VA(\text{Materials}) \qquad (1.19)$$

This proposal yields the production function of R&D simply as the missing part in the total added value chain after all other contributions have been taken into account. This method is as precise as the values added by the other business functions are known. We repeat the earlier statement that it makes little sense to optimise the R&D function without a thorough knowledge of the performance of all other business functions. Consequently, if there is sufficient quality and discipline in the accounting procedures of the more routine and repetitive business functions, this method does not require any additional work for the more difficult non-repetitive R&D function.

The productivity or efficiency of R&D is obtained from (1.19) as the ratio

$$E\ (R\&D) = VA(R\&D)\ /\ \text{Cost}\ (R\&D) \qquad (1.20)$$

Now the efficiency or productivity of R&D can be readily compared with that of sales and production. It should be expected that E(R&D) is the highest. If the product is only sold internally, the internal price must be used, provided that it is fair. It should not be distorted by manipulated internal exchange rates which transfer overhead, loss, or profit for reasons having little to do with the quality of R&D.

A second point of concern is the added value of sales, maintenance, and services. Often sales operate on a margin fixed by experience and tradition.

If that is, say, 20 per cent of the sales price, sales will automatically cost 20 per cent. The sales box will be a square no matter what kind of product or how difficult it is to compete in the market. Unfortunately, a fixed margin is often used. This ridicules R&D value accounting and optimisation of the value added chain. When, in addition, sales and engineering tasks are mixed to prepare tenders, we have a real sink for hiding the true value added. The objective of mentioning just a few bad practices is to point out how important it is to install and maintain accounting and controlling procedures which are on a par with quality standards expected from technology. The Value-Added Diagram is also a powerful tool to discover all kinds of deficiencies internally.

Sales and R&D have at least one factor in common, *ie* that each project or contract is usually unique. This is unlike production where repetition allows for economies of scale, learning and productivity curves, market prices, and, as a result of all that, figures for the value added for each product. Nevertheless, sales usually operate with a number of similar products so that it should be easier to arrive at realistic value-added figures than it is in R&D. Benchmarking with leading competitors is recommended here. If that is done for the entire value added chain, the total price allows calibration of scales.

Since the R&D efforts precede production and sales, all costs and values must be discounted to the reporting date as usual. In order to make the investment decision for a new product, the Value-Added Diagram should be drawn up for the entire product cycle (see Section 6.3).

Figure 1.8 presents an interesting example of establishing a Value-Added Diagram. The customers purchased parts from a software package for their specific needs. In this very simple case the customers determined directly the value added by R&D for each part by the volume sold, because the cost of each component consisted essentially of the lines of code costs plus a small volume dependent addition. The boxes (components) could then be ordered by their value added to cost ratio. Immediately, from a first glance at the Value-Added Diagram, a decision could be made to update only the winning components and to transfer the resources saved into a real step forward in the performance of some selected losers. In this case, transferring more R&D money into the right components made the difference between a 30 per cent loss and a 30 per cent profit. The cost of corporate R&D for making this change was negligible.

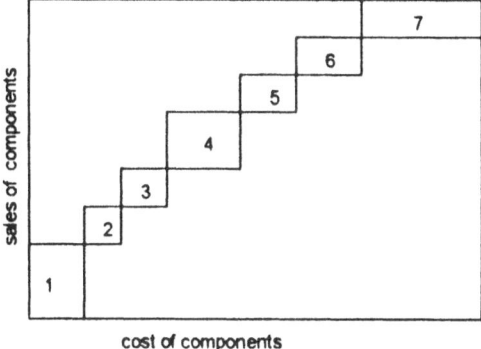

Fig. 1.8. Value-Added Diagram for a software package.

6 Innovation and Key Components

The performance of products and systems is largely determined by its key components. No system is produced from scratch. Innovation and research always concentrate on improving the key components. This even applies to software systems. Key components of software are, *eg* source codes and interfaces. Any make or buy decision must start with reaching a consensus on key components, and proceed by considering the strategy for the whole product, the required extent of innovation, and the risk-reward portfolio for innovation.

6.1 Key Components

If one asks the directors of research, production, sales, and policy to rank the components used in their systems unit in the order of their importance, the result may be four very different lists. For the Company of the Future it is necessary to specify what 'important' means, and to reach a consensus on the ranking criteria and their relative influence. The best ranking criteria are the dependence of the final product's or system's performance on the particular component, its uniqueness, and its value added. Equally important is the availability of the component in the market. Both criteria can be combined in the Component Chart, indicated in Figure 1.9.

This chart is helpful for making rational make or buy decisions. Components of high strategic importance, low availability in the market, and therefore no competitive market price, are typical key components (A-components). They will be produced in-house. They are indispensable for the defence of the system against competition. The opposite is true for the C-components, which are readily available.

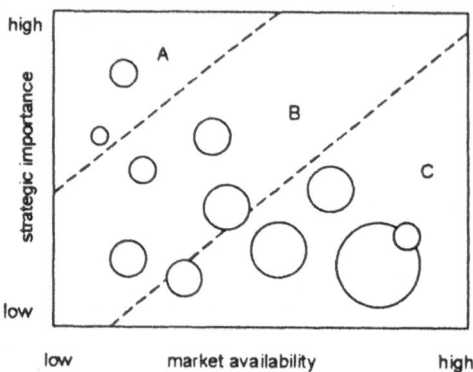

Fig. 1.9. The Component Chart.

B-components with intermediate availability and importance may be typical candidates for joint ventures: the market may not be large enough for competition, but the strategic importance is low enough to allow cooperation. The upper right hand corner is empty since high strategic importance and high availability in the market are mutually exclusive. The components can be placed on the chart together with their value (price), as determined by the management.

6.2 Product and Marketing Strategy

Independent of the type of component, there are the opportunities to innovate in the direction of low cost (C), high technical performance (A), or any intermediate trajectory (B). These alternatives are illustrated by Figure 1.10.

The disadvantage of strategy C is that it leads to a dead end; this strategy cannot be repeated with the same product. The advantage is that it can be combined with the final return on investment, *ie* the cash cow strategy. The advantages of strategy A are that it leaves all opportunities open, and allows the keeping of a technical lead. It is the most expensive alternative at the beginning, but in the long run, with the inclusion of the later products derived from the first, it is often the most economic alternative. It is evident that any decision on the best strategy requires close co-operation between sales, production and R&D. The Company of the Future will employ the optimum marketing strategy mix.

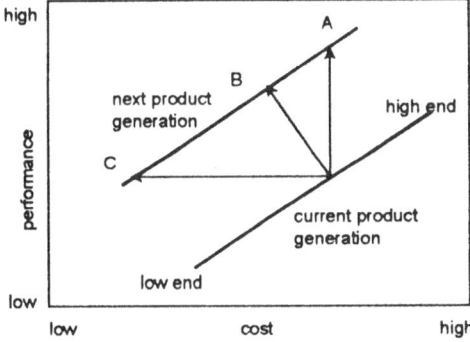

Fig. 1.10. Product and marketing strategy for components.

6.3 Continuous Accounting and Control

In a competitive market, the lifetime of one product design is limited by the emergence of a better design. Innovation is necessary just to keep the volume or to defend the market share. We are considering here products where R&D is substantial (as for microelectronics chips) in contrast to products where R&D is negligible compared to other innovative methods to defend market share (as in advertising for detergents).

For a single product without much competition, the textbook method is to compare the estimated costs with the estimated revenues discounted to the time of decision (present value). The decision is yes if the return on investment is high enough compared to other investment alternatives, unless entrepreneurial foresight overrides such decision rules. Before continuing, let it be clear that the latter is the force which keeps the stock market rising. Every insider knows that perfection in accounting and control has a remarkable potential for killing real innovation.

Unfortunately, single products without competition have become very rare in this world. In general we have a long sequence of overlapping product generations within one product line. Then the revenues of the current product generation must pay for the development of the following and sometimes even for next generation and so on, in order to avoid large fluctuations in the cash flow.

This general situation calls for a continuous accounting and control tool. In the best case it should present revenues and costs for each product generation as continuous functions over time in such a way that their overlapping sums add up to overall sales and cost curves which are as smooth and close to the desired levels as possible (convergence requirement). Continuous functions allowing also mutually independent adjustments of their heights (value), slopes (market speed of entry and exit), and shifts (generation succession time) would be particularly useful (independence requirement).

One set of functions fulfilling all these requirements are those used already to predict the markets of the Company of the Future. Equation 1.4 represents the overall sales, where Δa is the maximum sales volume per unit of time ($ per year or month etc.) for the whole product line, $\alpha\Delta a/4$ the steepest sales increase of the whole product line ($ per year or month etc.), and T the time where the product line reaches half its maximum sales volume. Since every S-curve is exponential for t << T, linear near t = T, and constant for t >> T, one can adjust the three parameters to fit any desired sales volume. The case of declining sales (if desired) just requires to reverse the sign of α. Cost accounting just requires to change the sign of the nominator.

As Figure 1.4 has already shown, the requirement of convergence with Equation 1.4 is automatically fulfilled by the set of Equation 1.8. There exists a converging set for any sales envelope a(t). τ is now the time where the individual product generation reaches half its maximum sales volume, and $\beta\Delta a/4$ is the steepest sales increase of the individual generation. Each curve like Equation 1.2 corresponds however to the sum of sales of its own and all future product generations. The sales of each product generation is therefore the difference between two successive curves. Only S-type curves have the property that the difference between two of them shifted in time converges for both ends simultaneously. This is why they are so suitable for the accounting of overlapping product generations. In this way the sales of all product generations add up automatically to overall sales and the same is of course true for all costs.

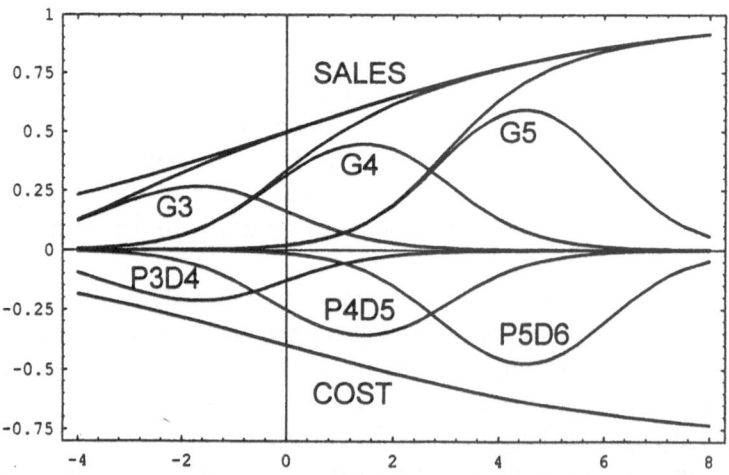

Fig. 1.11 Continuous accounting for overlapping product generations

In most cases the parameters are known. Otherwise it is very easy with a computer program like Mathematica to fit the parameters to the product line. Figure 1.11 shows an example for a chip product line with a generation succession time of 3 years, 80% overall cost of sales, nearly linear growth of sales, and 3 years market entry time for each generation. In this example the sales for each generation pay for its production cost and for the development cost of the next generation. If needed, discounting to present value can easily proceed by adjusting α and β.

6.4 Risk and Reward Portfolio

Large reward, low risk innovations have become very rare. Low reward, high risk innovations are to be avoided. The Company of the Future is therefore left with high reward high risk innovations (Type A), intermediate innovations (Type B), and low risk, low reward innovations (Type C). This portfolio is illustrated by Figure 1.12:

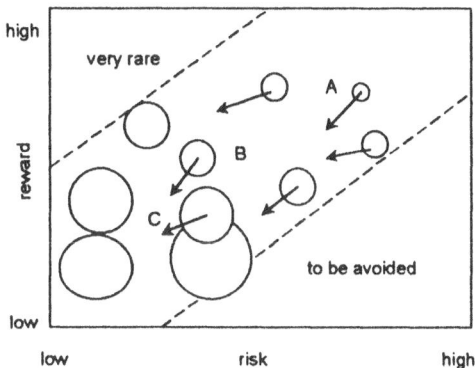

Fig. 1.12. Risk-reward portfolio of innovations.

For this portfolio, each business unit is required to assess its innovations (ideas, those in the process of being developed, and those already in the market) in terms of risk and reward. High and low ratings are assigned relative to internal experience and/or to competition. Categories for positioning in the portfolio are, for example, volume, market share, and added value for the reward, as well as development time, performance goals, and cost for the risk.

It is essential that there is agreement on the categories and the positioning of innovations in the chart. Otherwise innovation may reduce to gambling at one extreme or to money grubbing at the other.

Generally, a product will move down along the A → C diagonal of Figure 1.10, as it proceeds from the original idea to the cash cow. The innovation portfolio consequently needs continuous input. The distribution between Type A and Type B, the risk-reward mix, is an excellent monitor of the innovative strength of a company. It is one of its most valuable soft assets.

We used equivalent notations A, B, and C for Figures 1.8, 1.9, and 1.12. This allows to label components in a simple and effective way familiar from credit rating. A Triple A component or product e.g.

- is a key component with high strategic value and low availability in the market,
- is subject to the marketing strategy of performance improvement, and
- has a high risk high reward position in the innovation portfolio.

It is a straightforward exercise to assign notations to each of the products. When weighted with the value added per year, top management may obtain an objective rating of the balance of risks, the innovative strength, and the market value of different product lines, business units, and the whole company.

7 Creativity and Accountability

7.1 The Synthesis of Cultures

In Section 2 we saw that the phases of market pull and technology push are G7 history. For the Company of the Future's innovation the functions of sales, production, research, and service are all equally important. They must work in parallel. It is also essential to ensure that research and innovative ideas are not restricted to the traditional research function. Innovative ideas can and must come from every area of employment and from every function.

Research in the traditional sense owes its reputation to the amazing discoveries of the natural sciences and their technological use. These allowed the expansion of our productivity by orders of magnitude; but marketing research and software research have now become at least as important as these discoveries, even though they cannot claim to report to mother nature, the superior master. In most companies hardware, software, and marketing research are performed in different units. There is little co-operation at the working level. Communication of innovative ideas and results proceeds, if at all, *via* occasional management meetings or in special projects or task forces. For services, for example those which provide the systems for the information society, we do not even have a concept of how to do research for future business.

The Company of the Future will need direct co-operation at the working level between research from all functions. This is not as easy as it should be because our universities still cultivate the separation between the natural, engineering, computer, economic and social sciences to a far greater extent than is good for the realisation of human talent and is advantageous from an economic point of view.

A second factor which makes co-operation difficult is the creation in the 1980s of 'vertical' business structures. It was clearly necessary to overcome the inertia experienced when working in 'horizontally' structured organisations, but the other arrangement often leads to vertical frictional effects rather than smooth operations. The sales, production, and R&D functions tend to be regarded even more in serial order rather than as parallel functions of equal importance for the business. It follows that the early development of young specialists responsible for the innovative strength of the company across all corporate functions is a challenge of strategic importance for the Company of the Future. The responsibility for this can first be given to the R&D function. Later, a joint venture between sales, production and R&D might be a good alternative (see also Section 8.5).

7.2 Research for Services

After finance and sales, research, and production, the services are becoming the fourth pillar of industry. The main reasons for this have been stated before:

— The transition of the industrial society from the generation of new capital stock investment to the maintenance of investment. Industry is expanding into services to compensate for this decline in the mature G7 group of economies (see Section 3.2).
— The reduction of product cycle time, mainly through the impact of mircroelectronics and software. This discourages customers from buying large systems.
— The lack of capital and sometimes personnel of industrializing countries to buy and operate systems needed for fast economic development.

The development of the industrial society has been largely the result of successful hardware research. Marketing and software research has not matched this performance. In view of the growing importance of services, will service research lead to a new step forward for innovation?

In the G7 the fastest growing business areas are services, communication and information. There are no established concepts for research in its markets and products. Universities have not yet discovered this opportunity for their own innovation. Media companies must still recruit the most creative talents irrespective of their education, let them work in flexible teams, and just ask them to identify business opportunities.

The most successful recipe is the traditional sequence of ideas - hypothesis - controlled experiment - result - assessment for future action, known from hardware research. The need for experiments with uncertain outcomes is admittedly difficult for anyone to accept who has never experienced a real discovery or unexpected outcome from an experiment. There are large gaps between the experience of natural and computer scientists, not to mention market researchers. Research into new services has a large potential for a society where industrial goods increasingly derive from services. Service research requires real experiments with prototypes and customers. It is definitely not a discussion type of discipline. It takes real money, time, sensible supervisors, and protection from business fluctuations, as in hardware research.

7.3 The Human Element

The ingredients of creativity and innovation are unusual ideas, enthusiasm, and diligence. In general, these are not all strong or equally represented in any one person, that is only so for very creative people. Therefore it is necessary to form teams where each member has at least one ingredient as a prime quality.

Psychologists use a triangle with the expressions schizophrenic (unusual ideas), hysterical (enthusiasm), and pedantic (diligence) to describe the characters of people who excel in one of these ingredients. A good supervisor of creative teams is a person who is capable of assessing these qualities, picking the right characters, and making the work of the whole team successful.In contrast to this ideal, teams often conform far too strongly to only one point in the triangle. It seems also that our universities are producing less and less characters with originality.

We must make a blunt statement here: We can talk about innovation as much as we like, but if we do not accept unusual characters with non-standard modes of operation, we might as well forget about innovation. Without tension there is no force. A democratic committee is unlikely to produce an original idea or solve a real problem. We must learn again to live with inconvenient people.

7.4 Creativity and Remuneration

Really creative characters defy standard accounting practices. Standards are made for repetitive, reproductive work, measurable in quantity per unit of time. The best way to do justice to research and, to some extent also to sales, is to work with a base salary and a bonus system. The supervisors must be able to assess the uniqueness of the contribution to the innovation for a first bonus, and in case of an unexpected business impact for a second one.

Standard assessment forms are not suitable for use with innovative groups. It is necessary to develop management competence for assessing uniqueness. First level superiors of research groups are extremely valuable persons for any company and the best source for top management for the Company of the Future (see Section 8.3 below).

8 Role and Organization of R&D

8.1 The Size of R&D

Every company with an explicit strategy (see Section 4 above) needs research; companies without a strategy can forget about research as well. Research is a resource, an arm to catch opportunities, a consultant for decisions, and a source of new concepts and processes. This is just the set of four elements constituting our general strategy. Therefore the question of 'how much research is required' cannot be answered by saying 'as much as the strongest competitor'.

To a first approximation, we can look into the strategy and the efficiency of the strongest competitors and into their ratios of R&D to added value. Then it is necessary to correct this ratio for reporting differences and standards. Large differences are known, for example, for the cost of software production. In Germany they are included in R&D, in Japan in the cost of sales. The R&D officers know how to compare quantities and qualities of competition.

Secondly, it is necessary to consider R&D's integration into the company: How much research is performed in sales, service, production, subsidiaries, operations, or for acquisitions, mergers, and cultural change.

These questions are much more important than the distribution between central (corporate) and decentralised (divisional) research.

Thirdly, we require a breakdown according to the individual business, its product lines, and its market development (*status nascendi*, cash cow, declining, *etc*).

This discussion shows that a top-down approach including benchmarking with the competition may not give the best answer to the question of what is the right level of R&D. We propose to use in addition the 'bottom-up' method described in Section 6. Using the volume for innovation, the marketing strategy, the innovation portfolio, and the Value-Added Diagram of Section 5, each product line has direct control over the right quantity of R&D for itself. If the sum arrived at is close to the result obtained from the top-down approach, one can be satisfied.

8.2 The Distribution between Corporate and Divisional R&D

During the technology push period corporate or central research laboratories were naturally quite popular and well funded. As a consequence of decentralisation most of them became too small (under critical size) or disappeared altogether. Such excursions have little to do with effectiveness or efficiency, they are more or less a matter of fashion. Nevertheless there are clear guidelines which can be used for making the decision regarding whether or not to have a corporate research department, and for its size, and these depend on the nature of the business.

Corporate research departments make sense when

— the company strategy explicitly includes technical leadership
— top management stands united behind it,
— at least 50 per cent of the funding is by headquarters,
— the laboratory is productive with respect to producing ideas, inventions, and advice, for all groups, and
— the value added (see Sections 5.1 and 5.2) is positive.

These are necessary, but not sufficient conditions for corporate research. There are products and businesses with their own core technologies (Type I businesses), for example power plants or telecommunications. For companies consisting of only one of these types of businesses the question of a centralised or decentralised organisation does not exist. There are also products and businesses with overlapping, very broad range, or very new technologies (Type II businesses). These three factors are relevant remits for corporate research departments. Examples are businesses using a broad range of materials and processes such as medical technology, measurement and control technology, industrial automation, and transport. It would be too inefficient and ineffective to maintain several decentralised R&D laboratories for such a combination.

For very wide range companies, such as Hitachi and Siemens, which cover both types of businesses, corporate research centres may also include some of the Type I R&D.

The interface between corporate and divisional R&D is very flexible because there is no solid line to be drawn between the responsibilities of researchers and product developers. Innovation requires overlapping responsibilities. It is clear, however, that it makes no sense to have a central laboratory which has a negligible size compared with the largest divisional laboratories. The decision to have corporate research implies that it must be kept strong in a competitive sense and independent in its internal management (see Section 8.4).

8.3 R&D Supervision

There are three types of supervision and these depend on the kind of research performed: *Peer management* suits basic research of the discovery type where each researcher is more or less on his own. Area 11 of AT&T's Bell Laboratories and IBM Yorktown Heights exemplified this type of soft supervision *par excellence*.

Project management suits the generation of specified, expected results; the team is fully committed to its task for a given time.

R&D management is the art to mix groups for innovation, combining individual talents for originality and effectiveness, as described in Section 7.3.

The last type requires really capable supervisors. If they are weak, their group's style will degenerate into one of the other types, which are the stable minima of R&D management. The peer supervisor's role reduces to hiring the best researchers with little effort to unite forces for innovation. The project manager's function is to get the plan fulfilled in the specified time with little chance to follow up on unexpected spin- offs, which are the origins of really new products.

After employees have worked for five years under the conditions of project management they will find it very difficult to enter the other two types of research and be successful again. The development of leadership talent is only really possible in the last type.

8.4 Core Technology Focus

The number and variety of research projects to be carried out by R&D laboratories can be so large that these laboratories lose their identity. Any business unit has the right to decide whether or not it can accept or refuse an order according to whether it fits into its business strategy. Similarly, research laboratories must have their own identity. Otherwise they will not be able to combine efficiency, effectiveness, and excellence.

It is therefore in the interest of the company that research laboratories define their fields of competence. Naturally, they must satisfy the major needs of the company's next generations of products. But for a large company, checking with business units may yield several hundred technologies if every research team wants its speciality to be included. Sometimes, reduction by an order of magnitude is required. The relevant questions for this reduction are:

— Which technologies can be provided externally through co-operation with suppliers or academia, because they are not critical or easy to reproduce ?
— Which technologies are too special, and needed only for one business unit?
— Which technologies are mature, and should be standard practice?

The residue consists of endogeneous, growing technologies needed for many business units. These we call the core technologies of the company. Large bandwidth electrical engineering companies may have 20 to 40 core technologies. These must be continuously updated in order to minimise the cost of change.

In order to be over the critical size, there are generally 10 professionals per research group and one to five groups per core technology, depending on the scope of the business.

8.5 Innovation Centres

When a company has decided to streamline and focus its R&D, in order to meet the needs of the business, into core technologies, it must also do something with respect to long-range planning. Assuming that the organisation of R&D parallels the core technologies (the logical thing to do), this long range planning has to be organised by separate groups. We may call them innovation or foresight centres.

It is important that innovation centres do not compete with the core technology groups. The innovation centres create ideas for future innovation. They get a few per cent of the total R&D budget for outsourcing market studies, for temporary think tanks, or for consultants, but they do not perform R&D themselves. Consequently, their staff is recruited temporarily from the most creative sales, production, and R&D departments throughout the whole company. After one to three years experience in planning, these people are very valuable not only in their original department, but also in the entire company. This is particularly true for the managers of innovation centres. The topics for the innovation centres do not correspond to those for the existing businesses or divisions because new business opportunities are not usually found in the core of existing businesses, nor in cash cow or profit centres. They appear at the interfaces between different business fields. One way to achieve this is to use society's general needs instead of business fields to name the centres, *eg* health, safety, energy, transport, information etc.

The innovation centres produce road maps for products, technologies and business fields. They operate like think tanks, *ie* with postponed judgement/evaluation for the new ideas. These centres go as far as developing rudimentary business plans. If a responsible suitable business unit does not yet exist, the business plan must be fully developed, including the Value-Added Diagram for the product (see Section 5 above).

The innovation centres are the board's insurance policy for providing an innovative future beyond the existing businesses. The closer the business units are hooked into their market, the more important are the innovation centres (see also Section 3in Chapter V).

9 Management of Knowledge and Integration of Concepts

9.1 Inventory of Tools and Management of Change

Since industry is in a transitional state between the technology-push period and the next, still unknown period (see Figure 1.2), the ability to anticipate and to lead through change will continue to be a great challenge and asset. Innovation by the entire enterprise will be required with respect to its strategy, organisation and processes in any of its functions. So far, we have considered new tools which can be of most assistance in anticipating and leading a company through change. This section will complete this set by considering business communication methods.

Most of the classical management tools will of course remain. Some of them are listed by their key word in Table 9.1:

Table 1.2. Classical tools of production management and control

Production	Financial Control
Fixed Assets	Return on Investments (ROI)
Stock	Cash Flow
Economies of Scale	Profit
Productivity	Liquidity
Quality	Business Value

Every new tool must either be integrated into the existing set or replace one or several existing tools. It is recommended to periodically check the whole inventory of tools in use across all business functions, to relate them to each other, and to streamline the set for effectiveness and efficiency.

The Value-Added Diagram proposed in Section 5.1 is an excellent instrument for organising such an inventory for better integration of tools. Its fractional nature facilitates and enforces constructive co-ordination between the purchasing, R&D, manufacturing, sales, servicing, control, and strategy functions at any corporate level.

In this context a warning is appropriate concerning central control. There is the danger that control tries to be too good in the sense that it wants to lump everything together. A company which tries to integrate business units which are entirely different in their time horizons, customer attitudes, and vertical structures with the same set of control tools may find itself very soon on the bad side of perfection. Before a new inventory is made the question must be raised and answered by all divisions of how many different sets will be needed for enough freedom for each business unit to develop its abilities to the full.

During periods of steady, strong growth and long product cycles, ie during the technology-push period, the traditional tools and concepts were developed to very high degrees of perfection. However, perfection can turn out to be a problem when times change to unsteady or weak growth and to short product cycles. Such times require the employment of flexible tools and concepts which are, as has been stated before, easy to learn and easy to use, but should not be just fashionable or too simple.

The deeper the traditional tools are embedded into a corporate culture, the higher is the resistance to adapt to a changing environment. But the economic development (Section 4) and the ending of the East-West conflict, which was a convenient umbrella for stability in every respect, required fast changes.

The consequence of this were strong moves (sometimes over-reactions) to streamline business and to simplify business cultures, operations and organisations. One of the most successful, the core-business concept, will be discussed next. Simpler concepts, such as decentralisation, produced not always the expected success. When this happened, the next management in charge often felt the need to decentralise further. This may have facilitated mergers and acquisitions because top management had also more liberty to move. On the other hand it may be difficult to find any corporate goodwill beyond the sum of the goodwill of individual units. The former is the justification for a company's existence.

The *raison d'etre* of profit centres is to generate profit, not synergy. They intentionally acquire short term return on investment attitudes and avoid any long term charge to the balance sheet. Long term strategies are even considered adversaries of good performance. The profit centre is often too small for a competitive effort. Its management loses at first the experience and then the necessary confidence in its ability to tackle new, but particularly rewarding risks. In order to prevent irreversible decay, headquarters must either enforce innovation activities at profit centre level with the same vigour as it enforces profit, or it must provide for them at corporate level including the chain of start ups businesses. Evaluating both alternatives, we predict for the Company of the Future a return to classical entrepreneurship (see Chapter V).

9.2 The Core Business Concept and Management of Knowledge

The core business concept allows to streamline a business and to avoid the inherent problems of profit centres. The concept is to match core competences in technology, production, and marketing for core businesses with full responsibility for their operations. The companies represented by the industrial authors of this book have introduced this concept quite early. The selection rule is to concentrate on businesses which achieve a sufficiently strong market and technology position. Above this, the selection process considers

— corporate hygiene: the degree of correlation between the businesses, their 'distance' from the company's expressed mission, the distribution of unit size.
— competitive strength: it is easier to achieve economies of scale and a good market share by focusing on fewer but potent businesses.
— return on investment: the investment and profit horizon.

Once a core business structure is achieved, it is of the utmost importance to keep it moving. This refers to each business as well as to the whole set. New core businesses must be opened and old ones closed. A static portfolio of core businesses must be avoided. The concepts represented in this chapter are particularly selected and developed to suit that purpose.

An important feature of the core business concept is that it attracts top professionals in marketing, production, R&D, or finance/control. The 'General Manager' is a concept viable only for department stores. Professional knowledge is a real asset as it appreciates in value in contrast to equipment, which depreciates. The corporate goodwill is proportional to the corporate distribution of this professional knowledge.

Professional meetings across core businesses are not a luxury. They are absolutely necessary. Beyond that internal professional computer links may be helpful if secure and focussed to few, important knowledge areas. But a warning is in order, because what computer people promise does not always materialise. Four levels should be distinguished:

— *data* are just pieces of information where unlimited access is the prime issue
— *information* is a selection of *data* with a meaning to the holder
— *knowledge* is a selected *combination* of information with potential for action
— *leadership* is the ability to take the *initiative* and responsibility for action

With decreasing usefulness, computers can support professionals down to the knowledge level, but leadership and tacit knowledge are fortunately not accessible to computers.

9.3 Soft Assets

All changes described in the preceding Sections lead to the prediction that soft assets will dominate the goodwill of the Company of the Future. This is not trivial because tax systems and social networks are still based on hard assets such as added value, real estate, plant and equipment (capitalisation). The fact that some tax revenues are declining in an unexpected way is not only due to the migration and consolidation of industry but is also the result of industry's transfer into intangible assets.

Traditionally, the value of a company is determined by its fixed assets, its annual sales (multiplied by a factor depending on the type of business), and goodwill which allows adjustment for the reputation and other special values of the company. In the future, the value of a company will be determined essentially by its soft assets. We will have to develop yardsticks for measuring them. The most important items which will constitute the goodwill of the Company of the Future are indicated in Table 1.3. To assess one's own performance with respect to the items in this list is a useful exercise, in particular before mergers and acquisitions.

Table 1.3. Soft assets to be developed by the Company of the Future

---

Competence of Employees: Qualification; training; understanding of strategy.
Corporate Culture: Strategy and concepts; vertical and horizontal communication.
Information: Patents; learning curves (archives); competition; public relations.
Marketing: Customer, supplier, and component portfolio; image and market share.
Topology: Corporate structure; ownership; alliances; global networks.
Provision for Future Success: New markets and innovations in process; regional distribution.

---

10 Communication and Change

10.1 The Basic Asymmetry

The long period of technology push, economic growth and peace among the G7 nations brought about a complacent stability to enterprises. It is not surprising that structural unrest started in the US and migrated finally to Japan. The US started the information age, Japan has excelled at manufacturing excellence. As already stated, the management of change will continue to be one of the most important skills for the Company of the Future.

One fundamental problem with the management of change is the military history of command and report in hierarchical structures. Thus, bottom-up reporting is a well trained skill throughout one's career. Top-down reporting skill is not so commonly acquired by experience. What results is usually just giving orders. This asymmetry is at the core of problems with the quality of internal communication.

Since public relations (external communications) is in most cases headquarter's responsibility, we have the same problem there. It cannot be eliminated just by the 'order' to do away with it, because it is a deeply engraved cultural matter. The problem will not be resolved by a reduction of hierarchical levels either, because this would aggravate the asymmetry.

Generally a change of corporate features requires a revision of corporate communication - bottom up, top down and horizontal. Such an opportunity should not be missed to overhaul and improve corporate communications. We can and should learn from nature which had millions of years to develop high performance communication systems for the survival of genetic information.

10.2 The Example of Nature

The cortex is capable of processing only 100 bits per second (order of magnitude). At the peripheral 'working level' sensory input, dynamic output and local feedback add up to a level of the order of 1 million bits per second. The human communication system is capable of four orders of magnitude compression (bottom-up information) and expansion (top-down information) of the data flow. It is a balanced communication system with respect to the bottom-up and top-down. A company with 100,000 employees and 10 board members has an equivalent task.

Nature developed five hierarchical levels to master this task: The interface with the outside world, the connections at the peripheral level, the spinal cord, the cerebellum, and the cortex. Between each level there is roughly an order of magnitude compression and expansion of data. Obviously nature did not maintain any architecture (which it may have experimented with) of a higher or much lower 'span of control'. It seems that the error rate and cost of complexity in the communication system are minimised this way.

There is absolutely no justification for installing particularly lavish or lean hierarchies in corporate structures, and there is too much at stake for leaving a decision to fashion. Nature opted for approximately 1:10, but the most important lesson we can learn from nature is the bottom up - top down symmetry. This requires well architectured sub-routines for top-down expansion of information. The messages differ at each level not only quantitatively, they must be qualitatively different.

The quality of the top-down process is the dominant part in added value of management. Therefore, innovations in this field will be very rewarding for the Company of the Future. At the present time we can only point out that there is a large need for improvement, and the solution will not be as simple as in the case of horizontal communication. There a considerable improvement can be achieved if we learn to talk with each other and stop talking about one another.

11 Conclusions and Recommendations

*Economic growth follows very general laws which scale according to the skill of the economy and the company, respectively. They allow to predict for the first time the structural evolution of future markets from very few fundamental economic parameters which are constants since 1850. The bulk of growth follows a catch-up process with a slowly moving, innovation limited state of the art.

*The skill is embedded in the relevant knowledge of professionals which appreciates together with the procedural relevant knowledge, and in the relevant knowledge embedded in the infrastructure, which depreciates.

*The purpose of corporate strategy is to defy competition by organising the selection and renewal of relevant knowledge. This constitutes the competence and systematic order of the company. A general strategy focuses on the resources, opportunities, goals and processes of the company. Tactics are a liability and only necessary when the corporate strategy fails.

*The Company of the Future will acquire an inventory of management tools which is balanced between R&D, production, sales, and financial control. A basic set of new tools is proposed in this chapter. The central and integrating tool is the Value-Added Diagram.

*The role of R&D is stressed. An effective production function for R&D is developed for the first time by using the information contained in the Value-Added Diagram.

*While the G7 are in transition to service societies, the traditional industrial markets will experience a six-fold increase within the next two generations due to the skill of the Asia-Oceanian region. Unemployment will be the main source of trouble, not the limited resources of this world. The unemployment in fast recovery countries like Germany and Japan is quantitatively caused by the dynamics of their development which put three times the pressure on their educational and employment systems as compared to the gradually moving US economy. The problem is purely structural and not subject to any supply and demand policies, since their GDP per capita has reached the state of the art level.

*Soft assets will dominate the goodwill of the Company of the Future. Since Universities have not yet discovered that the world has changed more in the last two generations than in the last two centuries, top level education must be done increasingly in house. Here the Japanese tradition will be extended. With respect to other traditions we must anticipate social innovations of the caliber of the last two generation's technical innovations.

*We hope that by developing the tangible, practical approach described this chapter, readers will be able to formulate the best strategy for their Company of the Future.

References

1. A. Smith, 'An Inquiry into the Nature and Causes of the Wealth of Nations', 1776, reprinted by Oxford University Press, 1993, ISBN 0-19-281796-5
2. H. G. Danielmeyer, 'The Development of the Industrial Society' *Eur Rev.,* 1997, **5**, 371 - 381
3. H. G. Danielmeyer, to be published
4. C. von Clausewitz, 'Vom Kriege', ed. W. Pickert and W.R. van Schramm, Rowholt, ISBN 3-499-45138-7
5. J. A. Klein *et al,* R&D Management 1996, **26**, 5 - 15

Chapter 2 A
Research in the Company of the Future

Klaus Brockhoff

In this chapter we focus on research and long term development. The elasticity concept, derived from marketing and production functions, is found to be applicable to the relationships between Research and Development (R&D) and specific businesses within the company such as the chemical business. Technology leaders expect that in the long term a reduction in R will lead to a much larger increase in D, and that an increase in R leads to a much larger increase in sales than would be the case from the same increase in D. This contrasts with a strongly negative correlation between interest rates and the industrial research budget. The co-operation between science and industry clusters around the European 'hands on' policy, the Japanese 'active distributor' policy, and the low performers 'hermit' behaviour. One of our strongest recommendations is the use of project-based research funding.

1   Some Difficult Questions

Namehei Odaira, the founder of Hitachi and its research laboratories, re-marked in a calligraphy of 1930: "Though we cannot live 100 years, we should be concerned about 1000 years". This implies that management should take a long term view and approach goals steadily. Management cannot, however, take this literally as this would imply an almost unlimited time horizon for the planning of its activities. It would also imply the as-signment of very large sums of research money to exploring opportunities for the future. It is therefore best to diverge from this advice, as it makes better economic sense to focus the planning operation much more strictly. This would then imply that much smaller sums would need to be invested in research.

Even when planning for more limited time horizons, we can keep longer term objectives in perspective, and thus retain a certain degree of resis-tance to short term changes. In this sense, K. Matsushita provided an inter-esting example in a speech delivered to his employees in 1932. He sketched objectives for his firm and for the electrical industry in general over 250 years, but then broke down this time period until he eventually arrived at a plan for the eight years immediately ahead. This established a culture of buffering short-term fluctuations by offering long-term perspec-tive research.

On the one hand one might ask whether *any* funds should be allocated to research in a private company. It could be argued that a company should leave research to others, namely institutions like universities and research institutes, which are publicly funded. The results from such research are usually available to anyone, and should be obtainable if they are consid-ered valuable for the company. This may have the appearance of saving money and increasing the competitive position of the firm. The resources originally earmarked for research could beneficially be transferred for use by development departments in business units, where effective use is more readily visible.

On the other hand, some firms argue that their own research is the key to their success. If we again look at a Japanese company, Nichia Chemical Industries, which is a medium-sized organization located in Anan, we find that it recently developed a prototype semiconducting laser that emits blue light, a phenomenon which was not previously possible. The emergence of this product was made possible *via* 'niche research' based on previous experience with indium-gallium light diodes. The company expected its sales to expand ten fold between 1995 and 1996 as a result of these find-ings. Furthermore, expansion into other markets is foreseen if additional development work should prove to be successful [1]Nakahara from Sumitomo and Takeda from Hitachi both emphasize the importance of in-house research taking place within their companies (see Chapters IV and V). This is partly because in-house company research creates useful knowledge barriers between the company and its competitors, enabling it to maintain project leadership [2].

In a recent survey of German companies, 75% of the economically weaker firms complained about erratic objectives for R&D, whilst only 30% of the stronger firms voice the same complaint [3].[1] The history of DuPont can be used to demonstrate the swings of a pendulum between the relative strengths of its research funding as opposed to its development operations, and this in part reflects impatience with the ability of researchers to repeat past successes within a relatively short period of time [4]. Such swings of the pendulum can also result from a search for an optimum organizational structure or optimum funding levels, where 'hard facts' upon which to base decisions are lacking. Recent trends which favour decentralization do not favour research, as decentralized units tend to adopt more short term planning horizons. In Chapter VI it is demonstrated how research funding can be optimized using an approach which is derived from what a company will require in the future. Here we address the same topic on the basis of estimates of the relative potential of research in progress.

It is interesting that recent trends towards cutting back on research expenditure seem to be only a repeat performance of earlier and similar developments [5-7].[2] The director of an aerospace laboratory recalled that "For a time, decentralization proved to be an effective organizational solution to the problems caused by diversification and growth, but by the late 1950s there was a growing tendency within the divisions towards parochialism and interdivisional competition leading to redundancy and a concentration on short term problems. Each division had its own research staff...." [8].

Fluctuating shares of research expenditure relative to total R&D expenditure within countries raise additional concerns. In the early 1980s it was said that " basic science and intellectual capital seem certain to play a more fundamental role in relation to socio-ecomomic development than hitherto. Recognizing this, high-technology companies have been channeling increased resources into basic research, especially in areas where fundamental scientific breakthroughs are needed if emerging generic technologies are to realize their full commercial potential" [9]. It is ironic that a book of this kind on research foresight should be so much at odds with

---

[1] From a study of 98 firms conducted by Arthur D Little, Inc.
[2] For instance, considerable interest in this question arose in the late 1950s

what has happened recently in the US, *viz* "As a result of the restructuring of many companies, the levels of their efforts in basic research have been attenuated. Their dependence on university research has increased. Industry has increased its support for university research and entered into many hundreds of collaborative arrangements" [10]. By the middle of the 1990s even research centres with high reputations in basic research in the US and Europe, and which can point to a phenomenal track record of research breakthroughs that have changed the world, have come under pressure to undertake more applied research. One of the most prominent examples of this is the reorganization of the Bell Laboratories of AT&T [11].

These inconsistent policies lead to further questions: 'How can such rapid shifts of behaviour be explained?', 'How should one react to the behaviour observed?', and 'Do companies behave differently in competing countries?'.

The last question is of particular interest with respect to the phenomenal growth of corporate research in Japan. It has been observed that "Unlike the United States, where basic research flourishes in academia with Federal support, Japan lacks a strong public infrastructure for fundamental research. Stepping into this gap are Japan's major corporations, many of which have come to see the building of their own basic research as a necessary step in anticipating new technologies with commercial potential. Since 1985, just about every major electronics corporation in Japan has opened independent, and somewhat freewheeling, facilities in the suburbs of Tokyo which are devoted to fundamental studies in materials, electronics, and, oddly enough, biology" [13]. In Table 2.1 we present some illustrative data on major private research laboratories in the Japanese electronics industry. It shows that this industry was comparatively late to engage in research.

Table 2.1. Data for major basic research laboratories in the Japanese electronics industry (Source : Reference 12)

Laboratory	Date Opened	Number of Researchers	Annual Budget (mil $)	Fields of Research
Canon Research Center	1985	250	n.a.	Optoelectronics, advanced materials, biotechnology
Hitachi Advanced Research Laboratory	1985	114	41	Electron beam physics, software, molecular biology
NTT Basic Research Laboratories	1985	200	25	Quantum optics, computer science, materials
NEC Fundamental Research Laboratories	1989	100	35	Advanced materials, atomic manipulation, neurobiology

Thus, the lack of a basic research tradition in Japan has been used to justify a growing share of private research expenditure in that country, to be used as a strategic weapon against competitors [9]. This strategic weapon needed to be developed when the imitation strategy suffered from its own success.But even in Japan, some firms, like Hitachi, have chosen to integrate parts of their research laboratories into business functions in order to tie their research closer to business needs.

This leads to another question: 'Could the relevance and accessibility of university research play a role in explaining differences over time and between countries?'. An answer to this question is attempted at the end of this chapter.

It is difficult to draw conclusions from casual observations. Statistical information may provide a more valid picture of the situation in research in industrial firms. Consequentially, let us have a look at what happens in firms in major industrialized countries.

2 Characteristics of Research

2.1 Problems of Definition

An answer to the questions on whether and how much companies should invest to support research is much more difficult than is indicated by the few arguments mentioned above. In defence of in-house research, management may point to the relatively low cost of these activities. In fact, on average only a small share of the total research and development expenditure is devoted to research (see Figure 2.1). It is interesting to observe that this share is developing very differently in advanced industrial nations. It is stable and low in the US, it is rising in Japan, and in Germany it shows substantial fluctuations over time. In Germany, we observe a pro-cyclical relationship between the growth of the gross national product in the same year and two years ago and the share of industrial research. This could reflect rather rigid, standardized, and past-orientated budgeting procedures. If so, this is not a healthy basis for the generation of contributions from research.

Certainly, it is dangerous to argue with averages of research shares, as they are subject to more or less variance. Thus, leading companies in the electrical and electronics industries spent about 10 to 12% of their sales on research and development. These median values have had a variation between under 5% to more than 20% during recent years. In 16 interviews with European firms in this industry a median share of 9% was reported; in

20 Japanese firms we have noticed a median share of 19%. Differences in definitions of the term notwithstanding, the percentage shares represent large sums of money that - if saved - seem to raise the return on sales by one percentage point at least in the short term. Competitive pressure and impatient stockholders may exert pressure to reduce what appears to some of them as an expenditure without a return, and to some others as luxurious. The chapters in this book on research and development in the Company of the Future share the view that such short-term considerations are dangerous not only for competitive reasons but also because this reduces the potential for the long-term future.

Research is a carefully chosen combination of resources that is aimed at generating new knowledge. In this respect, it may not be distinguished from development. But while development is clearly aimed at immediately using the new knowledge in new or improved products or production processes, this is not expected of pure research. Where such a use of new knowledge is visualized rather broadly and not in very specific terms, one is used to speaking of applied research. In this respect, differences between research and development can be recognized. The OECD builds its definitions of research and development on this observation. They are used in its member countries for preparing statistical information (OECD, 1992).

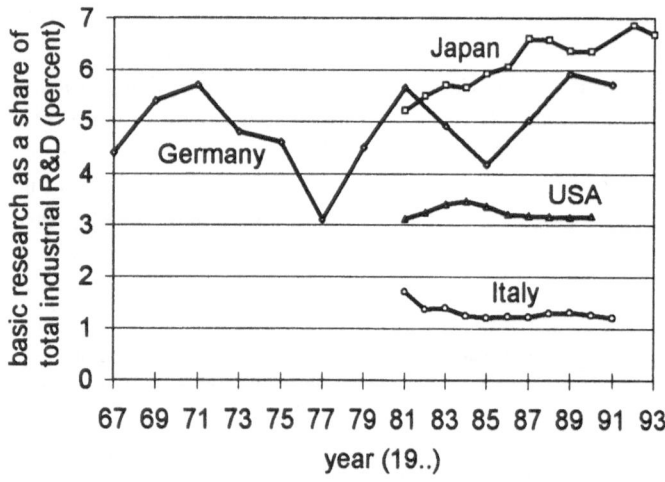

Fig. 2.1. Basic Research as a Share of Industrial R&D Expenditure in Germany, Italy, Japan and the US, 1967-1993 (Sources : References 14 and 15)

In practice, these definitions may not be entirely clear and they give rise to problems of demarcation. They also reflect different research or development cultures and this is manifest in the way that results from these activities are presented. Thus it can be shown that relatively more publications and patents result from research in Germany as compared with Japan [16]. It is argued that structural differences in property rights systems may have induced these differences. Such differences can have profound impacts on the way that research and development activities are coordinated or integrated [17].

The difficulties of definition have initiated a wide range of suggestions for more precisely defined terms. However, these problems cannot be totally avoided this way. For instance, funding and guidance by top management, a long time horizon, and an intent to support basic corporate objectives are considered as additional characteristics of corporate research [18]. Unfortunately, they can also become relevant objectives for development.

From the perspective of university research which is no longer limited to pure basic research, it is suggested that additional categories for a classification of research activities are needed, such as 'applied basic research' [19][3] or, from the perspective of industrial research, *'north star research'* (see Chapter IV). If the apparent need for such changes in definitions signals changes in the character of research performed in universities, it would indeed tie in with the observation of an increased interest by industry in collaborative research with universities, as was mentioned above. The effect of a broader definition can be gained from comparing Figure 2.2 with Figure 2.1. The share of basic and applied research on total industrial R&D expenditure is eight times higher in the US and four to five times higher in Japan than the share of basic research in the respective nations. The same applies within companies.

---

[3] The recent suggestions of this author were already critically discussed some 30 years ago [7]

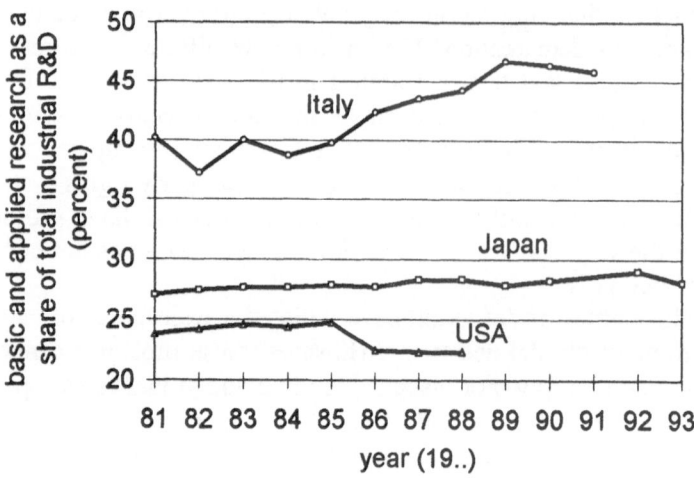

Fig. 2.2. Basic and Applied Industrial Research as a Share of Industrial R&D Expenditures in Italy, Japan and the US, 1981-1993 (Source: reference 14)

As an illustration at the company level (and as an additional indication of the growth of Japanese research activities that can be gathered from referring to Table 2.1 for comparison), let us consider some organizational aspects of Hitachi's R&D. This company spends 10.1% of its sales on R&D (1993), which amounts to $ 3.7 billion. 26% of this sum is spent in nine corporate research laboratories. Since February 1995, two of these laboratories have been assigned to business units, and by so-doing the share for the corporate research laboratories was decreased to 17% of the total R&D expenditure.

2.2 Relevance and Transferability of Research Results

To defend investment in privately supported research activities, a considerable number of arguments need to be used:

— the relevance and the transferability of research results,
— the specific risk of research,
— the specific benefits from research.

New knowledge generates economic value to the individual firm only if the firm can effectively exclude other companies from using the same knowledge. In theory, published research results can be used by an unlimited number of interested individuals or firms at no additional cost once they learn about these results. Rivals can be excluded from such free rider behaviour only if the results can be legally protected or if they are kept secret or if the cost of transferring the results is high enough to exclude others from their use. However, patenting is only very rarely available to protect research results, and keeping them secret constrains the derivation of economic benefits from the new knowledge[4]. The cost of transfer depends not only on one's own activities, but also on those of the potential users of the new knowledge. Thus exclusion of rivals is not a perfect option.

Consequently, it is often thought that universities or other public research institutions "are the proper places for the pursuit of 'pure' science, and for the establishment of laboratories, etc., devoted to it" [20]. Industry has only limited opportunities to influence their course of inquiry. In some countries, such as in Germany, freedom of research is a constitutional right. Influence can be exerted only indirectly through funding or moral persuasion. From industry's point of view, direct funding is a second best solution, given the above arguments on the relevance of the benefits from the new knowledge. Moral persuasion can be offered in general terms[5], or it may take the special form of suggestions for research topics. For example, the Association of the German Electrical Industries has produced a catalogue of such topics [21]. Clearly, there is neither guarantee that moral persuasion has the desired effects nor that the fields of greatest interest to industry are supported by public money. A stimulation of certain types of university research could also be achieved by presenting fascinating first results of new phenomena. "It is clear that this sort of strategy cannot be pursued with second-rate staff", is the conclusion drawn from Bell Telephone Laboratories' behaviour in the case of its successful stimulation of research into materials problems after the discovery of the transistor effect [8].

What could make things worse, is that industry cannot control the quality of publicly funded research. This may require contacts to the research establishment well beyond national borders. It goes without saying that this is often very difficult, particularly if foreigners are granted only limited access to other nation's research institutions in addition to the hurdles

---

[4]   Some researchers observe new organizational developments in innovation processes that lead to more patent protection of research results. This would initiate a stronger need for close interaction between science and technology for individual firms (Foray 1995:90)

[5]   Marshall (1927, p. 100: "...studies will loose nothing, and the world may gain much, by keeping in touch with some of the industries, whose methods maybe increased by increased knowledge..." For a more recent example, see the reports on the publicly funded research centres in Germany [21, 24].

resulting from differences of language, culture, etc. Countries that feel deprived of their basic research results react by establishing institutional barriers to easy knowledge outflow [22]. Economically speaking, the cost of establishing access to the research results is higher for foreigners than for nationals.

In reality, even knowledge that is documented and available to others cannot be transferred without cost. This knowledge has to be identified, it needs to be absorbed by the internal organization, and it needs to be used. Identification and absorption require some in-house research capacity. The specific character of research that provides this capacity has been called 'absorptive capacity' [23].

Use of knowledge can be achieved only if the 'not-invented-here-syndrome' does not stand in its way. It can be shown that increasing the cost of transferring new knowledge into a company reduces the use of external knowledge, but it increases the use of internal knowledge up to a certain level, because this broadens the basis for the internal integration of the external knowledge. Increasing strength of the not-invented-here-syndrome reduces the use of both internal and external new knowledge [25].

2.3 Risks of Research

It is generally thought that research is more risky than development [26]. This does not mean that the probability of completing a research project successfully is very different from that of successfully completing a development project. However, given the very loose relationship between the knowledge derived from research and its use in products or processes as compared with the much tighter coupling to development knowledge, the probability of achieving a return on the investment for a particular research project may be lower than for an equal investment in a particular development project.

Returning to company in-house research it should be kept in mind that planning procedures require the determination in advance as to whether the support of general corporate objectives can be achieved by such activities. This requires the demonstration of a link between present inputs and future results. To prove this point, a reconstruction of the contributions of new knowledge to product or process innovation is often attempted in hindsight. This is indeed very fascinating. A particularly interesting example of such studies is in a report prepared for the National Science Foundation on the antecedents in science of revolutionary new products, such as magnetic ferrites, the video tape recorder, the electron microscope, the oral contraceptive, and matrix isolation [27]. Similarly, the Naval Research Advisory Committee initiated a report that outlined the beneficial activities of the physical scientist I.I. Rabi and his group of basic researchers to the US Navy [28]. In more general terms, Alfred Marshall observed some 70 years ago: "History shows that almost every scientific discovery, which has ultimately revolutionized industrial methods, has been made in the pursuit of knowledge for its own sake, without having a direct aim of any particular practical advantage" [20]. Consequently, the General Electric central research laboratory estimates what the company could have foregone if it had not been there, and uses this result as one of many yardsticks for research evaluation [29].

It is a different question whether such advances and contributions could be forecast and planned. High uncertainty and long lead times "make for a poor fit with most planning systems", and managers lack the capability to "target research clearly on a specific product or ... on a specific field of business" [18].

Even favourable experiences with research within one company do not indicate future successes and thus cannot be projected into the future. This is exemplified very well by the DuPont nylon case. After Carother's success of finding nylon in his research laboratory, the company was supporting research and looking out for "new nylons" but these did not appear on command [4]. When impatience won an upper hand, development was again supported to a greater extent than research. The company's support for research in relation to development seems to follow a pendulum movement that is derived from the most recent experience on where new knowledge originates. A similar problem was faced by Howard Schneiderman, Monsanto's senior vice president for research and development. His belief that "out of great science will come unique insights that will lead to product opportunity" was countered by strong arguments that "all research should be parceled out to operating divisions: this would have created market focus at the expense of central research capability. Corporate Research had as yet produced no biotechnology products and the ones under development ... were several years away from commercialization" [30].

The relatively *high* risks of research would be welcome in getting research support, if most managers were risk-seeking. Experimental research as well as observations of managerial behaviour indicate that particularly if a company is profitable, most managers will make the decisions which have the lowest overall risk [31]. It should be noted that risk-aversion does not mean that managers would not invest in risky prospects. It only means that managers prefer an investment with a certain return somewhat smaller than the expected value of uncertain returns of an alternative investment that offers the possibility of earning more and the risk of earning less than the certain return. According to a report in *Business Week* [32] the contact-lens manufacturer Bausch & Lomb appears to have lost its technological and economic lead at the beginning of the 1980's because it put too much emphasis on less risky product improvements during the times of affluence.

2.4 Specific Benefits from Research

Generating income from new knowledge which can be translated into the design of new products and new processes is but one of the specific benefits that can be expected from research. Given the specific character of research and its high risk it may not even be the only benefit that companies could expect to derive from this activity. This argument may come as a surprise. However, as far back as December 18, 1926 Director Stine of DuPont sent a memorandum to the executive committee of his company that spelled out more reasons for supporting research: "First was the scientific prestige or advertising value to be gained through the presentation and publishing of papers. Second, interesting scientific research would improve morale and make the recruiting of PhD chemists easier. Third, the results of DuPont's pure science work could be used to barter for information about research in other institutions. Fourth, pure science work might give rise to practical applications. Although Stine himself believed that applications would inevitably be produced, he felt that this proposal was totally justified in any case by the first three reasons" [4].

The broad spectrum of reasons may explain why most companies that perform research appear to enjoy higher growth rates and stronger productivity increases than other firms in the same industries. While the statistical analyses that support this view [33-35] could be criticized in many respects [36], the underlying result does not seem to vanish.

Two important questions emerge from this view. First, it would be interesting to learn whether the enumeration of reasons for research is exhaustive or not. Secondly, how does corporate planning respond to such a diversity of reasons, particularly as most of them point to benefits that are hard to evaluate, to say the least. We shall deal with these questions subsequently.

3 Reasons for Research

From Stine's memorandum it is clear that research performs more than one function. For example, Nokia AB describes ten guidelines for Nokia Central Research:

"Explore and develop:

1. new technologies and their innovative applications and solutions for products,
2. new system and product concepts based on new or emerging technologies, including those falling between or outside the scope of current business units,
3. international patent rights and inputs to key standardization activities,
4. methods, tools and process know-how for enhancing the speed, productivity and manageability of the business units' products / processes,
5. key 'next best' alternatives and 'second opinions'.
6. Offer business units' product development sub-contracting and consultancy by providing means for technology transfer, leverage competencies in critical product development tasks, being a vehicle for interaction that builds mutual understanding and trust.
7. Provide an environment for the exploration of new business opportunities (including those falling outside the scope of current business units).
8. Present insight and learning on new technologies for the business units.
9. Provide skilled personnel to business units R&D-units.
10. Manage Nokia's interface to international R&D co-operation".

This is a very demanding list, and it leads to the question as to what degree it could be considered to be generic. Therefore, attempts were made to identify these functions more systematically. This led to the ten functions presented in Figure 2.3.

		New strategic direc-tions	Supporting of existing businesses
Innovation by	Improving and strengthening un-derstanding of technologies in use	Corporate diversifica-tion to new applications and markets	Product and process im-provements
	Discovering and developing new technologies	Corporate diversifica-tion to entirely new businesses	New processes for es-tablished products
Corporate service by	Intelligence	Windows on new sci-ence and technology	Assessing threats and opportunities
	Human resources	Recruiting new kinds of skills	Recruiting talented people with high poten-tial
	Technology transfer	Identifying acquisition candidates with needed technological expertise	From corporate research to operations

Fig. 2.3. Functions of corporate research. (Source: Reference 18)

On the one hand, it is interesting to note that some functions, and parti-cularly those that provide corporate services, do not follow from the cha-racteristics of research as identified above. The question remains, whether even more functions might be identified. On the other hand, some other functions that follow from the characteristics outlined above remain un-mentioned. Furthermore, no information is available as to the importance of these functions, except for the scattered evidence collected from a few interviews.

Interviews with German R&D managers have elicited a list of 12 func-tions that have substantial overlap with those listed in Figure 2.3, and they point to some new functions as well. Presenting these to a sample of 26 research managers from large German firms it was possible to rate the rele-vance of these functions. Results are presented in Table 2.2.

Table 2.2. Functions of Research in German Companies (scale values from 0 = does not apply at all to 6 = completely correct). (Source: Reference 37)

Our own research ...	Mean	Std. dev.
... is a source of innovation (1)	4.62	1.60
... helps us to understand the technology of our existing products or processes better (2)	4.27	1.40
... helps us to improve existing products and processes (3)	4.15	1.46
... improves relationships with universities and other research institutions (4)	3.85	1.67
... increases our alertness vis-a-vis new developments in science (5)	3.85	1.71
... simplifies the application of research results from universities or other research institutions (6)	3.73	1.61
... simplifies the evaluation of research results from universities or other research institutions (7)	3.62	1.98
... simplifies the acquisition of scientific know how and methods (8)	3.23	1.70
... improves our image (9)	2.96	1.87
... supports the hiring of new research personnel (10)	2.38	1.81
... is a side-product of our applied research and development (11)	1.96	1.97
... is pursued because it gets public funding (12)	1.00	1.33

The high levels of consent for the first three functions indicated in Table 2.2, with low standard deviations, indicate that research managers consider the innovation-supporting functions of research as more relevant than the service-related functions. Within this group, functions that support technology transfer are given higher relevance scores than those facilitating human resource management, image improvements or attracting public funding.

The impressions given by Table 2.2 could have been biased by high correlations among some functions. Consequently, we have tried to identify groups of functions that are largely independent of each other[6]. Three factors could be identified:

— (A) *Research as a source of innovation* (related to the functions (1) and - negatively - to (11)); this is meant to assure long-term competitive advantages;

---

[6] This was achieved by factor analyses, using the Eigenvalue criterion for the selection of factors and Cromach's Alpha as an indicator of their coherence.

- **(B)** *Research as a source of improvements* (related to the functions
  (2) and (3)); this is meant to maintain short-term competitiveness;
- **(C)** *Research as a service to the company* (related to all other functions) [37].

Companies from the electrical and electronics industries attribute higher
relevance to Factor A than to Factor B, which is followed by Factor C.
Even the service-related factor is relevant, but it is hardly used as an argument to support research activities, even though some of its important ingredients were mentioned in Stine's memorandum to the Du Pont directors
(see above).

Table 2.3. Actual and ideal performance of research functions as seen by research managers in Europe and Japan (N=38; scale values 0 to 6 as in Table 2.2)

Functions	Actual		Ideal		Sig
	Mean	Std.dev.	Mean	Std.dev.	
Provide a knowledge base for future development efforts - prepare for future products or processes	4.4	1.1	5.3	0.8	**
Provide information on emerging technologies to development	4.4	1.0	5.1	1.1	**
Provide information on emerging technologies to top decision makers	3.9	1.4	5.1	1.3	**
Observe competitive actions	3.5	1.2	4.7	1.1	**
Provide a knowledge base for easier implementation of external research results	3.5	1.2	4.2	1.1	**
Provide attractiveness to external research personnel	3.3	1.5	3.9	1.6	n.s.
Support the image of a company that contributes to technological progress	3.3	1.4	3.8	1.6	n.s.
Ease training of development staff in new skills and techniques	3.2	1.4	3.8	1.4	*
Socialize new staff members with the company culture for later transfer to other departments	2.7	1.3	3.5	1.5	**

Source: Interviews by J. Bardenhewer, 'Company of the Future Project', Kiel 1995 (see
Appendix II). Std.d.= Standard deviation; Sig.= Level of significance, with n.s. = not significant, ** = significant at a 99%-level * = significant at a 95%-level.

Evaluations of the present relevance of research functions may be different from their perceived ideal levels. In yet another interview study we asked 17 research directors of major companies in the electrical and electronics industries in Europe (with the majority from Germany) and 21 in Japan to evaluate the present relevance of research functions together with ideal levels for the same functions. European and Japanese responses differ significantly with respect to one item only: The ability of research to provide a knowledge base for future development efforts, which then leads to new products or processes. In the ideal case, European managers assign higher ratings to this variable than do Japanese research managers. With respect to the interpretation given to factor (B) above, one may say that European managers are relatively more interested in maintaining short-term competitiveness. Because of this high degree of agreement, we have decided not to differentiate the responses by the continent of origin. The results of these overall evaluations are given in Table 2.3.

All ideal states are rated higher than the actual states. Neglecting tied values, the rank orders of the responses are identical. Managers want to give each function more weight, but without changing their present rank orders. Interviewees were not forced to make trade-offs in their responses. The smallest differences in weights are observed for those research functions that support image-building and that increase attractiveness to external researchers. These differences are not significant. All other differences are significant.

The largest difference is observed with respect to information for top decision makers. This could reflect the observation that the top management of many companies has developed a critical view with respect to research in the company during the recent periods when extreme competitive pressure has been experienced by their companies. Research managers seem to think that a better service to the top management could improve its evaluation of internal research. It could reflect also a growing recognition of the fact that one technology could affect many of the traditional industries. This becomes apparent from the statistics reproduced in Table 2.4.

Table 2.4. The relevance of scientific fields to technology in the US (Source: *Reference 38)*

Field of science	Number of industries (out of 130) ranking scientific field at high relevance (5 to 7 on a 7-point scale) with respect to its	
	Skills	Knowledge
Materials Science	99	29
Computer Science	79	34
Chemistry	74	19
Metallurgy	60	21
Physics	44	4
Applied Maths & Oper.Res.	32	16
Mathematics	30	5
Agricultural Science	16	17
Biology	14	12
Medical Science	8	7
Geology	4	0

The differences in the observations of actual and ideal performance of research functions can be summarized by factor analysis. This leads to three mutually independent directions for improvement:

- (D) *Supporting development efforts.* This is achieved by providing information on emerging technologies and a knowledge base. It involves the two most important variables in Table 2.3.
- (E) *Supporting external visibility of the company.* Supporting the company image, providing attractiveness for external researchers, and providing a knowledge base for the easy implementation of external research results contribute to this factor.
- (F) *Servicing.* The third factor draws on two different components. On the one hand it comprises the socializing of new staff members and the training of development staff. On the other hand it relates to technological competitor intelligence analysis and the provision of an information base on emerging technologies to top management.

Factor (D) indicates a support for innovation similar to the Factors (A) and (B) that were identified earlier. Factors (E) and (F) point at different aspects of services that may be provided by research and that are similar to the Factor (C) that was found above. These factors indicate quite clearly that management is well aware of the necessary downstream-coupling of academic research, corporate research, and development as a necessary condition for achieving returns on their own research. This factor was widely neglected in the economics literature until very recently [39].

Although the functions evaluated in Table 2.3 are not fully identical with those in Table 2.2, we can see some common, underlying features. This is further supported by the similarity of the factors that could be identified. In the following we shall try to integrate such factors into a concept of 'potentials' that could be provided by research.

4 Research as a Source of Future Potentials

From the foregoing data it becomes clear that research managers agree that research performs not just one but many functions within the company, and that most of these functions need to be strengthened. This is particularly true for the so-called service-related functions.

The functions are not performed for their own sake. Rather, they help to develop *potentials* that could be used to strengthen competitiveness. Drawing on the characteristics of research as well as on the empirical studies in Section 3, we can partition these potentialities into primary and secondary potentials. The following primary potentials are presented in the order of an idealized flow of a research process:

(a) *Identification potential*. This enables the company to identify technological knowledge that can become relevant for its present or future products and processes. In short, this may be called relevance for entrepreneurial use. The importance of this potential has already been exemplified by the data presented in Table 2.4. In a case study a research director has remarked: "Many modern developments are so specialized that they can only be interpreted by someone who has a working familiarity in a new field. Thus, it may sometimes be of value to support a small research effort in order to keep an eye on the new field" [8]. The head of Hitachi's R&D, Yasutsugu Takeda, says in his contribution to this project: "In order to discover the seeds and ideas for industrial innovation outside the company, especially in academic societies, the company should retain selected top-level researchers, whose activities are highly regarded in the world" (see Chapter IV).

(b) *Absorptive potential*. This potential describes the ability to absorb external technological knowledge for possible entrepreneurial use. In other words, the potential enables or facilitates the transfer of new knowledge from external sources into the company. A strong not-invented-here syndrome reduces this potential. As was observed by one of our interviewees: "My experience is that in order to exploit external research more effectively some internal research in the relevant field is required. Keeping up with science in the library, as a secondary activity for a researcher, is ineffective. I expect these trends to intensify." This is a necessary condition for information exchange with other scientists. While this is common understanding, it has also been established empirically for the field of development [40]. There is no compelling reason to assume that the same behavioural conditions could not be transferred to the exchange of information on research. In earlier years, this was described as the active participation in an 'invisible college' [7, 41].

(c) *Creative potential.* If new external technological knowledge has been identified and transferred into the company, researchers need to make good use of it. This ability is described by the creative potential. Again, a strong not-invented-here-syndrome is a barrier to the creative potential. The creative potential may be used to support new business or existing business: "Such changes of emphasis are cyclic and are a response to prevailing business climate. For example, in the late seventies and early eighties, the emphasis ... was on generating ideas for new business. Now it is almost entirely on bringing in new science and technology in support of existing business", reports an interviewee.

(d) *Interpretive potential.* This potential describes the ability to evaluate existing technologies and to understand them better. It is not uncommon that some techniques are known, but the principles that explain them are not known. Were these principles known, the techniques could be employed more reliably and perhaps on a much broader basis. Take for example ceramics. Pottery was practiced thousands of years ago and continuously improved through learning-by-doing. A much better understanding and a higher learning rate could be achieved by research into the chemical and physical principles of ceramics, but this approach has been employed only in the last few decades.

(e) *Internal transfer potential.* Few research results can be applied immediately to new products or new processes. Very often they have to be adopted by more or less elaborate development processes. The transfer potential describes the ability of research to create favourable, necessary conditions for a knowledge transfer into development groups. It is a tragedy for researchers if they perceive that their offering valuable results to other groups in the company is passed unnoticed or cannot be accepted because of a lack of funds, the surprise that they create, or other reasons [8]. Certainly, unless appropriate conditions exist in development groups, effective transfers will not be achieved.

The internal transfer potential exists not only between different stages of a research or development process. It is also concerned in the transfer of knowledge within one stage but between successive periods of time as well. This is addressed in a very impressive way by Nonaka and Takeuchi when talking about knowledge conversion within a company [42]. They use the distinction between personal, context-specific, and therefore hard to formalize and to communicate 'tacit knowledge', and 'explicit knowledge' that is codified and transmittable in formal, systematic language, samples or documents. There are four modes of knowledge conversion: From explicit knowledge to explicit knowledge, which is called 'combination; from explicit knowledge to tacit knowledge, which is called 'internalization'; from tacit knowledge to explicit knowledge, which is the mode of 'externalization'; and finally from tacit knowledge to tacit knowledge, which the authors call 'socialization'. This is described as "a process of sharing experiences and thereby creating tacit knowledge such as shared mental models and technical skills... The key to acquiring tacit knowledge is experience..." [42]. The examples given involve solving particularly difficult problems. We assume that the transfer from tacit knowledge to tacit knowledge is an important activity in basic research, particularly as technologies that may be demonstrated and that need to be documented for instance for patenting are not yet available. Thus, this form of socialization can be of particular importance for the advancement of research processes.

Some companies explicitly address research potentials beyond the creative potential. For instance, supplementary to what was identified above, some Japanese companies have strengthened the training, planning, and administrative capabilities of their R&D departments. Let us look at two examples. Sumitomo Electric Industries has a 'Development Planning Department' that performs decision analysis for the evaluation of R&D projects, an 'Administrative Services Department' that teaches young managers technology management, and a 'Techno-Research Centre' that engages in technological intelligence analyses. Hitachi's 'R&D Promotion Office' provides technological intelligence analyses, helps in creating inter-corporate projects, and supports planning and business assessment tasks.

Two additional examples may be added from British industry. At BG plc 11% of the total R&D expenditure is earmarked for 'strategic research'. This includes 'technology foresight', 'technology acquisition', and 'maintenance of skills and competences' in addition to those activities that are process or product related. The activities mentioned match some of the support functions that were identified above. Another example is given by Rolls Royce Associates, Inc (Derby), where 'maintenance and development of skills'-contracts are entered into with major supporters of this laboratory. These support the identification potential, the creative potential, and the absorptive potential of their researchers. However, in none of these cases are all of the potentials used.

The primary or core potentials support what we choose to call secondary or peripheral potentials. From the empirical investigations we identify three peripheral potentials:

(f) *Image enhancement.* By this we mean an ability to create or to support a cor-porate image favorable to the competitive position. Companies that support publishing new research results or that demonstrate and advertise their ability to govern high technology in their field may look for image enhancement.

(g) *Human resource attractiveness.* For some researchers, the perceived working conditions and the day-to-day problems of the industrial production or development departments do not appear to be highly attractive. Industrial research laboratories may offer conditions that are more to their liking, and at the same time personnel attracted to the research laboratories become familiar with the company culture. This may facilitate their transfer to one of the other departments at a later stage that could not have been achieved otherwise. As was observed in our interviews: "Research has traditionally been a recruiting point for staff with technical background throughout the company. We used to maintain a flow of 5 to 10% per year into other areas of the business. With cutbacks throughout the company, this flow has almost dried up. This is in my view a serious problem, because research needs a continuing inflow of new blood." Here we observe that the potential is of substantial importance to research itself, and not only to downstream activities.

(h) *Support.* Research may offer the potential to win public funding more easily. While this may not have been of great importance in the past, except for those companies that were highly involved in defence business (see Figure 2.4), it could gain additional importance in the future. National and supranational institutions support co-operative research in the so-called 'pre-competitive' areas. Spreading risks, saving cost, and developing network abilities could be objectives that need to be met. This is very often achieved by research rather than by development work. Most often, winning support means not letting others get these funds. This could be an important argument in a highly competitive environment as it improves the relative competitive position even if the support won is only consumed rather than being invested.

Primary potentials and secondary potentials together define research potentials of a company. Figure 2.5 summarizes the view that is developed here.

From this presentation it is evident that looking for contributions to new product or new process developments from research is myopic. Research builds more potentials that need to be recognized and accepted by the top management of a company. For this purpose it is helpful to negotiate a 'master research plan', a 'research charter' or a 'mission statement' for the research group among its members as well as between its management and the top management of a company. The document should define "a shared understanding of the mission that research is expected to fulfil" [8, 18]. It should name the themes or fields that the laboratory intends to cover, and the potentials that it will try to support or to build. Such a document is the basis for choosing the strategic directions of research and the proposed projects.

On this basis, the potentials need to be addressed in planning. In Section 5 below, we demonstrate how this could be done.

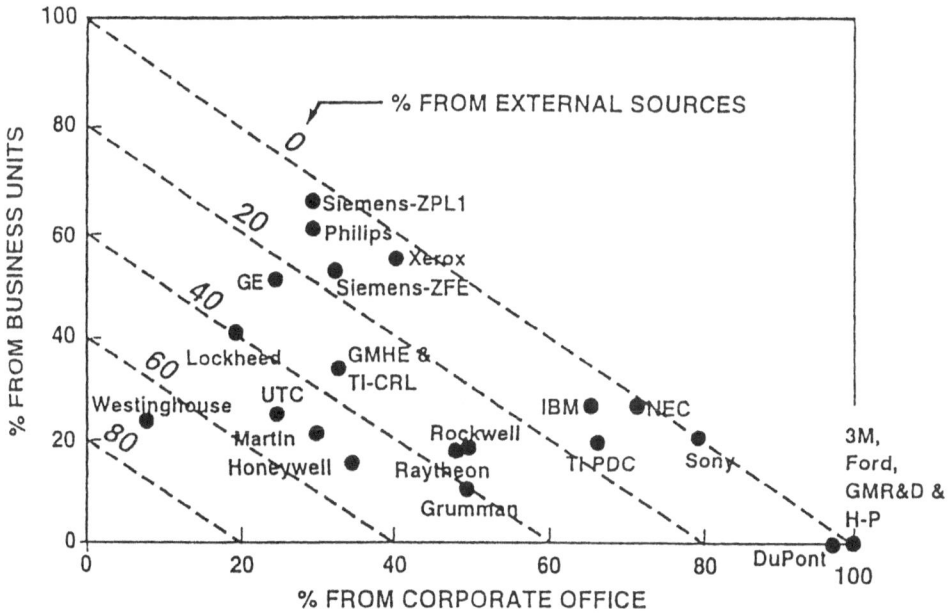

Fig. 2.4. Distribution of Sources of R&D Funds (Source : Reference 43)

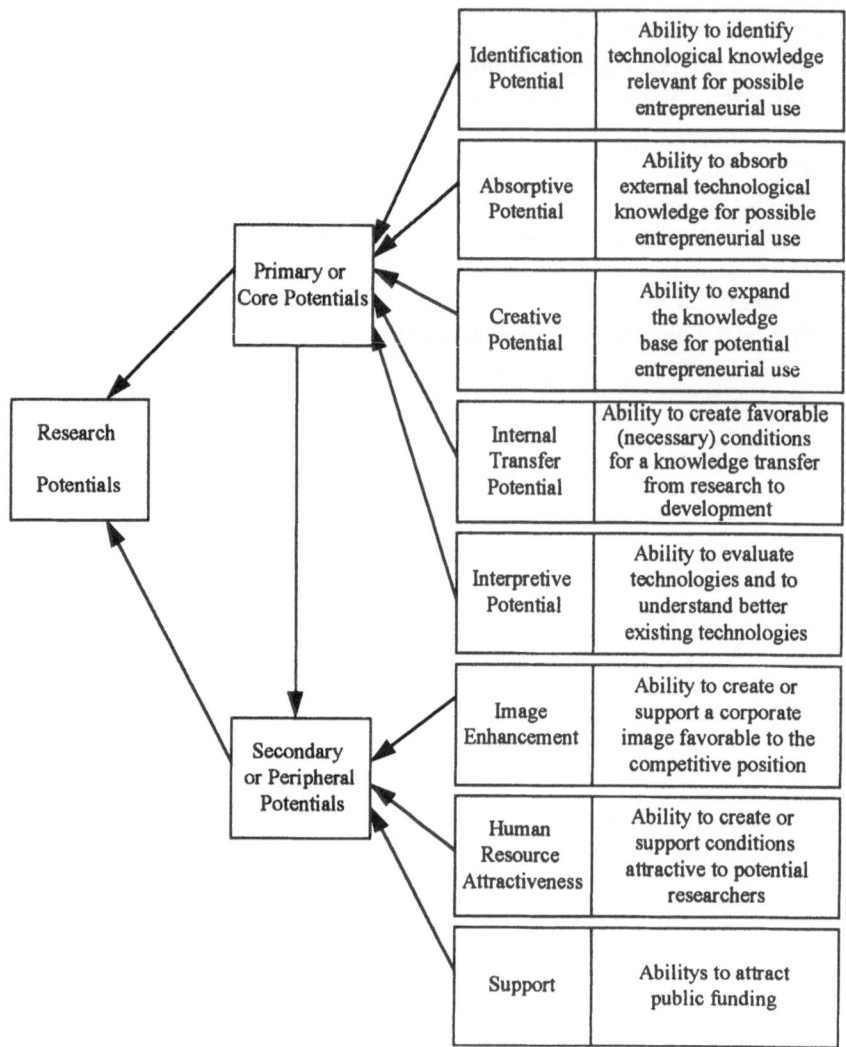

Fig. 2.5. The system of company research potentials

5   Research Potentials and Project Funding Decisions

At first, we shall restrict ourselves to the project level of research. Research projects should not be selected arbitrarily. Companies have to find out which projects are the more important ones for their future development and which are of little importance. Takeda, who is responsible for Hitachi's R&D activities, calls research that is performed in this sense '*north star research*' and contrasts this with 'blue sky research' (see Chapter IV). The north star and the blue sky are both far away from the earth, but only the former gives a definite direction. The blue sky would only signal that research goals are different from where we stand now but give no specific direction.

Whilst the concept of research potentials may be of interest for its own sake, it can also be used to plan the funding of research in a bottom-up approach. Empirical research indicates that this type of funding is quite common in some countries. The funding procedures for central laboratories of 53 large German corporations could be identified. These laboratories are engaged in research, although not exclusively. Four different funding rules could be identified:

— (a) Funding from company overhead.
— (b) Funding by taxing business units, not related to the level of support demanded by these units.
— (c) Funding by taxing business units related to the level of their support.
— (d) Funding by selling projects to business units.

It can be concluded from Table 2.5 that none of these strategies was applied in a pure sense. In this respect, funding by rules (b) and (d) is of particular interest. The primary funding source is substituted to a substantial extent by other sources. Research draws on 'subsidies' from some kind of overheads in the case of (d), and from project related payments in the case of (b). The highest proportion of research expenditure is reported for strategy (b), followed by strategies (d), (a) and (c). It should be remarked that the funding by rule (d) does not prevent performing research at a substantial level.

Funding in individual companies may deviate from the statistical data given in Table 2.5. At Daimler Benz 7.4% of the total R&D budget was earmarked for long-term 'precautionary' research, where equal shares have to come from the holding and the business units. It is known that this 'forces' some business units to spend on this type of research, while their management might prefer the use of the funds to boost their short-term earnings. During a one-day retreat with the whole board of directors the research plan is discussed. It had four sources of funds: (1) Funds for long-term projects suggested by central research, discussed with the business units, with priorities determined during the retreat; (2) Funds for medium-term projects suggested by business units, discussed with central research, and priorities determined by the research committee; (3) Funds for projects entirely determined by the initiative of business units; (4) Contributions to funds from outside sources that need to be integrated with internal funding. This provides an example of mixed approaches to the funding problem that is still almost entirely project driven.

Table 2.5. Funding procedures in central R&D laboratories of large German companies (% of funds coming from different sources) (Source : Reference 44)

Sources of funds	Group (a)	Group (b)	Group (c)	Group (d)
Company overhead	89.7	1.1	0.0	10.2
Taxing business units, unrelated to level of support	0.6	68.0	0.0	10.6
Taxing business units related to level of support	0.3	7.8	87.0	10.1
Funding on project basis	3.2	15.1	8.2	62.2
External funds	6.2	8.0	4.8	6.9
Relative number of units	30.8	17.3	9.6	42.3

The funding rules indicated in Table 2.5 appear to have weaknesses. Funding not related to performance is more frequent than other types of funding. Funding from overhead or taxing business units is correlated with non-favourable perceptions of the effectiveness or efficiency of central R&D laboratories. Other funding procedures could be more preferable.

We suggest the adoption of strictly project-based funding procedures that relate to all potentials that could be generated by the research. Furthermore, the time-horizon for funding decisions should be project-specific and not standardized to the usual one-year budgeting rules. This would imply that projects could be very long-term as well as short-term. This point needs to be stressed. A project funding mechanism along these lines was reportedly used by Philips but did not have this flexibility and had to be abandoned. Using this method, each project could be funded from more than one source. The share that the different sources contribute to a project would depend on the contributions of the project to the research potentials of the company.

Such shares are shown in Figure 2.6 for some artificially created sample projects.

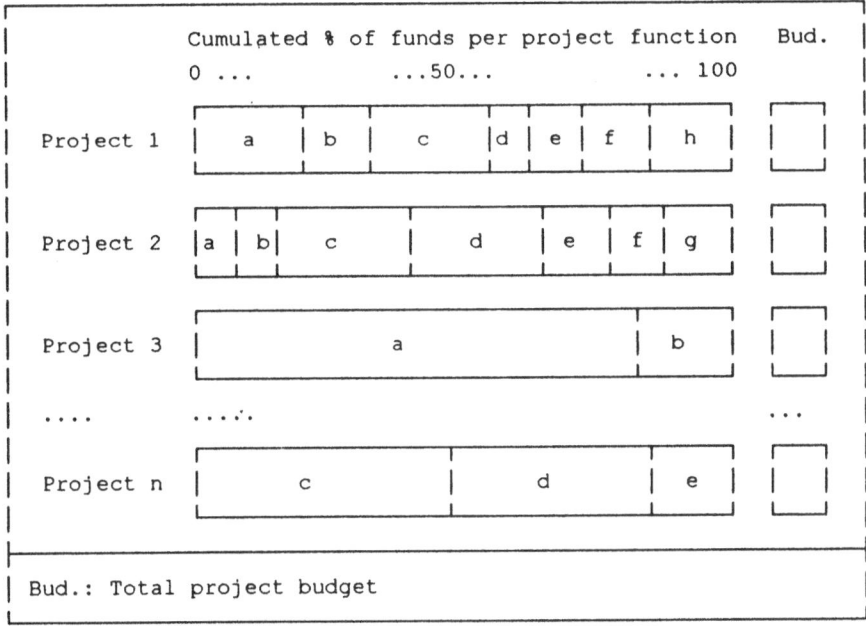

Fig. 2.6. Example for funding by projects and potentials

The project objectives, the total project budget and its time frame need to be planned as in all project management approaches. In addition, the shares of funds that need to be allocated to the different potentials that could be derived from the project objectives need to be estimated. By considering all research functions and potentials systematically, projects are given a much broader funding base. The funding is not narrowed down to the view that specific product areas need to be supported by new technologies.

Let us now consider the sample project. We begin with project n. We recognize a relatively high potential to expand the knowledge base (c) and to create favourable conditions for transfer (d). A small contribution of the project is expected from a better understanding of the presently used techniques (e). Funding for such a project could most probably be secured from one or more of the business units.

Project 3 suggests an increase in the identification and absorptive potentials of research. This addresses interests that are not likely to be shared by the management of existing business units, but rather by the top management of the company. This could be a long-term investigation of some technology that is considered relevant for the future development of the company, even beyond the presently defined technologies of different business units. Top management could fund such a project on a multi-year basis. This type of project can only attract funds if it falls within the charter or the mission statement of the laboratory. This exemplifies the interaction between this document and project selection decisions.

Project 1 addresses almost all potentials, and in particular it could be used to generate public funding. This may be due to the substantial possibilities in generating identification potential and absorbtive potential. Project 2 appears to be more company specific and product related, and is therefore unable to generate public support. It should attract the interest of at least one of the business units.

Figure 2.7 presents information in functionally-based project funding form that was developed on the basis of the ideas that were presented earlier. In its rows it lists the potential project functions. At first, it should be indicated whether such functions are likely to be supported by the respective project or not. Then, possible sponsors for such functions should be identified in the further columns. After that, funding shares for the respective functions and their possible sponsors can be entered, possibly as a result of negotiations between the project initiator and possible sponsors. The example shown is taken from a large number of test-runs for the form that were applied within co-operating companies. In some of the cases, the funding of completed projects could be replicated by the use of the form, whilst in some other cases the form initiated discussion on possible other sources for project funding than the ones being used hitherto. This suggests that the form may not only be used in the project planning phase, but also as a controlling device in later stages of project development, adding information on the divergence of actual from planned funding data.

Project funding is not made easier by this approach. However, correlating project contributions with their research potentials helps at the same time to identify potential project 'customers'. Research management and researchers should ask which potentials any one project supports, and as a result, which 'customers' should be approached for funding. Funding decisions should not be standardized with respect to the period of time for which funds are allocated. According to the project characteristics, long-term funding agreements and short-term funding agreements may co-exist at the same time. Top management may initiate projects which aim at identifying potentially important technologies by collaborating with universities and scanning the technological environment. Also, it may provide seed funds that help to integrate new researchers into the company. Alternatively, business units or their development departments may use the research group like a contract research institution. For example, Shell Internationale Research Maatschapij (SIRM) is considered "as contractor to other (operating) companies".[10]

Potentials/Functions of research	Contribution to these potentials?	% of Bgt.	Possible sponsors for the project budget													
			Internal sponsors (Top Mgmt., Business Units, Dev. Labs, Other Central Depts., ...)										External sponsors			
			Corporate		BU		DevLab		Central Lab		....		Government		....	
			1.000 hfl	% of Bgt.	1.000 hfl	% of Bgt.	1.000 hfl	% of Bgt.	1.000 hfl	% of Bgt.	1.000 hfl	% of Bgt.	1.000 hfl	% of Bgt.	1.000 hfl	% of Bgt.
Identification of external technological knowledge	o yes o no	10	314,0	30	523,3	50	104,7	10					104,7	10		
Absorption of external technological knowledge	o yes o no	10	314,0	30	523,3	50	104,7	10					104,7	10		
Creation of a broader knowledge base (new products/processes)	o yes o no	30					2512,1	80	628,0	20						
Creation of favorable conditions for transfer to development	o yes o no	20			1256,0	60	418,7	20					418,7	20		
Evaluation and better understanding of existing technologies	o yes o no	20					1674,7	80	418,7	20						
Improvement of image	o yes o no	10	418,7	40	628,0	60										
Improvement of attractiveness for new personnel	o yes o no	-														
Attraction of outside funding	o yes o no	-														
....	o yes o no	-														
Sum (Shares in %)	must add up to 100%			10%		20%		46%		10%				6%		
Sum (1.000 hfl)	10467		1046,7		2930,8		4814,8		1046,7				628,0			

Fig. 2.7. Project-Funding Form

The research department should help to evaluate presently used technologies or to develop creative ideas for future entrepreneurial use. This could involve projects performed by small groups in short time intervals.

Thus, project funding is tied closely to the needs of internal customers, and research management should be forced to identify these needs if it wants to sustain or to grow its research capacity.

The project budgeting procedures sketched above need organizational support. For example, the relationships between a central research laboratory and the business units used by Nokia are indicated in Figure 2.8. The scheme is made effective using 'informal technological relationships', and this policy is strongly supported by the management.

The approach described does not require the existence of a central research laboratory. For instance, Finmeccanica does not have a central research unit for historical reasons. Individual laboratories are run as centers of excellence for certain technologies. They identify three types of projects:

— Type A: Preliminary research (long term, highly innovative, high risk)
— Type B: Finalized research (mid term, innovative, medium risk)
— Type C: Development (near term, slightly innovative, low risk).

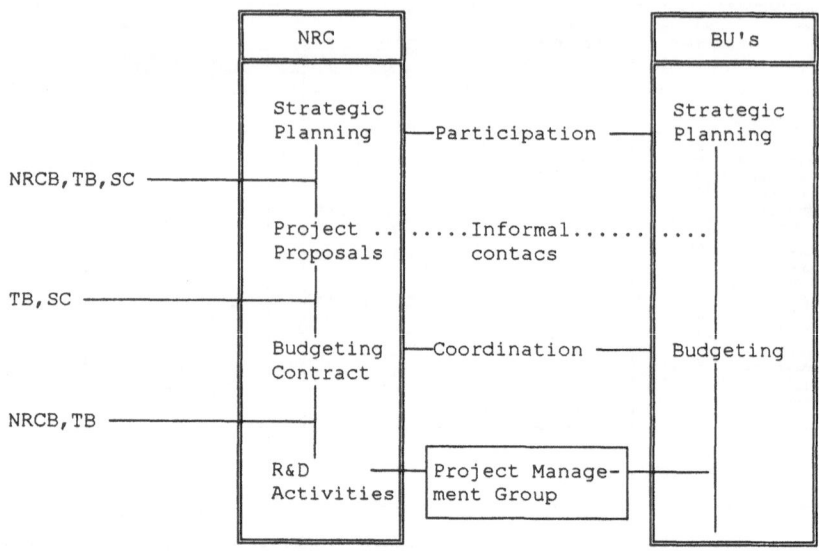

Fig. 2.8. Interdependencies between Nokia Central Research (NCR), top management and the business units (BU's). NRCB = Nokia Research Center Board, composed of CEO, top management representatives from Business units, top business units' R&D management. TB = Nokia Technical Board composed of top management representatives from Business units, top business units' R&D management. SC = Technical Area Steering Committee, composed of top and middle business units' R&D management.

In 1994, the expenditure on Type A and Type B projects was 32% of the Type C projects or 24% of the total R&D expenditure. The coordination among Type A and Type B projects is achieved by a Management of Technology Group that provides a *Technology Matrix* (where 860 technologies are related to 140 business units, including all the strengths and weaknesses of performing the technologies), *Technology Reports* (which assess internal know-how against the state of the art in relevant technologies), and a *Technology Plan*. Managerial processes have been established for coordination among the centers of excellence on the basis of the documents available for planning (see Figure 2.9). Type A and Type B projects may involve outside partners, and they may generate support from, for example, the European Union. Again, multi-functional and multi-sponsored projects are possible. However, when a central research unit is absent more coordination work is necessary.

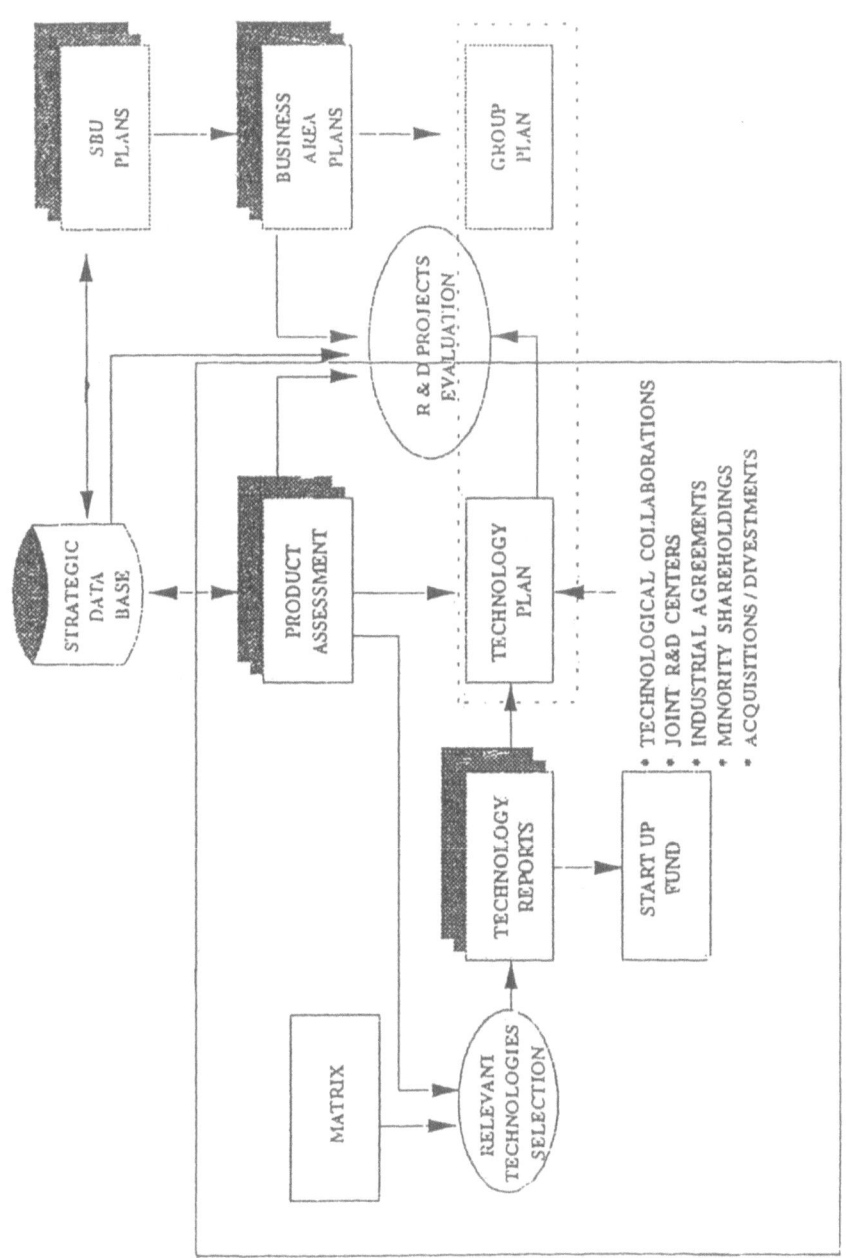

Fig. 2.9. Finmeccanica's Process of Technology Planning.

6   On Property Rights and Project Potentials

Projects that build on more than one potential should be funded by more than one source. This, however, leads to the question of who 'owns' the project. A convincing response to this question is that each funding source owns a share of the project, equal to its relative contribution to the total project budget, as agreed between the laboratory and the sponsors, unless some other sharing rule has been negotiated. Budget overruns or budget savings may be experienced due to the uncertainty that is inherent in research work. In our view, benefits and cost of uncertainty should be enjoyed or borne by the laboratory carrying out the work.

With respect to the character of the knowledge acquired, namely the possibility of using it many times without additional, or only marginal cost, another question has to be addressed. The conditions under which the laboratories or the sponsors could generate additional income from selling or leasing the new knowledge from a research project to third parties, be they internal or external to the company, have to be determined. The laboratories should be given the opportunity to offer different types of project contracts to their sponsors. If the sponsors wish to reserve the right to make multiple uses of the project results, the project budget should cover the laboratory cost, a surcharge for the consequences of uncertainty, and a possible laboratory profit. If the laboratory keeps the right to make multiple outside use of its results it should not try to add a laboratory profit to the other budgetary items, as it could derive such profits from the additional sales of the new knowledge. Laboratory profits could be used, at least partly, to sponsor projects that the laboratory feels are necessary for its own sake.

In this respect, it is interesting to return to the case of Shell. It is reported that "SIRM itself has a research budget (internally referred to as General Research) which is more or less equivalent to what elsewhere might be called corporate research. This budget is raised by a levy on the operating companies, the level of which is set by a Committee of Managing Directors. General research is often longer term and more generic. Increasingly in recent years, the business sectors and operating companies have been encouraged to participate in planning the General Research, but the decisions rest with SIRM, again at board level".

Our suggestion would be to include the right of potential sponsors to place projects at external as well as internal laboratories: Otherwise, the monopoly of the internal laboratory would lead to overcharging the sponsors. Certainly, the right of the sponsors to use of external knowledge suppliers should be buffered by a rule according to which the internal laboratories are given the freedom to develop and to make offers, as well as to select from competing offers. The latter may be difficult in practice. While criteria such as cost and duration of a project may be determined easily, the evaluation of competence and of credibility to solve a given problem are difficult to assess. However, the same problem is present in the choice of other types of contractual relationships as well. Consequently, this factor cannot be held against the suggestion developed here.

In fact, business units at Daimler Benz that intend to sponsor long term research projects may solicit proposals from outside, but they have to give their own central laboratory the right of last call. This comes extremely close to what is suggested here. Efficiency of research is continuously monitored by collecting data on customer satisfaction, while effectiveness is additionally the concern of audits that can even employ outside experts and that are performed as it appears useful.

7 Relative Share of Research in Relation to its Potentials

The identification potential, the absorptive potential, and the creative potential can all be made immediately relevant for use in an enterpreneurial fashion. They help to generate new business. In this section we concentrate solely on these potentials. The question arises as to what share of the total research and development expenditures should be earmarked for them. Thus, the minimum share of research is sought, assuming that the other functions play no role in this respect.

In economic terms, the ability to generate new business from the creative use of research can be expressed in a useful manner *via* the concept of the 'elasticity of research'. An elasticity is the quotient of the relative change of an output measure over the relative change of an input measure. The output could be sales or value added, while one of the inputs is research. This is taken as a proxy variable for the knowledge base derived from research (see Chapter I). Taking the high risk of research and its long lead time into account, the elasticity can only be determined in the long-term and at an aggregate level, and not for individual projects.

The concept of elasticities is an important one in economics. The reason is that companies are managed optimally if all the inputs used have the same marginal productivity. This marginal productivity can be derived from the elasticities of each factor which contributes to the generation of outputs. Consequently, elasticities are used as a basic source of information to determine optimal strategies in pricing, advertising, factor shares in production etc. Managers in these fields are used to this concept. This is less likely to be the case for R&D managers. Our interviews showed that research managers had to be strongly persuaded to think about an output elasticity of research, and the estimates that they then produced were then given reluctantly. At the end of this chapter we report on a Delphi-styled approach suitable for estimating individual elasticities (see Appendix I).

Elasticities have also been estimated from data produced by individual firms [25, 36]. This demonstrates that it is possible to use the concept at an aggregate level and for strategic decisions, such as the determination of a long-term budgeting strategy for research and development.

7.1 Mandatory Research

We will firstly consider a situation where without research no output can be generated. We call this mandatory research. It would be an indication that mandatory research is required, if the question is asked: "Why is it that we can no longer rely solely on engineering applications"? [8]

Assuming some generally applicable relationships between inputs and outputs (in the language of economics these are termed Cobb-Douglas-type relationships), important results on the optimum share of research (R) over development (D) expenditures can be derived. This share should be

$$\frac{R}{D} = \frac{l}{h} \cdot \frac{1}{(1+i)^k}$$

where
  l is the output elasticity of research,
  h is the output elasticity of development,
  i is the interest rate, and
  k is the time lag between research and its use in the generation of out put, while no such time lag is assumed for development [45].

The relative share of research depends on a quotient of elasticities, and a term that takes into account the effects of the time lag between research and its use. Relatively more will be spent on research, if its elasticity grows larger relative to the other elements of the formula. Relatively more will also be spent on research, if interest rates decline or the time lag declines. Both effects work in the same direction and reinforce themselves. If interest rates (or the cost of capital) increase, research will come under pressure, either to speed up the transfer of its results into new products or new processes or to reduce its share in the total R&D expenditure.

The relationship between research and finance is very interesting, and it is by no means only marginal. If the cost of capital rises from 10% to 12.5% and it takes 10 years from research to penetration of the market, this would result in a 20.1% decrease in optimal research expenditure. Alternatively, if the time lag could be reduced to just eight years, then the original level of research could be maintained.

7.2 Mandatory Research and Transfer Cost

Let us now assume that there is a cost attached to transferring research results into development. This cost is inversely related to the internal transfer potential. Consequently, the cost may increase as the level of research results to be transferred increases, and it may decrease as the level of development activities expands the absorptive capacity of development. Then, the share of research gets smaller than shown before, *ie*:

$$\frac{R}{D} = \frac{l}{h} \cdot \frac{l}{(1+i)^k} \cdot \frac{l}{1+z} = \lambda.$$

Here, z depends on the transfer cost parameters, the elasticities, the interest rate and the time lag. If transfer costs are incurred, z is larger than zero, and relatively less will be spent on research.

The level of the transfer cost may be influenced by very many variables. It may be considered in terms of the interface problems that exist between research and development departments. These problems may arise from the 'different orientations and expectations' of the roles to be played by the respective departments, which could be further nurtured by lack of communication [46]. Lack of communication may result from too great a distance between the research site and the development site or the location of other in-house customers of research.

A remarkable account of these problems is given by Xerox's Palo Alto Research Center (PARC): "Xerox hasn't cashed in on PARC's exciting research on computerized office systems, which was the center's original reason for being" [47]. Many reasons are mentioned for this: weak ties to the rest of Xerox, a loose management system that encouraged PARC to overstep its charter, lack of management attention, no channel for marketing products based on the researchers' efforts, and cultural differences nourished by the long distance between the East Coast, where Xerox' headquarters is located, and the West Coast of the US. More joint meetings and a joint hiring programme that brings new researchers to PARC during their first year, before they join other groups have now been installed to remedy the situation. The joint hiring policy is a good example of a secondary potential of research inin theategory of human resource attractiveness.

Similar considerations must be employed if research results are imported from external sources into a company. Again, being psychologically and physically close to the research site appears to reduce transfer cost. This is one of the reasons given by companies for placing research units close to where the most interesting university research is performed, and for choosing collaborative forms of research over merely supporting the development of new results by grant money. A major reason for Nokia AB setting up part of its central research laboratory in Tampere, Finland was the 'across the street'-closeness of the local university and the possibility of undertaking joint research projects with university staff in the departments there.

7.3 Supportive Research

Let us now turn to a different type of research, namely supportive research. Here, some output from product or process improvements may be generated without any direct involvement with the research department itself, whilst more radical new things can originate from a combination of research, development and other factors of production, as before. This makes it necessary to split total development expenditure into two shares, one to support radical innovations (D - F) and the other to support improvements (F). The optimal share of research expenditure is now determined by:

$$\frac{R}{D} = \lambda \cdot \frac{D-F}{D}.$$

For all values of F > 0 it is obvious that relatively less is spent on supportive research than on mandatory research, because development becomes more prosperous or productive.

Thus, an important question to ask in long-term budgeting is whether research is mandatory or supportive. The next question should address the level of transfer cost, particularly if the company wants to use external research results. Finally, time lag and cost of capital should be watched, as both reinforce each other in influencing the share of research. In any case, there is a need to come up with estimates of output elasticities of research and of development, and these are as important as those from other functional units in the company.

7.4 Tests of the Basic Relationships

We have no knowledge as to the relative importance of mandatory versus supportive research, and the level of the transfer costs that may arise. It is interesting to note, however, that the share of R&D will depend linearly on a variable $1/(1+i)^k$ which has no intercept and a coefficient which varies as l/h as well as the other parameters that may have to be observed. We will now test our analysis using data obtained from German industry.

We would like to determine a positive, unknown parameter b in the equation:

$$R/D = b \cdot (1/(1+i))^k.$$

The data for the dependent variable are available for the years 1965 - 1991 in Germany [48]. The independent variable depends on both the interest rate and the time-lag k. The interest rate was taken from data available [49]. A different choice of the interest rate variable would affect the level of b. As it is unknown whether, in its planning, management would consider the interest rate of the previous year or that of two or three years ago, we performed alternative calculations for these observations. Furthermore, we have no general information on the time-lag k. We will therefore choose to set $k = 1, 2, ..., 12$ and run alternative calculations. Then it should be possible to statistically select the best estimate of the unknown parameter b. The selection criteria are the significance of the parameter's difference from zero, and the coefficient of determination which indicates how much the total of variants in R&D could be explained.

It could be established that the relative share of the industrial research budget does in fact correlate very strongly with the level of the interest rate (see Table 2.6). This is evident from the high T-values, which measure the quotient of the parameter and its variance as well as the high coefficients of determination. Similar results can also be obtained on an industry level (see the Appendix).

The result is very interesting and it has substantial managerial implications.

Table 2.6. The relationship between the share of industrial research expenditure and the interest rate in Germany, 1965-1991

Time-lag of the interest rate variable (years)	-1	-2	-3
Time-lag of the research effect (k) (years)	3	6	10
Regression parameter (b)	0.063	0.079	0.106
Standardized regression parameter (beta)	0.988	0.990	0.995
T-value for the regression parameter	21.09	23.11	34.11
Level of significance for the regression parameter	0.0	0.0	0.0
Coefficient of determination (R-square)	0.9759	0.9798	0.9906

Assuming that the research budget is planned at least one to two years in advance, and that these plans are based on past observations of the interest rate or the cost of capital, we find that the most plausible estimate of the time-lag of the research effectiveness is between three and ten years.[7] In fact, the Shell organization reports that: "The planning process is based on a two year cycle. In year x, the programmes for years x+1 and x+2 are defined. In year x+1, high level reviews take place of the results of the previous cycle and of progress to date in year x+1. The programmes for year x+2 are then adjusted (in principle only marginally) in the light of the reviews and any intervening changes in the business requirements". We observe that the estimated time-lag is very sensitive to the assumed time-lag for the interest rate used in the planning procedure. Thus, more information on the actual planning processes are highly desirable.

If actual industry behaviour is close to optimal, the elasticities of research and of development should be equal to the respective intensities for R&D/sales-ratios. Assuming that approximately 3.1% of sales are spent on R&D in German industry (1991) and that 5.7% of total R&D is spent on research, then the ratio of the elasticities l/h should be 0.057. As only a minority of firms engage in research, the ratio should be higher for these firms. This ratio should be compared with the regression parameter b. The empirical data show higher values than 0.057. But taking the argument just raised into account, the results are in a plausible range. As the data used here are rather fuzzy, this empirical 'test' should not be given too much weight.

---

[7]   Alternatively, we have estimated both b and k from non-linear regression by the Levenberg-Marquard algorithm [50]. The best result using the sum of squares criterion is obtained with interest rated lagged three years. The results are very close to those given in Table 2.6. We obtain $b = 0.1090$ (T = 5.11); $k = 10.3923$ (T = 3.87); sum of squares = 0.000293.

8 Conclusions and Recommendations

A number of important recommendations can be drawn from this study:

* Companies should not neglect research. Company histories indicate that fluctuations in research expenditure can have detrimental effects on competitiveness.

* Research does not only support new products or new processes. Rather, it supports a large number of primary and secondary potentials.

* Potentials can be used to support the funding of research projects, where the term 'Project' should be interpreted in a broad sense.

* R&D elasticities are a significant aid to R&D management for planning and setting R&D budgets. In Appendix I we demonstrate how such elasticities can be estimated.

* To make good use of elasticities it is also important to know whether research is mandatory or supplementary to development. In the latter situation relatively less is spent on research.

* The higher the transfer cost from research to development the less will be spent on research. Consequently, it may pay to seek organizational or other help to reduce the transfer cost.

* Long time periods needed to get a new product to market and high interest rates reduce relative research spending. The first can be influenced by the choice of projects, while the latter is determined by the financial markets, which are outside company control. The interaction of both these factors needs to be considered when determining the composition of research programmes.

References

1 *Frankfurter Allgemeine* (1996) 3 February 1996, p.19
2 E. Konecny, C.P. Quinn, K.Sachs and D.T. Thompson, 'Universities and Industrial Research', Royal Society of Chemistry, Cambridge, UK, 1995
3 C. Foos, *Top Business*, April 1995, pp. 92-96.
4 D.A. Hounshell and J.K.Smith, 'Science and Corporate Strategy. Research and Development at Du Pont 1908 to 1980', Cambridge, 1989
5 C.C. Furnas, 'Research in Industry', 5th ed., Princeton/N.J., pp. 1-14
6 A.B. Kinzel, *Proceedings of a Conference on Academic and Industrial Basic Research*, National Science Foundation, Washington/D.C., pp. 15 et seq.
7 K. Berthold, Dissertation, Mannheim, 1968
8 A. Ruedi and P.Lawrence, in 'Strategic Management of Technology and Innovation', ed. R.A. Burgelman, M.A. Maidique and S,C, Wheelwright, Harvard Business School Case 9-474-164, Chicago, 1995, pp. 507-521
9 B.R. Martin and J. Irvine, Research Foresight. Priority Setting in Science, London, New York, 1989

10 P.H. Abelson, *Science*, 1995, **267**, 435

11 J. Schmitt, *USA Today*, 22 September 1995

12 D.P. Hamilton, *Science*, 1992, **258**, 570-71

13 OECD, 'Proposed Standard Practice for Surveys of Research and Experimental Development', *Frascati Manual*, OECD, Paris, 1992

14 OECD, 'Basic Science and Technology Statistics', OECD, Paris, 1991, 1993

15 SV-Gemeinnützige Gesellschaft für Wissenschaftsstatistik (1985-1991), *Forschung und Entwicklung in der Wirtschaft*

16 D. Foray, in 'Intellectual Property Rights and Global Competition', ed. H. Albach and S. Rosenkranz, Sigma Verlag, Berlin, 1995, pp. 75-117

17 M. Aoki, 'Information, Incentives and Bargaining', Arthur D. Little, Inc., Cambridge, 1959; 'Basic Research in the Navy', NONR - 2516(00)

18 R.S. Rosenbloom and A.M. Kantrow, *Harvard Business Review*, January/February 1992, pp. 115-23.

19 J. Mittelstraß, 'Stifterverband für die deutsche Wissenschaft (edt) Von der Hypothese zum Produkt', Essen, 1995, pp. 18-24

20 A. Marshall, 'Industry and Trade', London, 1927

21 ZVEI (Zentralverband Elektrotechnik und Elektroindustrie e.V.) , Frankfurt, 1994

22 'The New Reality' President's Commission on Industrial Competitiveness. Global Competition, Vol. I, II, Washington/D.C, 1985

23 W.M. Cohen and D.A. Levinthal, *Administrative Science Quarterly*, 1990, **35**, 128-152

24 H. Weule *et al*, 'Zusammenarbeit GFE/Industrie', Stuttgart, 1994

25 K. Brockhoff, *Zeitschrift für Betriebswirtschaft*, 1995, Supplement **1**, 27-42.

26 K. Brockhoff, 'Forschungsprojekte und Forschungsprogramme. Ihre Bewertung und Auswahl', Wiesbaden, 1973

27 IIT Research Institute, 'TRACES, Technology in Retrospect and Critical Events in Science', Vol. 1, 1968; Vol. 2, 1969

28 Arthur D. Little, Inc, 1959

29 W.L. Robb, *Research Technology Management*, March/April 1991, pp. 16-21

30 D. Leonard-Barton and G. Pisano, *Harvard Business School Case*, 9-960-009

31 K.R. MacCrimmon and D.A. Wehrung, 'Taking Risks. The Management of Uncertainty' New York, London, 1986

32 *Business Week*, March 30, 1987

33 E. Mansfield, *American Economic Review*, 1980, **70**, 863-73

34 A.N. Link, *American Economic Review*, 1981, **71**, 1111-12

35 Z. Griliches, *American Economic Review*, 1986, **76**, 141-54

36 Z. Griliches, *American Economic Review*, 1986, **76**, 141-54

37 O. Eggers, Funktionen und Management der Forschung in Unternehmen, Wiesbaden, 1996

38 R. Nelson, 'Understanding Technical Change as an Evolutionary Process', Amsterdam 1987

39 K. Pavitt, *Research Policy*, 1991, **20**, 109-19

40 S. Schrader and H. Sattler, *Die Betriebswirtschaft*, 1993, **53**, 587-606

41 D. de Solla Price, 'Little Science, Big Science' New York, 1963

42 I. Nanaka and H. Takeuchi, 'The Knowledge-Creating Company. How Japanese Companies Create the Dynamics of Innovation', Oxford University Press, New York, Oxford, 1995

Research in the Company of the Future

43 A.N. Chester, *Research-Technology Management*, 1995, **38**(4),14-22
44 K. Warschkow, 'Organisation und Budgetierung Zentraler FuE-Bereiche',
   Stuttgart, 1993
45 K. Brockhoff, *Technovation*, 1995, **15**, 591-600
46 R.A. Burgelman and L.R. Sayles, Inside Corporate Innovation, New York, 1986
47 B. Uttal, *Fortune*, 5 September 1983
48 H. Echterhoff-Severitt *et al.* 'Forschung u. Entwicklung im Wirtschaftssektor in
   drei Jahrzehnten', Essen, 1988
49 Dresdner Bank 'Historische Statistische Reihen, Durchschnittsrendite
   festverzinslicher Wertpapiere', May, 1991
50 J.C. Nash, 'Nonlinear Parameter Estimation', New York, 1987

Appendix

The relationship between the share of industrial research expenditure and the interest rate in Germany, 1965-1991, for three industries:

Industry	Chemical/ Plastics/Pharma ceutical		Steel con- struction, Machinery, Automotive		Electrical, Electronics, Optical, Fine mechanics	
Time-lag of the interest rate variable (years)	-1	-2	-1	-2	-1	-2
Time-lag of the research effect (k) (years)	3	6	9	9	4	5
Regression parameter (b)	0.093	0.116	0.085	0.085	0.080	0.087
T-value for the regression parameter	11.8	12.5	8.9	9.1	8.4	8.6
Level of significance for the regression parameter	0.0	0.0	0.0	0.0	0.0	0.0
Coefficient of determination (R-square)	0.927	0.934	0.878	0.881	0.864	0.871

Chapter 2 B
Empirical Results on Research Elasticities and on the Integration of Industrial Research with the Scientific in Europe and Japan

Justus Bardenhewer

Based on a sample of European and Japanese companies, an approach is presented for the quantification of industrial research. A Delphi-styled approach is employed for this investigation, involving both personal interviews and self-guided computer questionnaires. This technique provides information on research elacticities, *ie* the relative impact of changes in research and development in relation to prospective future sales. Results include indications of substitutional effects within R&D activities. An ideal ratio for R&D budgets can be estimated quantitatively

The empirical evidence also indicates that industrial research must be integrated with the scientific environment as a whole. Results obtained from personal interviews in European and Japanese companies show that these can be classified into different types, dependent on their degree of commitment to share and distribute research results. These types are correlated with different degrees of overall research success. Companies which use a 'hands on' approach towards the distribution of research results experience the best overall success rate in a comparatively short time. More traditional communication methods may produce similar success rates but the time taken to make an impact on the business will be longer. The results show that European industrial researchers are more dedicated to in-house transfer of their achievements, whilst their Japanese equivalents show stronger commitment to external communication, for example towards potential customers for future products.

1 Research Elasticities

1.1 Study Design

The elasticities of research and development are described as a necessary input for the calculation of optimal budgets for industrial R&D activities,[8] and these can be estimated for individual firms from long-term data [1-4]. It is even possible to differentiate between research elasticities with respect to overall measures of output and development elasticities [5-7]. Consequently, the question arises as to whether R&D managers can make subjective estimates that reflect their knowledge of the present and their expectations for the future. We asked a wide range of industrial research managers for their personal estimates of the impact of changes in research or development budgets on future outcomes, such as sales.[9]

When the study was started we had to realize that the concept of quantifying the impacts of research within a company was not familiar to the respondents. Research is often treated as an expense instead of an investment for the future. Hence, it is often financed from the company's overhead. Precise justification by return on investment is therefore rarely available. If an evaluation takes place, it is most likely to be based on qualitative information. This situation does not allow us to determine optimal budget levels.

We adopted a two-step Delphi-style approach for this study [8]. In a first step we performed personal interviews with the research managers. This enabled us to clarify the concept. Three relationships were investigated: (1) The impact of changes in the research budget on the development budget, (2) the impact of changes in the research budget on future sales, and (3) the impact of changes in the development budget on future sales. Questions were presented for the cases of decreasing and increasing the budgets by 10%.

The results obtained from this first step provided insight into the general direction and size of relative changes, and these had substantial variances. To achieve more reliable figures, a second round of interviewing was undertaken, and the results of the first step were included as feedback information. To facilitate the estimation procedure we used a computer program

---

[8]   The elasticity is the relative change, in per cent, of a dependent variable, y, resulting from a relative change, in per cent, of an independent variable, x. Thus, an elasticity of '2' means that changing variable x by 1% will lead to a change of variable y by 2%.

[9]   Interviewees were selected mainly from the electrical and electronics industries in Europe and Japan.

which displays the accumulated results from the previous interviews on the computer screen. The interviewee could then build his own reaction function interactively at the PC, and compare the results instantaneously with the accumulated results from the total sample. In addition, the set of questions was extended at this second stage by asking for reactions to 5%, 10%, and 20% changes of the R&D budgets. This program has been distributed by mail to the interviewees of the first round. It could easily be read directly from a diskette by most computer systems.   Most of the participants are from the electrical and electronics industry. In the first round we received estimates from 30 participants (77%), while nine felt unable to give any quantitative estimates. In the second round, 17 participants returned the diskette with their estimates (44%), while 22 did not respond.

1.2 Results

1.2.1 The Relationship Between Research and Development

From theory, we expect that the efficiency of development work can be raised if the company has significant research activities (Brockhoff, 1996). In this sense, research provides a lever for improving development efficiency. Thus the impact of changes in research activities on the company's development budget is a central point of interest: If this leverage effect does actually exist, then it would be expected that expenditure for development would need to be raised in case of *decreasing* support for research. Contrary to this, a traditional chain model of the company's functions would indicate that *raising* research expenditure would lead to raising research output and hence raising inputs for development departments. To make use of these inputs an increase in development budget would be necessary. It appears to be extremely important whether the relationship between research budgets and development budgets is part of a positive or negative feedback loop if the same level of output from R&D is sought. The results from our survey that relate to this question are shown in Figure 2.10. They support the hypotheses of a negative loop. At least in case of cuts in the research budget, a clear majority of the respondents expects that development expenditure would have to be increased. Several respondents mentioned the fact that development staff would in this case have to perform parts of the work which was originally located in research. Since development staff would not be specialists in that kind of work, this shift from research to development would usually be associated with a loss of efficiency. Consequently, the necessary increase in development budgets could be expected to far exceed the amount cut from research. This is illustrated in Figure 2.10. A decrease in research by 10% results in an average increase in development budgets by 2%, the absolute size of which is much bigger than the research budget.

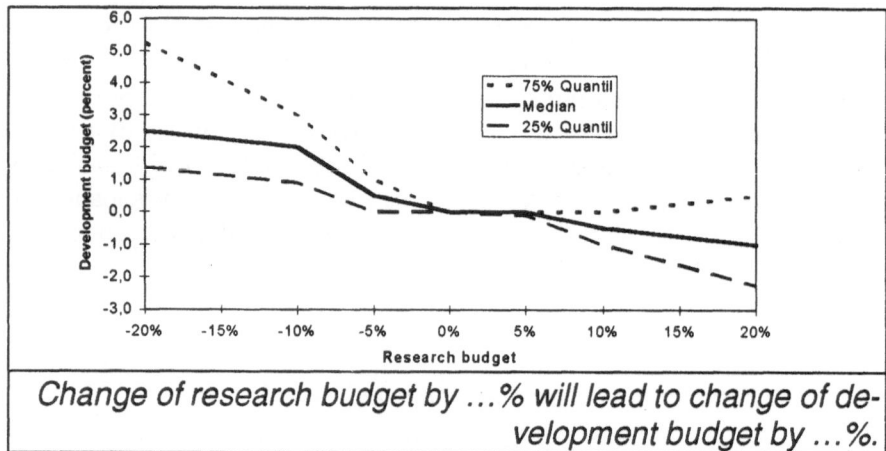

Fig. 2.10. Impact of research budget changes on development budget.

In Figure 1 75% Quantil is the upper quartile and 25% Quantil is the lower quartile. In Table 2.7. we give some sample results. From these it can be seen that the necessary increase in development budgets is relatively higher if the share of development gets larger. We assume that the respondents had in mind situations that reflect their own experiences, with a 10 to 12% share of research in the total R&D budget.

Table 2.7. Numerical consequences of a 10% reduction in research expenditures on development expenditures, if output is to remain unchanged

Share of research in the total R&D budget	5%	10%	15%
Changes of R&D budget due to...			
...10% reduction of research	-0.5%	-1.0%	-1.5%
...resulting change of development	+1.9%	+1.8%	+1.7%
Total R&D budget change	+1.4%	+0.8%	+0.2%

When considering research budget increases, the majority of the respondents expects smaller reactions in the development budgets. There is a general trend which suggests that development budgets could be reduced if research budgets are increased.

In interpreting the relationships one should keep in mind that not all the results emanating from research departments can be realized in development groups.

1.2.2 The Impact of Research and Development on Sales

Research can be expected to have impact on company sales in the long run. Research is expected to have a positive influence on sales, and this is regarded as an indicator of company success. To get an idea of the strength of this effect we asked for the direct impact on future company sales generated by changes of the research budget, as indicated above. In fact, substantial positive effects on company sales are expected to follow from increasing research budgets, and the reverse is expected from budget cuts. Figure 2.11 shows that decreases in research activity produce larger effects than increases. Nevertheless, with an average research expenditure of about 1% of a company's annual sales, an elasticity of 0.5 for the increase of research budget is a strong indicator that research expenditure is far below the optimum level (see Figure 2.11). In absolute terms, these figures suggest that the additional research budget would result in an increase of 50 times in additional sales.

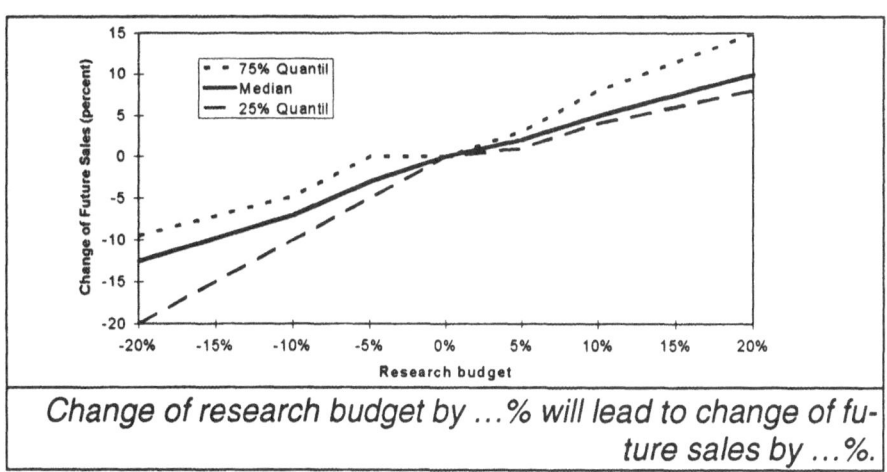

Fig. 2.11. Impact of research budget changes on the company's future sales.

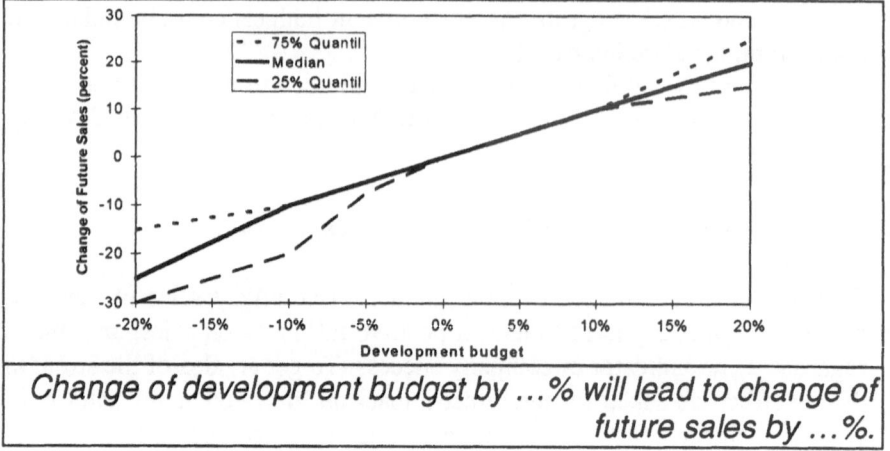

Fig. 2.12. Impact of development budget changes on the company's future sales.

Finally, the impact of changes in the development budget on the company's sales has been investigated. Figure 2.12 shows the responses received for this question. The expected reactions are more or less proportional, *ie* a 10% change in the development budget will result in a 10% change in future sales, in other words an elasticity of 1.0. Starting with a development budget of about 10% of a company's sales, these figures mean in absolute terms that the additional development budget would result in about 10 times the quantity of additional sales.

1.3 Integration in a Model

We will now attempt to integrate the elasticities identified above into the model for calculation of optimal relative shares of research and development in the total R&D budget (Brockhoff, 1996). The simplest model developed there is the one for mandatory research, *ie*:

$$\frac{R}{D} = \frac{l}{h} \cdot \frac{1}{(1+i)^k}$$

where
   l is the output elasticity of research,
   h is the output elasticity of development,
   i is the interest rate, and
   k is the time lag between research and its use in the generation of output, while no such time lag is assumed for development.

In our case we found that the research elasticity is about 0.5 and the development elasticity about 1.0. During the same interviews we asked for the average time lag between completing a research project and its use in new businesses. The median of the answers was about 4 years. With an average project time in research of 2 years, let us assume an average lag of 5 years between research expenditure and its impact on the market. For the interest rate we assume an average of 15% (because of the relatively high risks involved). Thus we arrive at the equation:

$$\frac{R}{D} = \frac{0.5}{1.0} \cdot \frac{1}{(1+0.15)^5} = 0.249$$

For the optimal share of research in the total R&D budget this implies:

$$\frac{R}{R+D} = 0.20$$

Assuming the levels of output elasticities of research and development received from our interviews and the interest rate and time lag proposed above, the optimal share of research in total the R&D budget should be 20%. This is far above the average share employed in practice. If one assumes a time lag of 10 years and an interest rate of 20%, the optimal share of research in total R&D would be 7.5%. When taking into account the more complex models which integrate transfer costs and parts of development, and are completely independent of research activity, these optimum shares will, however, further decrease. In conclusion, we can state that the average shares of research in total R&D budgets is consistent with our model if one assumes either that very high interest rates or that very long time lags and high transfer costs are characteristics which must reasonably be employed. If a smoother transfer process can be implemented and/or the time lag shortened, one should *ceteris paribus* increase the share of research.

2 Integration of Industrial Research with the Scientific Environment

2.1 Problem Definition

Research inside a company cannot be treated as an autonomous activity. If the company expects a positive impact from its investment in research the scientists must leave their ivory tower – not only once in a while, but regularly. The company will be able to make the best use of the positive results from its research activities only when proper communication with development and construction and marketing departments takes place, as appropriate. This will happen only if the final results of research projects are not only written in report form but are also delivered to these other departments. For successful transfers it is essential to implement a system of continuous communication in both directions. This then enables researchers to receive information regarding the probability of market acceptance for new ideas as well as the likelihood for inclusion of new knowledge in the company's products and processes.

Furthermore, internal researchers might be searching for contacts with the external scientific community for a number of reasons. The first is to identify and bring in-house relevant results which have been produced externally, *eg* in universities or other companies. A second is to convey knowledge obtained from the company's own research programme to appropriate parts of the community outside. These contacts can take place with varying degrees of formality or reciprocity, varying from merely scanning publications to entering into collaborative research projects. It is necessary to carry out internal research both to enable a company to assimilate external knowledge and to act as a yardstick for the efficiency of internal research.

In the following discussion we will consider empirical results which provide evidence on the role which external partners and their research may play in relation to an internal research departments' work as well as the impact on success which different strategies have when making ones own research results available to selected outside organizations.

2.2 The Relevance of External Knowledge

University (basic) research has in the past been interpreted as a kind of free benefit for industrial R&D laboratories. Their researchers could look for relevant results available 'on the shelf', and these could then be readily adapted to the company's needs in-house. A large part of the necessary input for a company's development could thus be imported from outside, minimizing the need for in-house investment in such long-term research projects. Data from industry seem to support this assumption. For small firms in the UK it was found that during the period 1970-79 almost twice the percentage of innovation-initiating ideas was derived from external research than in the preceding period 1949-69 [9]. Another study found that the share of innovations that were derived in some way from academic research amounted to 5.1% of major firms' sales [10]. Savings arising from the use of academic research results are estimated, in the same study, to be as much as 2.5% of these major firms' total costs. In the light of such figures, E.M. Scolnick [11], president of Merck, Sharp & Dohme Research Laboratories, states that "In my experience, the most important aspect of research management is the ability to access the scientific information emanating from academic and industrial laboratories throughout the world, to discern its importance, and to integrate it rapidly into our research".[10]

Despite all the optimism regarding use of external knowledge rather than doing the research work in-house, several important questions still remain: (1) To what extent are universities and public research institutions performing research in fields that are relevant to industrial R&D departments? Some *north star research* is certainly suitable for the university environment (see Chapter IV). (2) Is it possible for companies to access the knowledge achieved in research elsewhere, or are there specific prerequisites which have to be met in order to be able to import this knowledge? (3) How does a company identify relevant partners for its collaborative research? (4) Are there changes in the policies of these potential partners regarding openness and research strategy? (5) Is there a relationship between a company's strategy in disseminating research results and its success in research? We should bear in mind at the outset that some companies perform basic or *north star research* (see Chapter IV) in-house in order to create advantageous knowledge barriers between themselves and their competitors.

---

[10]   In an earlier study, Hermes [12] found that the tendency of companies to co-operate with external partners in R&D projects was especially strong only in projects very *close* to the market. Those projects having high *strategic* relevance were usually performed in-house. Our own results do not, however, support these findings.

As part of the 'Company of the Future' sub-project on the management of industrial research these five questions were directed to 40 managers responsible for research planning in major companies in Europe and Japan. They were selected mainly from the electrical/electronics industry.

The research activities in universities and public research institutes do not usually receive unqualified approval from industrial managers. In both Europe and Japan, the value and the relevance of external research is assessed as being in the middle on a scale from 'no value' and 'very high value' (see Table 2.8). The Japanese respondents qualified their rating to being based on the *worldwide* research environment. From Japanese publicly funded research alone they have not until recently expected a significant impact on their businesses, except for the provision of skilled personnel.

Table 2.8. Value and relevance of external research results.

'To what degree is research *performed strictly outside* your company...'	All interviews			Europe			Japan		
	∅	SD	N	∅	SD	N	∅	SD	N
of value/relevance for the company?	3.6	1.8	38	3.5	1.9	18	3.6	1.7	20
SD=Standard Deviation; 7-point Likert-type scale: 0=no value, 6=very high value. *Independent Samples t-test, unequal variances, 2-tailed: no sign. Difference.*									

Earlier studies have interpreted the low relevance of Japanese university research as one possible reason for the tendency of lower rates of return from Japanese industrial basic research than those found in western countries [13].[11] In the light of our recent interviews this interpretation does not hold. Many Japanese research managers mentioned that, due to problems of the Japanese research system, they rely on research activities from abroad, especially in North-America, but also in Europe. This is supported by the fact that several research laboratories of major Japanese companies are located close to the sites of major US and European universities.

Another indicator of the ability of Japanese companies to compensate for the relatively poor performance of their domestic universities' research by collaborating with other universities abroad can be found in the frequency of their co-operation with different partners (see Figure 2.13). The most frequently contacted partners in *both* sub-samples are universities, followed by other public research institutions, non-competing and com-

---

[11]   Results were based on comparisons between US and Japanese Companies.

peting companies, and polytechnics. Whilst the order of frequency is the same on both continents, a look at the differences in frequency shows that for Japan the universities are even more favoured than the next nearest type of institution than in Europe.

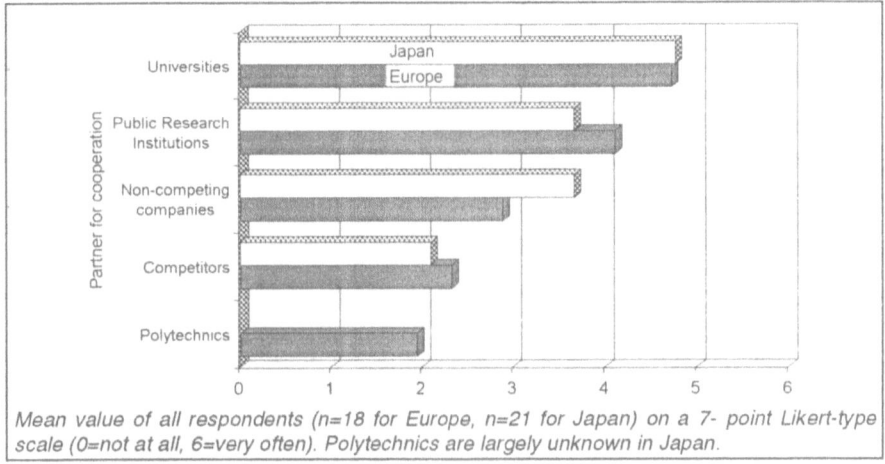

Fig. 2.13. Frequency of co-operation with external partners.

Furthermore, the willingness to co-operate with non-competing companies is much higher in Japan than in Europe.[12] This occurs as frequently as co-operations with research institutes, whilst the latter are sought relatively more frequently by European firms.

2.3 Relevance of Internal Capability for Understanding External Knowledge

The idea of research results being a kind of a free bonus was mentioned earlier. In addition to the question of whether or not universities and public institutions are able to supply the kind of knowledge required by industry or not, there is a second question 'Is industry – or are industrial companies – in a position to define their requirements in a suitable form for universities?' Since the seminal work performed by Cohen and Levinthal the concept of 'absorptive capacity' of a company has been progressed and modi-

---

[12] Non-competing companies were mentioned with the same frequency a public research institutes.

fied by several authors [14-16]. The idea is mainly that the use of external research is not only a substitute for in-house research activities but is very often complementary to it [17].[13] The thought that internal research has a kind of leverage-function with respect to the effectiveness of investment in external knowledge acquisition received clear support from research managers (see Table 2.9).

Table 2.9. Leverage effects of research.

'Can you agree with the statement that internal research provides a **lever**...'	All interviews			Europe			Japan		
	∅	SD	N	∅	SD	N	∅	SD	N
a. for integrating external research results	1.7"	1.5	39	1.2	1.4	18	2.2	1.4	21
b. for supporting development	0.8"	1.2	39	0.6	0.9	18	1.1	1.5	21
SD=Standard deviation; 7-point Likert-type scale: 0=fully agree, 6=fully disagree. Indep. Samples t-test, unequal var., 2-tailed: Sign.:=90%, **=95%, ***=99%, *=not sign.*									

The nature of the interaction between internal research and external research is mainly that any "transfer of technological knowledge is not a one-sided phenomenon ... but a two-fold process where the interference and cumulative effect of information from both parties provides solutions ..." [19]. This co-operation may be the primary advantage that a company gains by investing its own money in long-term research, which cannot be assigned to any marketable products at the time of decision in many cases. This leverage effect is illustrated by the value that research managers expect to draw from external research in the presence or absence of internal research activities (see Figure 2.14) – accessibility seems to be better *with* internal research than *without* research. In other words: Those who want to use external results should provide an internal basis for their identification and integration.

---

[13]   Brockhoff [18] has developed a theoretical model for the allocation of budgets between research and development using R&D elascticities.

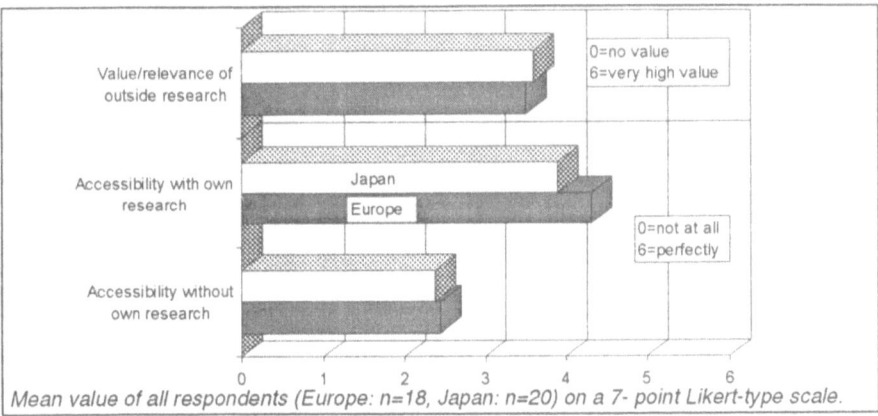

Fig. 2.14. In-house research and accessibility of university research.

2.4 Dynamic Changes in Public Research

It is often said that publicly funded and especially university research does not receive the greatest approval from industry. This is particularly true as far as business relevance of the research programme is concerned or its easy accessibility to interested industries. The only exception typically mentioned by managers is that they trust in the ability of universities to produce highly skilled future employees.

In the light of these comments, it is surprising that so many universities are the partners for co-operative research projects with industrial research laboratories.[14] It can therefore be expected that the large number of the contacts resulting from these co-operative projects will also lead to some beneficial changes at universities. During co-operative projects the industrial participants will also learn more about university work. The university participants can also be expected to get a closer appreciation of the needs and interests of their industry partners.

---

[14] 'Co-operative research' does not only mean that industry is trying to benefit from the results of university work, but also that the joint activities are long-term and mutually beneficial (see Konecny et al).

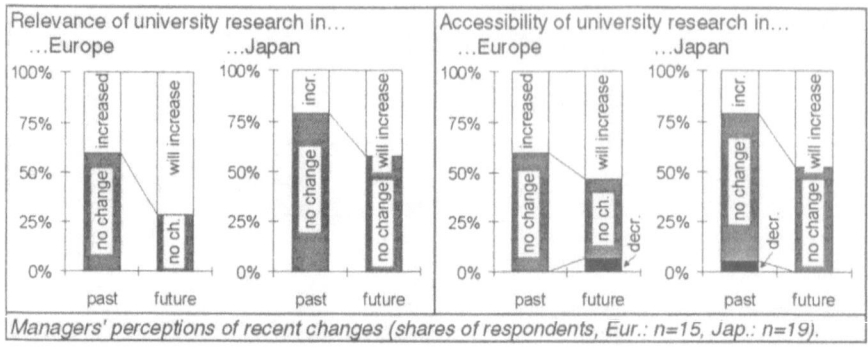

Fig. 2.15. Perceived changes of relevance and accessibility of university research.

Improvements of this kind seem to be well advanced in Europe (see Figure 2.15) whilst a smaller number of Japanese research managers have observed relevant improvements in the development of their relationships with universities. As universities move their research programme towards the needs of industry, the share of co-operative research projects may grow. Each time a university enters contractual agreements with one company this may increase opportunities for technology transfer and fruitful exchange inside this partnership; but for other researchers outside the partnership (companies or universities) it might become more difficult to access the output from this co-operation because of the industrial partners' interest in withholding information that could be exploited economically. Also, the *sticky information* [20] incorporated in research results will probably be available only to the direct project partners. In Europe this idea is beginning to spread. In Figure 2.15 we show that a few respondents indicate this expectation of a decreasing accessibility to the results of research as it increases in relevance.

2.5 Dissemination of Research Results Internally and Externally

The transfer of knowledge and technology has often been looked at only from the perspective of one company/laboratory transferring something from outside more or less successfully – and relating this transfer to a number of aspects of the situation existing with respect to each partner. We will now look at this process in more detail.

A necessary condition for the success of a research laboratory is to transfer the accumulated knowledge–produced internally or externally – to the downstream departments of the company. A large variety of communication tools may be employed to accomplish this task, and different approaches to using these tools may lead to varying degrees of effectiveness. Major influences can also be expected from the degree of active involvement of the 'receiving' departments. Thus, knowledge transfer by personal interaction (personnel transfer, workshops, informal contacts) will be more successful than transfer which is attempted *via* written reports and conference presentations.

Furthermore, it could be in the interest of the researchers to communicate the results of their research work – or at least the knowledge of the existence of their results – not only inside their own company but also outside. This external dissemination of knowledge may at first be stimulated by the personal interest of the researcher in obtaining a good reputation in the scientific community, and this could be achieved by publications in scientific journals or attending scientific conferences. These methods not only raise the standing of the researcher and spread knowledge of achievements outside the company, but also, in return, the company will use these opportunities to discuss results or problems with colleagues from other companies or from universities. In these informal situations it is easier to solve specific problems together without entering into formal agreements between companies, and at least some information on the activities of competitors and universities in relevant fields will be transmitted at the same time. Many scientists are consequently boundary-spanning people, and this kind of activity can be undertaken without any specific effort having to be made by the company towards co-operation with others [21].

McMillan, Klavans and Hamilton [22] have analysed the incentive for a company to open its own research results to the public in a theoretical approach based on a game concerning a prisoners' dilemma. In a proposed situation, unco-operative behaviour of player one (*ie* one company) may yield higher returns in the short-term because of the secrecy of knowledge, but in the long term the scientific community will punish this behaviour by withholding knowledge of their future achievements from player one. This punishment may even occur unknowingly since without any presence in literature the community will not consider player one as part of its relevant network.

Let us now look at internal information dissemination regarding research projects. In our survey we provided a list of nine possible methods for the dissemination of research results, and asked about their frequency of usage. In spite of the problems connected with it, 'written material' seems to be the most important and most frequently used method, employed by all the companies. It therefore seems that the written documentation of research results is a necessary basis from which to build further communication. For *internal transfer of research results* the following methods have preference (see Figure 2.16):

1. *Discussion of results*. For example, internal conferences are used to discuss and explain the achievements of the research.
2. *Personnel transfer*. *Personnel* move in both directions between research and other departments (usually development). This can arise from researchers staying with their projects when these move down the value-added chain, are there are also temporary assignments for training reasons.
3. *'Hands-on' information*. *Results* are handed over to potential internal customers in a more concrete form for demonstration of their potential uses (*eg* distribution of samples and joint workshops with development departments).

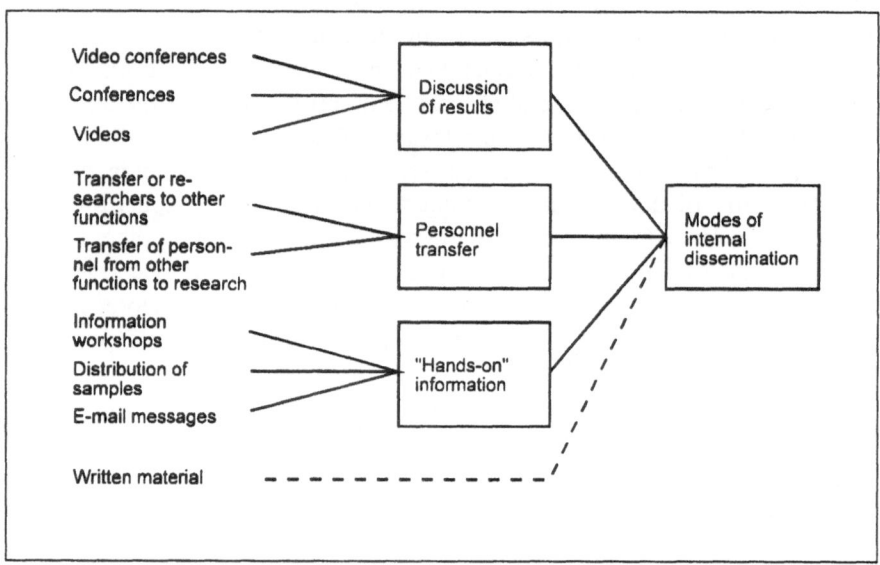

Fig. 2.16. Factors used for internal dissemination of research results.

Use of these three factors produces a highly significant differentiation between the European and the Japanese sub-samples.[15] The Japanese respondents are usually far more engaged in the discussion of results and – to a slightly lower degree – in the transfer of personnel than are their European counterparts. On the other hand, we find 'hands-on' information to be very important in Europe, whilst this level of importance is not reached in Japan. It seems that these differences in dissemination methods for research results may be correlated with the influence of business units in research budgeting and research programme selection. In both these areas, business units are more involved in Europe than in Japan.

A similar list of tools was used to evaluate their effectiveness for *dissemination of research results outside the company* (see Figure 2.17). Again, three factors could be identified:

1. *Transfer to support economic exploitation.* The principal objective here is to demonstrate possibilities for the integration of its results with the products or processes of possible customers using joint development projects, *via* presentation of samples or workshops.
2. *Scientific knowledge transfer.* This represents the scientifically motivated transfer of research results and involves presentations at conferences, publications and informal contacts between scientists. The latter could be quantified by the frequency of e-mail contacts, but it should be noted that such contacts are not allowed by some major companies, for security reasons.
3. *Personnel transfer.* Company staff to work outside the organization temporarily or part-time (either in joint research projects, or in part-time professorships), or temporarily host external researchers/scientists in internal laboratories (*eg* doctoral students are employed on specific projects, or researchers are exchanged between companies).

The three factors are again of different importance to managers in Europe and Japan. Whilst the means that support economic exploitation are far more frequently used in Japan than in Europe, the reverse applies to the external mobility of personnel. This is more accepted in Europe.

---

[15] Discriminant factors on all three factors relating to origin of respondents is highly significant (Sig.: 0.0064).

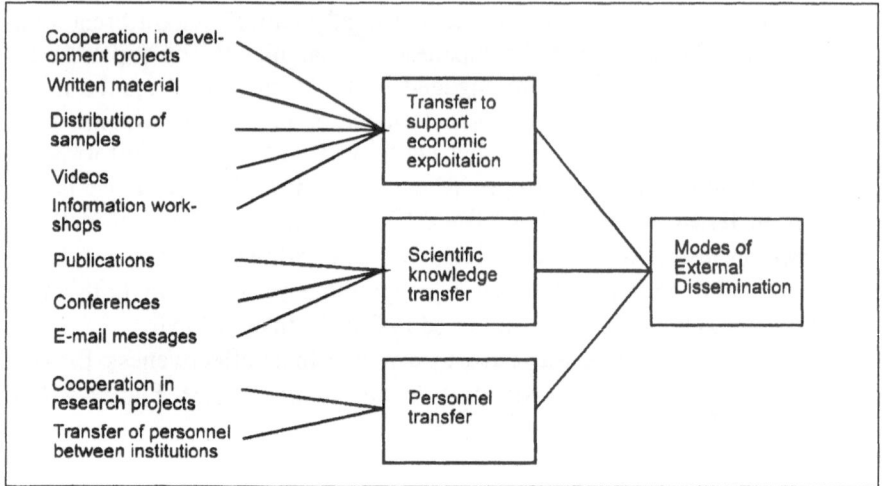

Fig. 2.17. Factors used for external dissemination of research results.

Looking at both the aspects of result dissemination investigated above, it is surprising that internal and external activities of similar kinds are somehow inversely distributed between Europe and Japan. Whilst 'hands-on' internal transfer is especially frequent in Europe the exploitation-orientated external transfer is significantly more frequent in Japan. And whilst internal transfer of personnel is more important in Japan, external transfer of personnel is significantly stronger in Europe. Reasons for these differences may in part be found in the higher reluctance of Europeans to move into different types of jobs (*eg* from research into development) while Japanese show less interest in changing organization than in changing their type of job.

In addition to identifying differences in result dissemination methods, we would like to learn more about the existence of transfer-clusters of companies and geographical distribution of their appearance. Clustering all companies in the sample according to their ranking of internal as well as external dissemination factors leads to three general clusters – with the companies being quite well distributed between the clusters:

1. *'Hands-on' transferers.* In these companies special interest is laid on the interactive hands-on transfer of results to other departments. However, they tend to refrain from abstract discussion of such results. Furthermore they seem to dislike the ordeal of making presentations of their work outside their own organization.

2. *'Hermits'.* These companies' research departments tend to avoid any contact with their scientific environment, but in addition only very limited contacts seem to exist inside the company.
3. *'Active distributors'.* Companies of the third cluster are strongly engaged in discussing their research results with both insiders and outsiders. Their only shortcoming appears to be that of direct co-operation with other internal departments, aimed at the implementation of research output in future products or processes, *ie* 'hands-on' transfer.

The above findings on the importance of the transfer channels, derived from the two sub-samples in the three clusters of companies, differs strongly between Europe and Japan. The European respondents are mainly 'hands-on' transferers, whilst the Japanese are mainly 'active distributors' - but a considerable number in Japan has also adopted the hermit approach, which does not seem to be a very promising situation (see Table 2.10 and Figure 2.18).

Table 2.10. Geographical distribution of the clusters of result dissemination.

	All interviews		Europe		Japan	
Companies:	N	%	N	%	N	%
(1) 'Hands-on' transferers	13	37.1%	11	73.3%	2	10.0%
(2) 'Hermits'	9	25.7%	2	13.3%	7	35.0%
(3) 'Active distributors'	13	37.1%	2	13.3%	11	55.0%
Total	N=35		N=15		N=20	

The diverging orientation of researching companies on the two continents leads to the assumption that differences may be found in respect of indicators of success of those research departments. Special advantages are expected for those companies where close co-operation with other departments takes place.

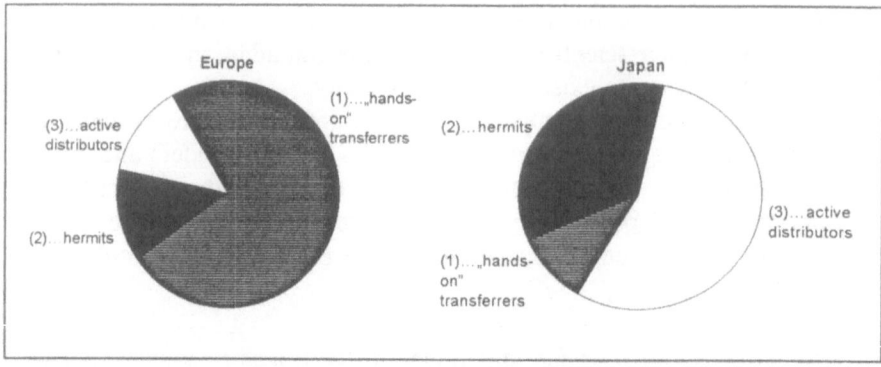

Fig. 2.18. Frequency of the clusters by continent.

2.6 Relationships between Success Factors in Research

It is difficult to find adequate criteria to measure the success at the research and departmental level. The overall company success seems to be an inadequate indicator for two reasons. Firstly, there are many factors in addition to the output of research. Research may have only a minor *direct* impact on success, but there are many *indirect* paths which lead from research to success and are realized *via* other functions. Thus any direct coherence identified between an activity in research and overall success may be accidental. Secondly, the time-lag between research activities and future sales is usually very long and difficult to quantify.

We will now examine two other factors for assessing the success of research. These have been discussed during the interviews:

1. An important factor influencing the value of money invested in research activities is the time-lag between investment and impact on the sales. The longer is this interval, the lower is *ceteris paribus* the present value of the returns, and this effect is growing as interest rates increase. Bearing this factor in mind, any shortening of the time needed to market research results will greatly affect its success (Brockhoff, 1995). We have therefore used the time-lag from availability of research results until its employment in both development departments and new businesses as indicators of research success (see Table 2.11).
2. Successful research will produce both interesting results and also produce knowledge which is valuable for the business of the company. For this value to be realized in the market place it has to be transferred into successful development and construction. Our second indicator of re-

search success is therefore the share of finished research projects which have been successfully used in products or processes in subsequent years (see Table 2.12).

The best results in both categories are reached by the companies in the first cluster which are focused on co-operation with other departments in-house using 'hands-on' transfer methods. The time-lag for research results being used in further development work is estimated to average only slightly above half a year. This figure is especially encouraging when looking at the average 2.5 years for the companies of cluster two or three. The tighter contacts with business units seem to pay off. Similar results are obtained for the time-lag before the research results are taken up by new businesses. Here the mean values for the other two clusters are again almost twice as high as those for the 'hands-on' transferers, which estimate that they can usually reach this target in less than three years.

The success rate is especially low for the second cluster (*ie* the 'hermits'). This may be an indication that ignoring activities within the scientific environment increases the risk of producing knowledge that is irrelevant for the market. On the other hand, we conclude from the results of our interviews that the success rates for companies from the third cluster are almost as high as for those from the first cluster. It may be assumed that since these companies put less weight on 'hands-on' transfer, they give considerable emphasis to interaction with the scientific environment, and are usually engaged in longer-term orientated projects than are the companies from the first cluster.

Table 2.11. Success indicators for research in the three clusters.

Clusters:	1 (N=13) Hands-on		2 (N=9) hermits		3 (N=13). active dis-tributors	
Direct measures of research success:	mean	SD	mean	SD	mean	SD
Time-lag: use of results in development (*years*)	0.65	0.80	2.39	1.29	2.65	1.56
Time-lag: use of results in new businesses (*years*)	2.85	2.60	4.67	2.60	5.65	3.10
Success rate of research projects (*per cent*)	47	20	31	20	44	24

The longer time-lags probably indicate that the research projects' results are a more suitable input for the more radical innovations rather than for short-term and incremental developments. Hence, in the long run, this strategy might be preferable. Managers of the companies from the third cluster perceive the overall technology dynamics to be higher than do representatives of the other companies.[16] The overall conclusion is that the hermits' strategy leads to the poorest results for all the measures of research success which we investigated. The two remaining strategies give comparable results for the project success *rate*. The intensive use of 'hands on' information in-house, however, significantly speeds up transfer to development and new business. The questions that relate to differences in the levels of innovation cannot be answered here.

Table 2.12. Credibility given to research.

Clusters: *Satisfaction with credibility given to research by...*	1 (N=13) *hands-on*		2 (N=9) *hermits*		3 (N=13). *active distrib.*	
	mean	SD	mean	SD	mean	SD
...top management	4.2	1.7	3.4	1.5	4.4	1.3
...others within the company	4.3	1.0	3.4	1.4	3.4	1.4
...outsiders (relevant fields of research)	5.0	1.8	3.9	1.0	4.5	1.0
7-point Likert-type scale: 0=not at all, 6=completely.						

An additional indicator which might be relevant to measuring the success of research is the credibility research departments receive elsewhere in their company and in the external environment. One could have expected that the 'hermits' would not have much credibility in the *external scientific community*. Only if they decide to cut themselves off from external contacts for strategic reasons, will the company have problems with this. Nevertheless, the figures show a different picture. Satisfaction with credibility given to research by outsiders varies significantly amongst the three clusters.[17] It is especially low for the 'hermits'. This strong dissatisfaction could be an indication that the cut-off strategy is not actively supported by researchers but is only forced upon them by top management's fears for loss of valuable information. On the other hand, the credibility

---

[16] Median: 3.5 for the active distributors, and 3.0 for each of the other clusters, but no significant differences between the clusters can be identified.

[17] Discriminant analysis on all three factors relating to the origin of respondents is significant (Sig: 0.0635)

given from the external environment is especially high for the 'hands-on' transferers, and the 'active distributors' are found to be somewhere in the middle between the other two. The question remains, however, as to whether the first cluster overestimates credibility given by outsiders simply due to their high success rate.

Looking at the satisfaction with credibility given by *top management*, it is now surprising that for the companies of the second cluster the credibility given by these strategic decision makers is relatively low. It seems that those people whom we expected to be the reason for the unfortunate closeness of research departments evaluate research by the low success rates, which in turn result from top management's decision not to open research to the outside world. If this success rate is really connected with the closeness, these research departments will not be able to improve and to gain credibility, unless there is a decision at the top level to change in policy.

Business units ('others within the company') seem to indicate high degrees of contentment only with those research departments which practice 'hands-on' co-operation. At the same time, top management tends to evaluate more abstract output and to transfer projects into development, as cluster one and cluster three receive relatively high credibility. A considerable share of difficulties in coordinating top and business unit managements' ideas and in selecting research programmes may be due to this difference in accepting good results for their own sake or only in counting transferred results.

3 Conclusions and Recommendations

A number of recommendations can be derived from this study:

* Research and development elasticities can be estimated using a Delphi-styled approach.

* The results of our study are based on the electrical/electronics industry. For application in other industries, the process would have to be repeated using an appropriate sample and the results may differ.

* There seems to be a strong positive impact of variations in research expenditure on future sales.

* Changes of a company's research budget inversely influence its development expenses, due to substitution effects.

* The system of elasticities which has been derived here can be employed to derive an optimal distribution of the overall R&D budget on research and development. Actual budgets should be carefully reviewed on this basis.

*We can conclude that knowledge from external sources is playing a crucial, and perhaps increasingly important, role in industrial research. Thus, co-operation with the academic sphere, and especially with universities, is the most frequent form of external co-operation entered into by industrial research departments. Attempts by university laboratories to improve with respect to the industrial relevance of their research seem to making progress. However, closer co-operation with single industry partners may bear the risk of privatizing parts of the publicly funded research results. Increasing relevance may in this respect be connected with decreasing accessibility for other companies.

*Further, we were able to identify three clusters of companies, classified according to their strategies for internal and external dissemination of their research results. Whilst the companies focusing on 'hands-on' transfer dominate in Europe, in Japan the group which actively distributes results clearly dominates, and even the 'hermits' play an important role in Japan. Relating these clusters to success indicators for research, we see clear disadvantages for those companies that do not allow their researchers to make external contacts. Focusing on hands-on transfer leads to high success rates in relatively short time spans, whilst the activity in transfer of results of a more traditional kind incurs similar success rates but connected very long time-lags.

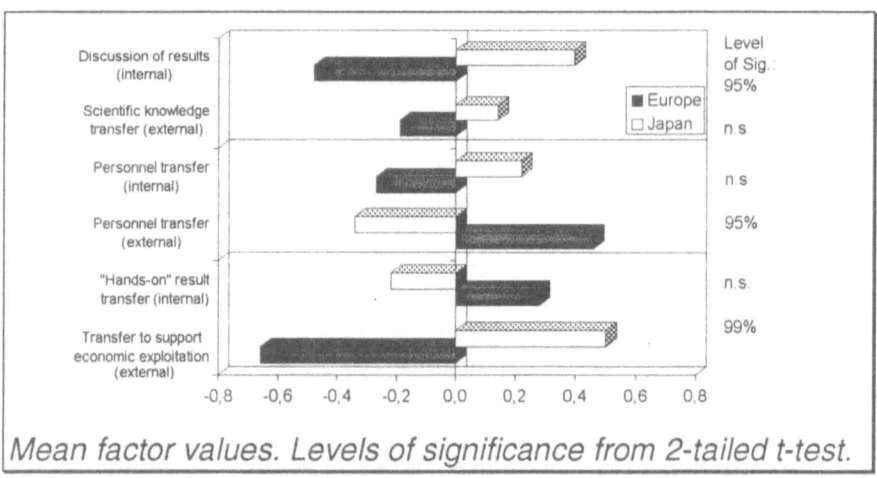

Fig. 2.19. Relevance of factors of dissemination of research results by continent.

*Returning to the European - Japanese comparison, Figure 2.19 highlights typical strengths of the companies operating in the two continents. We see the Japanese to be stronger in the more theoretical discussion of results internally. This might be due to the presence of a higher proportion of the more basic parts of research being in Japanese companies. Internal exchange of personnel is slightly more frequent in Japan. At the same time the exchange of personnel with external institutions is significantly more frequent in Europe. The most obvious differences, however, are found in the activities at the 'business interface': While European companies are more active in presenting 'hands-on' results of their work internally, Japanese research departments are much more involved in the presentation of their achievements to the market and thus in supporting the marketing of the companies products.

*Future research must, on the one hand, be directed towards a more detailed evaluation of success indicators for research; and on the other, results from this study should be evaluated on a larger sample to increase its validity and reliability.

*External research can be advantageously used by companies to effectively extend the range of their research programme.

*Some in-house research effort is necessary to provide a basis for assimilation and integration of research results obtained from outside .

*To increase the speed of transfer of research results, practical cooperation with development departments is indispensable.

*Open and active transfer activities (both inside and outside the company) have a positive affect on the success rate of research departments.

*The management of research should be aware of the strong dependency of research success upon its co-operation with partners inside and outside the company. An overall culture of secrecy has negative effects on most success factors.

References

1. R. Bardy, 'Die Produktivität von Forschung und Entwicklung. Eine ökonometrische Analyse der Abhängigkeit industrieller Wertschöpfung von Forschungs- und Entwicklungsausgaben aufgrund von Produktionsfunktionen, mit empirischen Ergebnissen für die deutsche Chemiewirtschaft', Meisenheim a. Glan., 1974

2. K. Brockhoff, *Jahrbücher für Nationalökonomie und Statistik*, 1972, **184**, 111-120

3. K. Brockhoff, *Zeitschrift für Betriebswirtschaftliche Forschung*, 1972, **24**, 709-723

4. K. Brockhoff, 'Forschung und Entwicklung, Planung und Kontrolle', 4., erg. Aufl., München, 1994

5. E. Mansfield, *The American Economic Review*, 1980, **70**, 863-873.

6. A.N. Link, *The American Economic Review*, 1981, **71**, 1111-1112

7. Z. Griliches, 'Productivity, R&D and Basic Research at the Firm Level in the 1979's, *The American Economic Review*, 1986, **76**, 141-154

8. H.A. Linstone,and M. Turoff (eds.), 'The Delphi Method, Techniques and Applications', Don Mills, Amsterdam, London, 1975

9. R. Rothwell and M. Beesley, M., 'Barriers to Growth in Small Firms', ed. J. Barber, J.S. Metcalfe and J.S., Porteous, London, 1989

10. E. Mansfield, *Research Policy*, 1991, **20**(1), 1-12

11. E.M. Scolnick, *Research-Technology Management*, 1990, **33**(6), 21-26

12. M. Hermes, Dissertation, Kiel, 1995

13. E. Mansfield, *American Economic Review*, 1988, **78**, 223-228

14. W.M. Cohen and D.A. Levinthal, *The Economic Journal*, 1989, **99**, 569-596

15. W.M. Cohen and D.A. Levinthal, *Administrative Science Quarterly*, 1990, **35**, 128-152

16. W.M. Cohen and D.A. Levinthal, *Management Science*, 1994, **40**, 227-251

17. O. Granstrand, E. Bohlin, C. Oskarsson and N. Sjöberg, *R&D Management*, 1992, **22**(2), 111-133

18. K. Brockhoff, *Technovation*, 1995, **15**(10), 591-599

19. A.-P. Hameri, *Technovation*, 1996, **16**(2), 51-57

20. E. v. Hippel, *Management Science*, 1994, **40**(4), 429-439

21. M.R. Sheen, *R&D Management*, 1992, **22**(2), 135-143

22. G.S. McMillan, R.A. Klavans and R.D. Hamilton, *R&D Management*, 1995, **25**(4), 411-419

Chapter 3
The System Company

Luigi Paganetto

In this chapter we describe the characteristics of a System Company and the variables which need to be considered for decision making within such an organization. High quality technology management and system integration are key factors, but the configuration of the market and the nature of contracts involving component suppliers are also important. The factors involved in 'make or buy' decisions are reviewed. Total control of the technology is the most desirable situation, based on vertical integration; and the degree to which this can be achieved in practice is discussed along with other factors which also bear on management decisions which need to be optimized.

---

1 Definition of a System Company

In many industries a new form of organization is emerging, and this we can call the *System Company* (SC). It may be defined as a company which is somewhere between a general contractor and a vertically integrated organization. The system of management in these companies is neither totally hierarchical, nor totally market based, but is characterized by networks which have high levels of dependence and trust between partners. The actual structure of a SC will depend on its position along the value-added chain. The critical parameters are the degree of vertical integration and the nature of the system integration activity. In fact, most of these companies are moving up along the value-added chain and are reducing their manufacturing activity in favour of their system integration activity. Due to the complexity of the strategic space, SCs tend to change their organizational boundaries quite frequently by means of acquisitions, mergers, alliances and non-equity agreements. For these companies it is vital to know a) how to manage innovation in products that they do not produce themselves, b) how to evaluate their own investments without controlling the whole chain of value, c) how to protect their know-how from component manufacturers who could become competitors in systems, d) how to maintain their capabilities of innovation in systems without controlling innovation in components.

System Companies produce final products that show an inherent systemic nature in terms of the knowledge used to develop the product itself. These products, which can be defined as *complex systems*, result from a great variety of components and sub-systems with high technology content.

On the market demand side, products are realized in small series or as single models and exhibit a high degree of customization that reflects the heterogeneity of users' requirements. With respect to technology, systems exhibit high levels of interdependence between the functions of individual components. This makes the design and manufacturing of each component heavily dependent on the definition of the characteristics of other components. The interactions between components cannot be solved using a fixed set of physical parameters at the beginning of the process, because they change over time during the process. Due to the combined effect of demand heterogeneity and technical interdependence, companies that design and produce such complex systems are organized on a *project basis*.

Some common features with respect to organization and strategies are present in these companies and for this reason they can be described at a global level as large, multi-business, multi-technology, divisionalized corporations. Often, they are also characterized by a relevant degree of internationalization and by strong and evolving relationships with governments.

These characteristics can make strategic management in systemic industries rather complex, and consequently the achievement of strategic superiority depends crucially on the ability to control the rapid pace of technological change and to manage the activity of system integration.

2   Technology Management within a System Company

System companies operate in technologically turbulent environments, characterized by rapidly changing organizational boundaries. As already mentioned, the strategic management in systemic businesses is characterized by the need to control the system technology, as well as to anticipate and influence the development of individual technologies. This goal can be achieved only by anticipating technological trajectories for both the overall and the constituent technologies and identifying the relationships between them in the long term.

For a better understanding of the meaning of the term 'technology management' it is useful to recall whether and to what extent possession of technology has been perceived to be a competitive advantage. In the first half of this century, technology was considered to be nothing more than a 'black box': the use of physical and human resources would produce technological innovation, often in an unpredictable way. In other words, technological innovation was produced by sporadic and lucky intuitions made by isolated 'researchers' who, in many cases, suffered financial distress without coming close to the foreseen objective. After World War II, the isolated efforts of a few pioneers was organized *via* a more structured environment by the emerging big corporations. R&D Departments and Research Offices were created whenever market competition demanded 'up to date' products and refinements to them. Over this period, technology was seen only as a component of the production process, subject to a budget and to a strict timetable. During the 1980s, this 'control approach' evolved into a 'strategic approach'. "Strategy driven approach to technology management is achieved by bringing both technologically knowledgeable executives and the firm's chief technology officer into the strategic formulation processes of the company" [1]. In other words, decisions about technology are taken at top-executive levels and technology itself is seen as a strategic variable rather than just a production variable.

Companies will benefit from changes in the management guidelines and tools used previously. The 'strategic approach', which considers technology as a key component of the company strategy, and was used with the old 'control approach' (where project budget, timetable and estimated returns were the only variables to be considered) is now becoming less important and a 'fourth generation' approach is gaining prominence. This looks at technology in terms of *'technology management'* rather than just *'technology knowledge'*. Whilst the technology knowledge approach addresses the application of scientific and engineering knowledge to the solution of problems, technology management produces integration of technology throughout the organization as a source of sustainable competitive advantage.

Technology management is thus the new strategic approach used to deal with the main opportunities available within an SC, in a way which combines and coordinates the various inputs from the partners involved, in order to deal with the uncertainty of the technology development process, and to manage the distribution of ownership and production among different institutions, firms, and individuals involved. As long as these aspects are handled successfully, companies will be able to produce sustainable competitive advantages.

Over recent years, *technology* has become a key factor in determining a company's competitive advantage and managers have learned to manage this resource. However, now that technology has started to be spread and communicated more cheaply and rapidly amongst competitors, the deployment of a particular advanced technology is still a necessary condition for obtaining a competitive advantage, but this is often destroyed after a very short interval by new competitors who have access to the same technology.

In order to obtain a competitive advantage that lasts for a long time, companies should achieve new standards of quality and novelty, ready for when competitors threaten them *via* product imitation. There are basically three ways of obtaining such a *'sustainable competitive advantage'*. The first, which may be unrealistic, is to believe in the existence of a continuous flow of innovations from within the organization that guaranties continuous movement towards higher levels of excellence; and the second, which is more realistic, is to conceive this movement towards excellence as capable of being determined by the management, which is able to analyse a wide range of information such as market trends, real (suppliers) and financial constraints, needs (consumers) and technology evolution. The third, and recommended, way is to consider a combination of the two.

As a consequence of these considerations and making the assumption that successful firms should endeavour to realise an *endogenously determined sustainable competitive advantage* (EDSCA), it is essential to ensure that care is taken with the management of technology evolution and how managers understand this evolution. In fact, market trends and real and financial constraints and needs strictly depend on technology evolution.

During the 1980s the NEC Corporation sustained a competitive advantage with respect to GTE because its management was able to foresee technology evolution and, based on this, to review supplier agreements and to anticipate or, even better, to generate consumer needs. This winning strategy was possible because NEC thought about technology in two parallel ways, *ie* acquisition and deployment. According to Werther *et al* [1], among others, "to successfully acquire and deploy a specific technology may well lead to a competitive advantage. But a sustainable competitive advantage comes from the organization 'learning' how constantly to improve its technology acquisition and deployment capabilities".

The ability to blend acquisition and deployment of technology and to adjust a company's organization according to the various blending thought to be necessary is what in the recent economic literature is called a *'relational good'*, This relational good is something that is neither easily observed nor quickly duplicated by competitors. Consequently it has all the properties to be considered as an *endogenously determined sustainable competitive advantage*. This approach should be based on only a few subjects and these should be operative over a significant period.

In its broader definition, a System Company can be considered an entity whose main objective is to achieve an *endogenously determined sustainable competitive advantage* in an environment where there is severe pressure for changes not only in individual technologies, but also in the architecture of the system and the relationships amongst the components of the system itself. In this context, *technology management* becomes the instrument for achieving such an objective *via* the interrelationships between acquisition, development and deployment of technologies.

In order to attain a better understanding of how SCs and technology management are inter-related, let us look at the scheme depicted in Figure 3.1, which we have defined as *'Company's Technology Pattern'*:

---

[1]   The notion of a *relational good* has been described in its earlier development by Lieberstein [2], Aoki [3] and Morishima [4]. In our context a relational good can significantly influence market outcome *via* its external effects. The importance of such external effects is in determining different development patterns is widely recognized in a growing body of literature on endogenous growth theory, started by the seminal work of Romer [5]. In our new approach the relational good investigated refers to the management of technology in a complex organization rather than the technology itself.

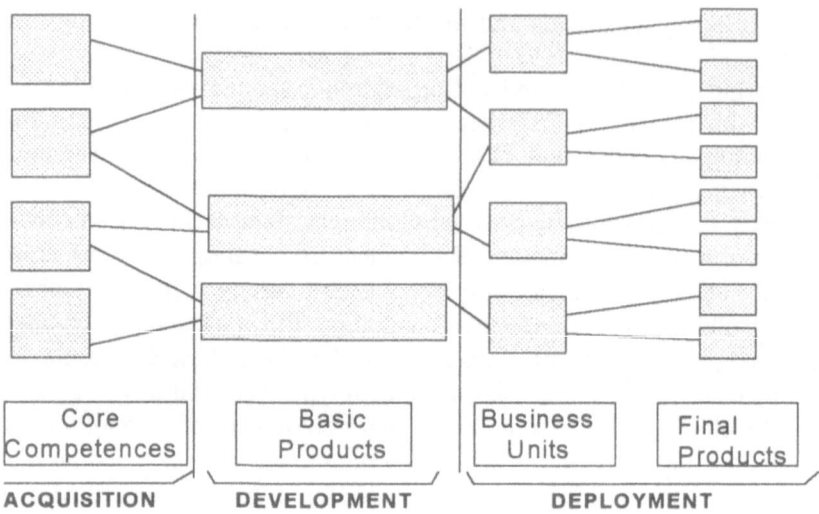

Fig. 3.1. Technology pattern: the case of total control.[2]

With this concept we mean something specific to a company which characterizes its structure for a significant period of time. In other words, it can be interpreted as the company's DNA, where all the relevant information about the organization's future development for the next 10-15 years is written.

In the Company's Technology Pattern we can distinguish the *'core competencies'* or what the organization learned at all stages of its management activity: this is not only its knowledge of pure technology, but also how the technology can be compatible with the whole of the organization (including production, finance, marketing, etc.). These competences are the more valuable to the company, the bigger the number of component parts in the goods produced.

From the point of view of effective technology management, once a company has acquired a core competence, the next step is to make it tangible, and to develop it and obtain some *'basic products'*. The development of basic products is one of the most important activities in the management of a company. In fact leadership in the basic product market allows the control of manufacturing standards and evolution in the final product markets for a long period of time.

---

[2] Figures 3.1. and 3.2. are based on reference 6, but have been modified according to our new interpretation.

The *'deployment'* phase is implemented through strategic *business units* and through the production of *final goods and services*. In this phase it is possible to implement four strategies which tend to prolong competitive advantage: value added, lock-in, pre-empting and blocking. Whilst the first two are used to attract customers and to keep them on a long-term basis, the remaining two are used to maintain competitive advantages. The over-all objective is to transform and raise the company's technical standards and to prevent or at least to make unattractive the entrance of competitors into the market.

When companies produce goods with a high systems content, technology management is particularly difficult due to the necessity of controlling the technology of the whole system, as well as to anticipate and influence the development of the individual technologies. In other words, the goal of maintaining control of the system cannot be achieved by simply looking at the single technologies of the components or at the technological architecture of the system alone; but rather by anticipating the trajectories of both and highlighting the existing reciprocal relationships in the long-run: this is what we define as *'Total Control of Technology'*.

When control of the technological pattern is total, the company is said to be *'Technologically vertically integrated'*. Situations of this type are quite rare and the probability of maintaining total control decreases with the complexity of the goods produced. For instance, a company may not always have access to some competencies for one of the following reasons: technology exists but is secret; technology is patent protected and not generally available; technology is available, but it imposes some standards that do not conform with company standards; technology is available but the company does not have the expertise to handle it or technology is available and can readily be implemented, but is expensive. In all these cases, control of the technology pattern is partial (the part below the dotted line in Figure 3.2) and the company can loose the opportunity to be present in the market for the final goods in some cases.

A further non-trivial factor related to the control of technologies is the rate at which the availability of links between parts of the technology pattern change with time. There are some competencies that for a particular period should be proprietary, but after a limited number of years these can easily be obtained from elsewhere.

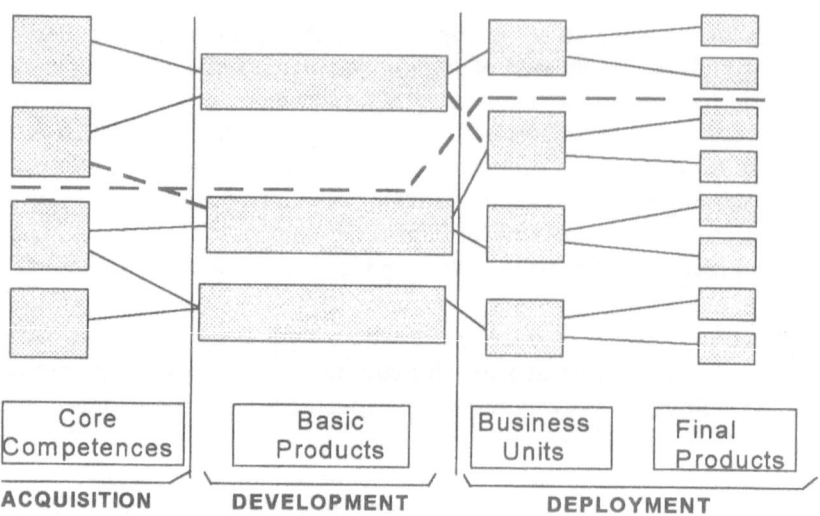

Fig. 3.2. Technology pattern: the case of partial control.

This aspect of their technology opens SCs to a wider set of problems, merely the degree of coherence of technological trajectories that imposes the management of different types of strategies across time. In fact, the higher the level of technologies involved in the system, the higher the polymorphism of the evolution of the system dynamic. Each system represents the result from the simultaneous solution of many technical and economic trade-offs, most of which can suddenly change. Trade-offs are also influenced by the development of basic scientific research which continuously modifies the distribution of technological opportunities.

In the new approach "managers should think about investments more in terms of their capacity to build new capabilities. Rarely, if ever, is a strategically worthwhile capability created through a one-shot investment. Capabilities that provide enduring sources of competitive advantage are usually built over time through a series of investments in facilities, human capital, and knowledge" [7].

3   System Integration

A system company has a distinctive management capability, which requires cognitive skills that are different in some ways from those typical of the management of traditional manufacturing. The company must develop a specific competence for integrating its system which distinguishes it from its competitors, and for modelling its relationships with component firms, thus allowing the consideration of its system as something more than that of the sum of its own parts. In particular, a system company has to manage a network of partially separable productive units, characterized by high levels of diversity, complementarity and inter-relatedness, both with respect to existing technologies and future ones. However, it is from the capacity to manage these multiple interactions across different components, sub-systems and levels that increasing overall returns originate. There is thus a *super-additive* profit function which can be attributed not only to economies of scale but also to the presence of relevant technical, financial, and technological functions. For SCs, the cost of the system integration activity may overcome the costs of the development and manufacturing of components.

According to these considerations, a successful system company possesses two forms of knowledge: component knowledge and knowledge about the ways in which components are integrated and linked together into a coherent whole. In other words, a system company develops what is defined as *architectural knowledge* around which problem-solving strategies, information filters and communication channels are usually organized

In controlling the component-system dynamics, the SC is faced with the strategic problem of guaranteeing a long-term convergence between its own technological development plan and the specific technological trajectories of component manufacturers. The SC has to put component technologies into a hierarchy of levels of criticality, where the importance of components is normally defined according to the complexity and uniqueness of their technology and availability in the market. Accordingly, SCs have to decide whether to produce a certain component internally, or to obtain it from an outside company by establishing an appropriate contractual relationship with the component producer. The outsourcing process can produce short-run benefits but be costly in the long-run, due to the future inability of the system company to manufacture the component itself and to control its technological impact. However, when the choice to go outside prevails, the system company must ensure that the business relationship with the other company is firm and that adequate contractual arrangements are made so that the uncertainties in the relationship are minimal. The SC then has to consider asymmetric information and it has to choose the optimal contract which allows it to accurately evaluate the component producer's skills. Moreover, if the system product requires that some components are on the frontiers of technology, the system company must develop competencies which enable it to be an 'intelligent' buyer of this technology. This means that companies should possess in-depth knowledge of the technology in question, and the capability of developing and preserving this knowledge in order to acquire and maintain the necessary competencies to enable it to make the most appropriate decisions. Accordingly, suitable investment in research is made in order to understand the role played by the specific component within the total technology and the system architecture.

As far as the system company's choice to integrate strategically is concerned, this can be based mainly on technology management considerations. When a specific technology is identified as critical for the technological development of the system company, the marginal cost of production tends to be progressively irrelevant in the decision to integrate. Thus, this choice differs from that made within the standard definition of vertical/horizontal integration, which is based mainly on cost considerations.

Our analysis suggests a new approach to investments, which should be evaluated according to their capacity to build new capabilities. Managers should think about fixed investments and R&D expenses in terms of their capacity to create or maintain the 'core competencies' of the system company. In other words, the investment in competencies should be considered as a growth option on the future development of the company which gives it the right to expand in the future into new product or geographic markets. This kind of investment captures the importance of investing rapidly in the opportunities critical to the growth and success of new businesses. The lack of early investment in an area of expertise may foreclose the future development of a technical capability in that area. As in a cumulative and path-dependent process, a low initial investment diminishes the attractiveness of investing in subsequent periods even if the firm becomes aware of technological opportunities. In other words, companies cannot afford to miss a generation of technology and expect to remain competitive.

Finally, it is important to stress that the SC, independently of the degree of vertical integration, tends to maintain its own *'Total Design Capability' for* product-systems. This does not mean that the SC plans the whole design activity but that the company has the management capability to do so. Possession of this capability means that the SC is still a competent buyer of sub-systems and can develop deverticalization strategies with just a little loss of knowledge. Thus, the manufacturing and design activity for the same components follow different patterns of evolution. SCs also control the production of those components whose realization may interact with the design activity.

4 Some Examples of System Companies

In this section some examples of system companies are given in order to illustrate how they operate in practice. Most of this information was obtained by my colleague Simone Tani during interviews in both Europe and Japan with managers of company R&D or Technology Planning Departments. Forty companies were visited, most of them twice and some of them three or four times.

The key determinants shaping the evolution of the company's value-added may be clustered around three main topics: the nature of technological evolution and the knowledge the system company needs in order to develop a new product-system, the history of the company, and the business in which it is involved.

System companies generally focus on more selective and specific technological areas / businesses (system integration), but appreciate the multiple links between systems and components. These links may be cognitive in nature: it is impossible to develop systems without knowledge of components (risks in losing the complex cognitive representation of the system), as well as strategic: *eg* companies look for systems configurations that may allow the selling of as many components as possible. System companies are however focusing on customized components, because they cannot usually afford to develop general purpose high volume components. According to Walker [8] "Perception of where their special advantage will lie in the future appears however to be changing. Increasingly they are coming to regard themselves as systems companies, reflecting the growing interconnectedness of technologies. Increasingly they are operating at the top level of the product hierarchy - integrated systems ... This is substantially due to the impact of the new generic technologies".

The average value-added of industrial activities of system companies (the value of the industrial activities developed in-house for the most relevant complex system), according to the mean of the estimates of the company managers, was 56% in 1980 and 50.5% in 1995. The following companies, taken from the total sample highlight some key trends. Thus, system companies are still far from becoming 'virtual corporations', even though their share of value-added is decreasing slightly. This trend may be interpreted as arising from the trend to focus increasingly on core business, as well as the advent of digital technologies, which turn many components into commodities. A thorough analysis of the whole sample of companies leads to the following general conclusions:

Europe versus Japan. The Japanese companies are more stable than the European. The main changes in taking make or buy decisions and in division of innovative labour take place within the borders of each group, between the parent company (the system company) and the subsidiaries. During the eighties the value-added of the system companies increased, due to the use of a widespread strategic approach to master the technologies previously licensed from abroad, particularly in systemic heavy business. An approach based on increasing procurement is gaining some popularity in Japan, mainly due to contingent yen appreciation, but this is a new fashion rather than an already established practice. On the other hand, EU companies have been much more willing to get rid of component manufacturing. Furthermore, at least as far as leading companies in heavy industries are concerned, there seems to exist a sort of time-lag between the two economic areas. The Japanese companies arrive later to master whole systems and to develop proprietary technologies, and this also means starting the outsourcing processes later.

Complex systems versus high volume products. Four multi-business system companies argued that it is better to be more integrated in complex system business than in the high volume products which they also produced. The value-added of electronics mass produced appliances is particularly low in comparison with complex electronics systems. This feature as determined by the specific nature of the system / component relationship in complex system business.

Qualitative vs quantitative changes. A sub-sample of companies argued that while their share of value-added is substantially stable, major changes are happening in the composition of this value-added. Among the determinants of this qualitative change are: (a) the relative weight of mechanics versus electronics in heavy systems; (b) the hardware versus software division; (c) the relative proportion of manufacturing to services. Even though the quantitative importance of services must not be over-emphasized (particularly in Japan), it is also true that the ability to deliver key services is increasingly a *conditio sine qua non* for getting contracts.

Differences in complex product generations. The systems of the previous generation and generally all the new complex systems show a significantly higher degree of value-added developed in house in the same company. Established systems show a relatively high degree of outsourcing. By developing new product generations in-house, the system companies may also control the evolution of the outsourced subsystems of the previous generations. This issue, which is related to the single product to be developed, must not be confused with the general trend in companies to be less integrated in new business areas than in past company business areas.

Amongst the different value-added activities, pursued in order to maximize profits, the first priority, as identified from the responses of ten Japanese companies was the optimization of the purchasing activity. The effectiveness of that strategy is however linked to the quality of the basic system design (an effective design allows the optimal use of components, increasing their quality and reducing their number) and the engineering of the business process, which are the second and third relevant items. The manufacturing activity is also considered to be of key importance for added-value, to a greater degree than by the EU companies. Out of the seven EU companies that discussed this topic, the first item was again the optimization of the purchasing activity. However, four companies claimed that R&D is the key value-added factor, *via* various means: R&D to reduce costs of materials (Snecma and Framatome), R&D optimization by compressing development time of complex systems, in which manufacturing is relatively less important (Matra), and R&D for getting a competitive edge in the product to be sold (Thomson CSF). EU companies were definitely more concerned about the effective use of R&D for value creation.

System companies' value-added is changing either from the qualitative or from the quantitative perspective. From the qualitative aspect the issue is linked to the changing division of innovative labour. This issue can be analysed from both the aspects of the *evolution of the supply chain*, and from the *evolution of companies between systems and components, ie* evolution along the value-added chain. Top-down evolution is usually a deliberate strategy, whilst bottom-up evolution is an emergent strategy, arising from particular market and industry structure constraints.

In the aerospace, railway and energy industries, integration activities previously developed at the final system integration level are increasingly developed at lower stages of the supply chain, without major shifts in companies ranking along the value chain. In those cases the company involved in subsystems development adds new systemic functions, but remains in the subsystems business, but there are exceptions. On the other hand, the evolution from components to complex systems development is a key factor in the electronics industry, especially in Japan.

The common element among the different situations is the competition to control the system integration activity. Sometimes this is attempted by replacing the incumbent system company (a goal very hard to pursue in the heaviest businesses, which require massive investments and established interfaces), and sometimes by absorbing system companies' functions, *eg* by exploiting changes in the nature of the value-added chain.

In the following examples the most relevant issues for SCs are highlighted:

Aerospace Company, Europe. This system company stresses that key suppliers have tried to gain power by developing subsystem integration. They want to be considered subsystem integrators by the system company.

They do not want to replace the system company, but their goal is to increase the value they add to the components they develop. The problem is the vertical division of labour, more than eventual changes of role in the industry. The system company's goal is the total control of the system, which may contrast with the goal of the key suppliers. In order to be able to control the evolution of the whole system, the final integrator gives directives that are driven by the future possibility of technological changes. Directives on methods are critical for managing future system evolution. Even though bigger and bigger subsystems are outsourced, the system company feels more and more that it is a system integrator and not just an assembler. The main goal is achieving flexibility in relationships with suppliers by maximizing the software content of components, in order to allow for retrofits during the aircraft life-cycle. The stronger protection of system companies is the fact that system know-how is usually built through exclusive relationships with key clients which are rooted in well established inter-organizational routines. Rising *development costs* are a key factor underlying the trend in change of emphasis from systems to components.

Railway Company, Europe. In the railways industry subsystem developers are highly specialized companies, which supply many system companies. Specialized suppliers gain substantial economies in understanding what is required. They are not interested in competing at the final system level, while their goal is to add value through more responsibilities in the division of labour at the subsystem level. Furthermore, system integration is an industrial activity that requires hard investments in plants and heavy technical infrastructures. Component companies are usually 'softer' companies, for example electronics firms. The stability of the railway business is a further reason for hindering movements from components to systems or *vice-versa*; but the total system integration may be achieved *via* mergers between mechanical and electronics companies.

Aero-engine Company, Europe. This industry is characterized by subsystem companies which are trying to become total system integrators. BMW aero-engines, for example, in the merger with Rolls-Royce, will become a system integrator, and it is a new task for that company. Companies such as MTU and some Japanese enterprises are working in the same direction. The behaviour of incumbent system companies is critical for subsystem companies willing to become system integrators, as new aero-engine models may emerge from a partnership. On the other hand, shifts from systems to components is quite an usual situation for companies entering the civil aero-engine business from the military business. This company is almost fully integrated in the military engine business, but decided to enter the civil engine business by creating a partnership with an incumbent system company, and just a few components were developed by the entrant.

Energy Company, Europe. The evolution along the supply chain and the evolution of the supply chain itself may be linked. This system company is involved in the integration of meter boxes for energy applications. The key electronic components are provided by a leader component company. The competitive advantage for this company is its relationships with the customers, while the key strength of the component company is the quality of the equipment provided. The product-system is increasingly composed of electronic and telecommunication modules, and is increasingly networked into higher complexity systems. The strategy of the component company is not to get the system integration level of the system company, but to by-pass it in order to manage the new emergent system. For the component supplier the target system is not the meter box in itself, but the whole communication system between meters and utilities, of which the previous system becomes a component. The goal of the former component company is to provide the final customer with a total package that contains one of its boxes. Furthermore, the box is becoming more and more standardized, due to the nature of the components provided by the supplier. The advantage of the supplier company is also based on the fact that its 'commodity' culture is closer to some of the customers than the specialized culture of the system company.

Electronics Company, Japan. In the electronics business, components are progressively absorbing systems functions, and this may result in difficulties in dividing systems from components. In fact, *systems on silicon* are devices which are becoming increasingly similar to systems. To design such devices, the concept designer is a system engineer, with a system knowledge. Furthermore, if some components are increasingly similar to systems, most of today's systems will be components of the even more complex systems of tomorrow. Distinction between systems and components, accordingly, must be assessed from a dynamic perspective.

Two Electronics Companies, Japan. Both companies support the relevance of the evolution from components to systems. In the first case it is the outcome of a diversification effort in systemic business applications. In the second case it is the outcome of the exploitation of particularly effective component technologies. However, most of the Japanese companies evolving towards more complex products do not leave components development, which often remains the heart of the business and an effective base for diversification.

Electronics Company, Japan. This company is evolving from being a traditional component company, and its goal is to reach the system integration level of the network (monitoring systems for power transmission lines) from the network terminals. The systemic task is to achieve the optimal combination of components. However, entering the system business is a major breakthrough for this company. It was not held back by technological barriers, but rather by changing sales channels and social nonverbal constraints. In fact there is a problem of social control in Japan, both at the level of people and competitors, and not all of the strategic options are easily available.

Two Examples from the Radar Industry

This final example comes from the work of two other members of my group, Vincenzo Atella and Marco Cucculelli who studied the impact of market structure on the system company.

Following the strong process of acquisitions which took place in the early nineties, the radar industry has shown an increasing degree of concentration. In 1993, the world market share of the first eight producers was approximately 80%. At present, US producers control half of the world market for radar while European producers supply the remaining share. The world leader is Thomson (France) and its influence is present in almost all the segments of the industry.

Reflected in the new development programmes of these companies is the fact that avionics radar is the most dynamic and innovative product. Concentration in this avionics segment is increasing at a speed faster than in the industry as a whole: the first four producers represent half of the whole supply of the segment and the concentration ratio is close to 85%. In the avionics radar industry, US producers are the leaders: first of all Hughes, followed by Westinghouse and Texas Instruments. The leading producers in Europe are Thomson (France) and GEC (UK), after the acquisition of Ferranti.

The relevance of the avionics segment in the radar industry is also evident from the dynamics of mergers and acquisitions. In recent years, the most important acquisitions have been focused in the avionics sector. Examples of this can be seen in such leading companies as Finmeccanica (FM) and Fiat, GEC and Ferranti, Westinghouse and Norden. Furthermore, collaborations and joint ventures established in recent years by almost all the leading companies in the world underline the relevance of the avionics segment to the future of the radar industry (joint venture between GEC-Thomson, technological collaboration FM-GEC-DASA, *etc*).

The technological content of the products can be used to divide the radar industry into two sub-segments: ground-based radar and avionic radar. The technology of the most important components and subsystems for ground-based radar is 'mature' and easily available in the market. On the contrary, system technology and knowledge are less standardized and producers tend to maintain a (total or partial) design capability in house. Avionic radar is the more innovative product: given the operational condition in which these devices usually work, the importance (in terms of reliability) of component technology is very strong. Furthermore, system knowledge and system design play a significant role in integrating the single component technologies in the most efficient way. The systemic side of the product is surely more relevant to avionic radar than ground-based radar.

According to one system company leader in the radar industry, the evolution of component technology has produced an increase in the share of outsourced components and design, at least for standard ground-based radar. The reason for the increasing outsourcing of components has been related to its availability on the market at a lower cost. Some of the components are not as application-specific as for ground-based radar, and the trend in the last ten years has been towards outsourcing of both manufacturing and design. On the contrary, customized components and application specific subsystems continue to be produced internally, as in the case of the subsystems for the avionic radar.

Past and future trends of the main components are indicated in Figure 3.3. Components and systems are listed on the right. The Figure gives evidence for two clearly distinctive patterns of technology management evolution within the company. The trends for components above the dashed line are those that can produce a technologically competitive advantage, while the others are the 'mature' technologies that are outsourced or acquired from the market.

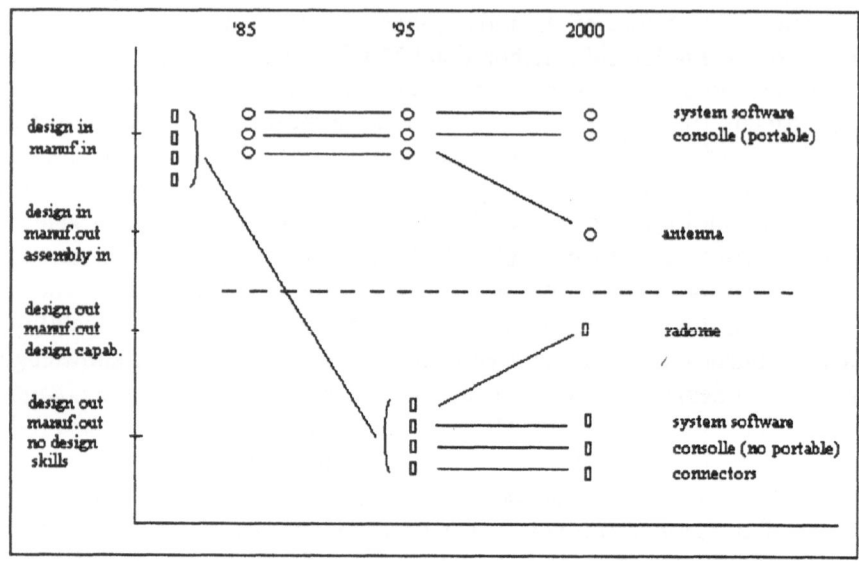

Fig. 3.3. The pattern of evolution in selected technologies within a radar company.

Another system company in the radar industry, agrees that the main difference in radar technologies is related to the distinction between avionic radar and ground-based radar. For example, in avionic radar the signal processing system is usually made in-house and probably in the future will be integrated *via* gallium arsenide (GaAs) circuits, in contrast to the chips and other components for signal processing systems for ground-based radar which are available on the market. For ground-based radar systems there are three or four times more outsourced components than for avionic radar systems radar. One of the critical technologies in the future radar industry will be gallium arsenide and this company has decided to control its own technology in that field. While GaAs is produced internally, silicon technology and some processing technology are purchased externally as for a commodity. The decision to invest in the internal manufacturing of components, such as GaAs circuits, and in-house design of the antenna will lead to a dominant position in the market.

In avionic radar almost everything is supplied in house and the only things which are purchased from outside are designed internally. There is thus total design control on everything supplied from both inside and outside the company. For ground based radar, on the other hand, this company buys computer systems, displays and consoles from outside and produces only the computer software internally.

Regarding the increasing trend towards manufacturing only high value-added components and subsystems for the radar, the company is going to focus on software, system technology and design knowledge as its strategic competencies rather than on single components or subsystems. It will subcontract a larger proportion of the assembly work outside while retaining responsibility for the systems and their configuration.

5 Decisions within SC Management

The achievement of the 'total control of technology' which many SCs would like to have, requires a decision from company's management. For example, this could be between 'in house' and 'external' sources of R&D, especially in a context of technologies rapidly becoming more advanced. In this situation, the logical steps which managers can take in order to arrive at the best decision are the following:

1. Write down the 'Company Technology Pattern' (CTP);
2. Evaluate the availability and feasibility of all the links between the parts of the CTP;
3. Decide between in-house and externally sourced R&D, when necessary, according to some pre-existing behavioural models such as 'Transaction Cost', 'Path Dependency', 'Firm Size' and 'National Origin'.

Regarding Step 3, several solutions are possible according to the model used. A company should bring its R&D in-house when the number of suppliers in the market is small. In this case, if for any reason it is necessary to change supplier, the cost of this may become too high. Problems can arise when there is strong competition in a particular sector. In this case, the supplier can easily use the acquired knowledge in a different, but related project, entered into with a rival firm. Path dependency suggests that a company is more likely to bring an R&D project in-house when it has accumulated more in-house R&D experience. 'Company Size' and 'National Origin' models do not give an unambiguous answer. For example, Anderson and Schmittlein [9] found that in the electronics industry the likelihood that a company would use an internal sales force (rather than independent representatives) increases with the company's size. In another publication, by Clark, Chew and Fujimoto [10], contrasting results were obtained.

The above analysis has sketched the structure of a System Company, without paying too much attention to the external environment. We will now consider the market structure within which these firms operate.

There are many internal and external constraints that could prevent SCs from achieving *Total Control of Technology*. Two of the most important constraints are the input and output market structures.

It should be clear by now that only companies which produce complex systemic products are suitable for SC management. Very often, these companies are large multinationals which operate at world-class level in a monopolistic or an oligopolistic environment, rather than in a perfect competitive environment. The nature of the market environment is crucial for the business relationships that the SC can enter into with other SCs or with the sub-system/component suppliers. In this sense, a two-way interaction exists between the SC and the market structure, as long as market structure can influence SC operations, or these operations can modify the market environment. Assume, for example that a hypothetical company plays a game. With this game our company is committed to run a train from point A to pont B of a railway, obeying the following rules:

a) the train must stop at all stations along the line;
b) at each station a predetermined number of passengers must get on;
c) the train cannot leave a station for the next, unless a pre-determined number of passengers has joined the train.

This game is analogous to the production process faced by companies. At each station you need at least a certain number of inputs; and without these inputs the production cannot go further and the process cannot be completed. The game by itself is not interesting and the solution can be found as long as the number of passengers waiting at each station is greater than the number of passengers getting on the train. In other words, the solution will exist as long as the system producers can find sub-system/component producers willing to get on that train.

We may need to overcome two problems which can arise. The first is that the system producer cannot find passengers at some stations; and the second is that some of the passengers (sub-system/component producers) cannot find a place on the train. In the first case, the system producer will try and secure the minimum number of passengers waiting at the stations by means of subscriptions or other forms of contractual agreements. This is equivalent to taking in-house that part of the production process. In the second case the sub-system / component producer has no choice due to the monopolistic position of the system producer. In this case, the monopolistic position of the system producer is able to a considerable extent to shape the sub-system/component producer market.

A different situation emerges when two different lines (two SCs) are available to move passengers from A to B. In this case both players play the same game (they produce the same goods) and both must obey the rules listed above. What are the differences from the previous situation?

First of all some of the sub-system / component producers which operate in a monopolistic market can seriously affect the behaviour of the system producer. The relationships between producer and supplier are now developed on different grounds. The supplier is now able to choose between producers and this opens up a wide range of opportunities for the supplier in the future. In this case, in-house R&D decisions by the system producer can become a winning strategy.

6   The Changing Boundaries of a System Company

The theoretical framework developed in this chapter contains several interesting assumptions which should be verified on empirical grounds. The final goal is to find a general rule that we can consider as the driving force for System Companies, and we already know that this will be operating within a highly dynamic environment. The main findings that can prove the basic theoretical framework developed in this chapter are:

— System Companies appear to be a clearly *distinctive category* of firms. They are not mass-production companies;
— System Companies *exhibit high turbulence in their vertical boundaries*, which are subject to considerable mobility in the long run;
— The most important transition path is *deverticalization*, either complete or partial;
— System Companies try to maintain some *degree of control* over strategic components, even when manufacturing is outsourced;
— In general, System Companies appear to be *more integrated* with respect to strategic components than mass-production companies;
— The dominant organizational configurations, at the end of our period of analysis, are two *intermediate forms*, *ie* partial control of components through design and partial deverticalization through design capability; intermediate forms seem to be successful in the long run as the system evolves.

Technology by itself cannot be considered as the only determinant in System Company behaviour. Market structure and financial constraints are also very important for the development of System Company activities. In this sense, we have found that a large part of merger and acquisition activities carried out during the 1980s and 1990s was mainly driven by willingness:

— To achieve control of the full scope of core and related activities (strategy);
— To expand the range of core and related activities and to achieve synergy between these activities (market and strategy);
— To realize the goal of Total Design Capability through the acquisition of new knowledge.

7 Conclusions and Recommendations

In this chapter we have considered the main issues related to the concept of a System Company, *ie* technology management and system integration. Far from being a self-contained study on the subject, its main goal has been to present in a systematic way this comparatively new topic of industrial economics and industrial organization. We think that these concepts will attract significant attention from both researchers and managers in the near future.

The optimal configuration of a SC at the business unit level is determined by the nature of the technology and its dependence on system integration; and by the rate of change of knowledge bases and of technology in system integration and in critical component areas. It will also be affected by vertically related industries which produce key components.

Amongst factors which must be considered by SCs is their strategic behaviour, by considering the company's position along the value-added chain, using as critical parameters the degree of vertical integration of the company and the nature of the system integration activity. The strategic behaviour can be determined by consideration of three important perspectives, *ie* the quality of the technology, the configuration of the market, and the nature of the contracts involving component producers.

Technological strategies must be established in order to take 'make or buy' decisions based on the evolution of organizational boundaries during the last 10-15 years and to forecast this evolution for the years to come.

Consideration must also be given to the investigation of the relationships between the SC and other companies that may be technology partners in R&D, competitors in the same market, and component producers or suppliers. It is possible to verify the existence of a dynamic consolidation process which arises from a weak variant that consists of situations of strategic alliances and forms the networking phenomenon, and a 'strong' variant that consists of operations of merger and acquisition. Empirical analysis shows the difference between the European and the Japanese situations, but there is a general tendency for SCs to prefer the weak variant. Some illustrative examples have been discussed to illuminate these and other aspects of System Company strategy.

References

1. W.B. Wherther, E. Berman and E. Vasconcellos, 'The Future of Technology Management', *Organizational Dynamics*, 1992, **10** (1), 20-32
2. H. Leibenstein, 'Allocative Efficiency *vs* "X-Efficiency"', *American Economic Review*, 1966, **56** (3), 392-415
3. M. Aoki, 'The Co-operative Game Theory of the Firm', Basil Blackwell, London, 1984
4. M. Morishima, 'Cultura e tecnologia nel "successo" giapponese', Il Mulino, Bologna, 1984
5. P.M. Romer, 'Increasing Return and Long-Run Growth', *Journal of Political Economy*, 1986, **94** (5), 1002-38
6. C.K. Prahalad and G. Hamel, 'The Core Competences of the Corporation', *Harvard Business Review*, 1990, **43** (1), 7 - 21
7. R.H. Hayes and G.P. Pisano, 'Beyond World-Class: The New Manufacturing Strategy', *Harvard Business Review*, 1994, **47** (1), 77 - 86
8. W. Walker, C. Schultze and T. Shergen, in 'The Relations between Defence and Civil Technologies', ed. P.Gummy and J. Reppy, Kluwer Academic Publishers, London, 1988
9. E. Anderson and D. Schmittlein, 'Integration of the Sales Force: An Empirical Examination', *Rand Journal of Economics*, 1984, **15** (3), 385-95
10. K. Clark, B. Chew and T. Fujimoto, 'Product Development in the World Auto Industry', *Brooking Papers on Economic Activity*, 1987, **3**, 729-71

Chapter 4
Technology Management
in the 'Company of the Future'

Yasutsugu Takeda

In this chapter we consider technology management in the 'Company of the Future'.The mission of this company will consist of three ideas, *ie* to contribute to global society *via* company competence which leads to value-added innovation, to create this competence *via* the activities of intellectuals including R&D people both inside and outside the company, and to achieve healthy and stable financial results over a long period. It is important for managers of the company to watch the balance of Profit, Cash Flow, and Fund for Future Growth as management indices. Clear priorities should be set for R&D resource allocation and each project within this, and managers should be sensitive to the pattern and status of the life cycle for each innovative project. The company's business strategy should be well defined and its ability to establish appropriate global partnerships nurtured.

1 Introduction

Now is the time for managers in the industrial sector to reconsider the meaning of company management in relation to that of technology management. Judgement as to the value of R&D in business has been changing greatly over the past several years in most parts of the world. Indeed, there are quite dramatic examples of large or prestigious companies that have drastically reduced the proportion of their budget and staff numbers devoted to R&D in order to ensure profit in the short term. In particular, in the systems and software fields, many young and active companies have no separate research of their own.

In Japan, as in other parts of the world, business attitudes are changing. In the early 1990s, the bubble economy crashed. Since then attempts have been made to pursue more effective approaches towards technology and business development. Nevertheless, when looking forward to the 21st century we should be fully aware of the core competence [1] of a company, which is created by the company's intellectuals, especially its R&D people. A company will thrive best if it maintains its competence, especially if this gives it an advantageous lead over its competitors. This will force companies to design a new concept of technology management, to be used to the best effect in the coming age.

In many countries people believe that R&D, or advances in science and technology, are fundamental to the future prosperity of their societies. For example, in Japan 'the fundamental law of science and technology' was established in November 1995 and 'the mid-range plan for science and technology' was approved by the cabinet in June 1996. The Japanese government decided to allocate to science and technology a total budget of 17 trillion yen for the succeeding five years, intentionally providing support for 10,000 postgraduates per year. Most of this was allocated to universities and public institutes. It is hoped that this large investment in R&D, or science and technology, will bring a new vitality to society.

In order to meet these expectations, it will be necessary to feed back to society within a finite period the results produced by the technical programme. A powerful driving force helping to realise this feedback will be the activities of private companies, especially those orientated towards future markets. However, many private companies are apt to overreact to the current market conditions, including the demands of stockholders, and this results in short-range management. There is consequently a danger that a divergence of interest will emerge between national policy and the management of private companies, and this may cause a new danger, *ie* the 'unemployment of high-level intellectuals'.

One of the most important tasks for managers of a leading company of the 21st century, *ie* 'The Company of the Future', will be to utilise its intellectuals effectively, thus avoiding this danger. In other words, one of the most important social missions for the managers of the Company of the Future is to provide opportunities for its intellectuals and let them use their knowledge and wisdom to bring about progress within society. Progress within society includes both an increase in the GDP and a decrease in negative aspects such as environmental problems.

This chapter focuses on management concepts for the Company of the Future based mainly on my own first-hand experience, working in Hitachi. For several years I have been responsible for a high-tech business division, the annual sales for which have reached 100 billion yen, as well as being responsible for all R&D activities at Hitachi Ltd. This has provided good experience upon which to base guidelines for the most effective technology management of a company which makes a meaningful contribution to society worldwide, but at the same time pursues rewarding financial objectives. These are achieved *via* the competence and excellence of the company operations, giving it a distinguishing role derived from well-motivated activities of its innovative employees, involving scientists and engineers (R&D people).

2   Mission of the Company of the Future in the 21st Century

In the early 20th century, most of the company's products were considered to be the fruits of the capital invested and the work of the employees. For a first-rate company in the 21st century, *ie* the Company of the Future, however, a company's activities and its products must to a great extent be based on its intelligence and wisdom, and the results of its activities must be accepted on a world wide basis.[1] Consequently, the Company of the Future is defined as 'the company whose mission is to create added value using every kind of resource at its disposal, including capital, human resources, and information networks'.

As Walter L. Robb, General Electric's former Senior Vice President for corporate R&D, stated, "The most productive place a company can invest its money is in the brains of its brightest people" [2].

---

[1] One visible example is the SuperH microprocessor developed by Hitachi.

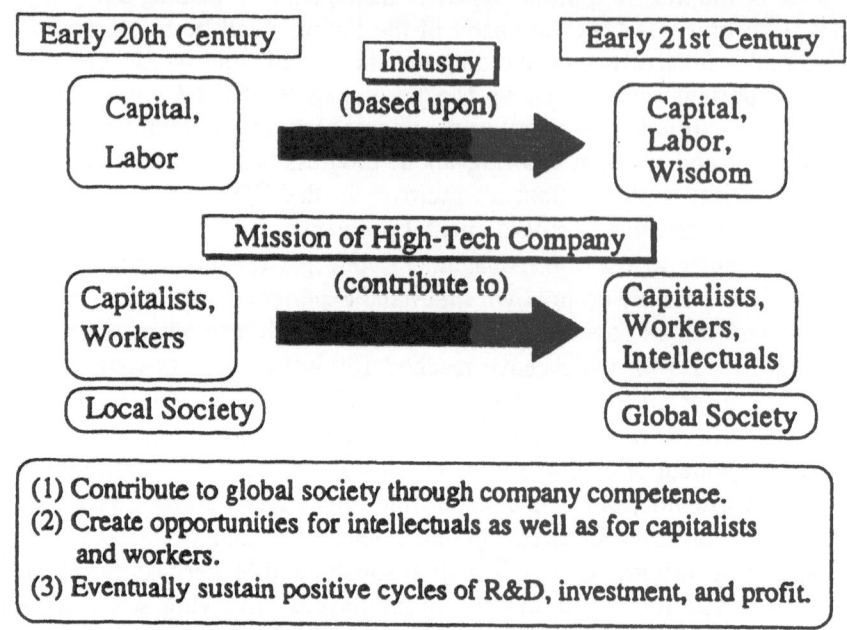

Fig. 4.1. Diagrammatic representation of the mission for the Company of the Future.

The essence of the mission of the Company of the Future is encapsulated by the three ideas listed in Figure 4.1. These involve contributing to global society *via* value added innovation derived from the company's competence, creating this competence through the activities of intellectuals, including R&D people, and eventually achieving healthy and stable results over a long period. In order to accomplish these objectives, the Company of the Future will need excellent technology management with enforcement of 'concurrent engineering' beyond section boundaries in the company and 'global partnership' which overcomes the boundaries between sectors and nations [3]. In other words, the technology management of the Company of the Future not only fosters integration of the technological expertise within the company, but also acts as an active agent promoting synergy between intelligence and wisdom of the world for product innovation, as depicted in Figure 4.2. Global information infrastructure can be used as a support function for concurrent engineering and global partnerships.

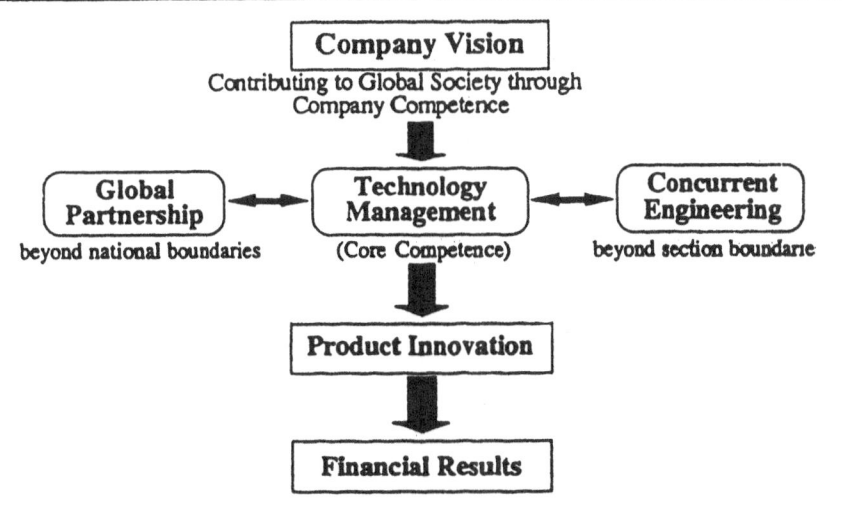

Fig. 4.2. Technology management for product innovation.

Most leading companies are very good at integrating their core activities such as marketing, sales, procurement, production engineering involving logistics, and development and research, as depicted in Figure 4.3. Their products are offered to the customers one step ahead of their competitors and, moreover, such products nicely meet the leading edge of customer demand. Outstanding products or businesses can usually be traced to a specific strength which can be called a 'core competence'. Such core competences may for instance be good 'channels for sales', 'marketing ability', or 'production excellence'. The intellectual property which is acquired from research activities can also be a strong source of a company's core competence, and can often provide an advantageous knowledge barrier between itself and its competitors [4].The skill of being able to control all these business elements simultaneously, *ie* the possession of 'concurrent engineering technology' then becomes a powerful core competence for the company. It is especially true in the systems business that distinguished 'concurrent engineering' can be the core competence of the company.

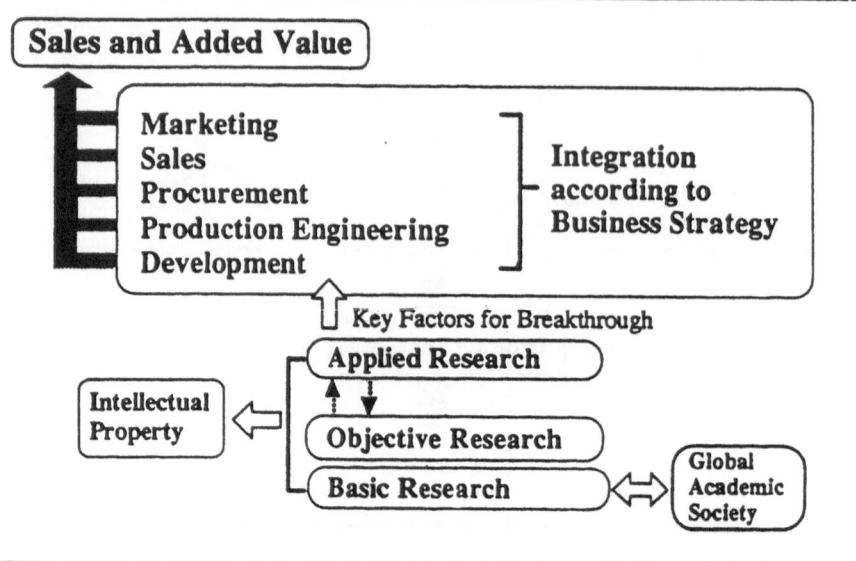

Fig. 4.3. Concurrent engineering in the Company of the Future.

It is also true that the possession of a core competence will enable a company to affiliate with strong global partners to create new business opportunities and to strengthen the position of its products in the market. Each company will try to maintain and improve its own core competence, and to offer to the market place the best products or business opportunities in its sector. Although there are many products and businesses in the market, there are only a few which deserve to be described as excellent. The situation is similar to that in the Olympic Games, where all competitors dream of getting a gold medal but only a few athletes can achieve this goal. Consequently, company managers should strive to recognise the comparative strengths of all businesses and products in his/her area, and the relative importance of each product to the company, and at the same time bear in mind the necessity of forging global partnerships.

In short, top executive managers of a company should always strive energetically to construct the best strategies for identifying and improving the competence of the company.

3   Key Management Indices and their Optimum Balance

The business situation in a company is measured *via* data provided on its sales, profits, and assets. These are summarised in their P/L (profit and loss) and B/S (balance sheet) statements. Since the 1990s, there have been demands for the inclusion of new concepts which describe a company's potential for future growth, as well as its earning capability. One response is to define the Fund for Future Growth (FFG), which takes into consideration not only today's profits but also today's expenditure designed to provide profit in the near and distant future.[2]

In Figure 4.4 we indicate the three management indices for the Company of the Future. The important concepts are (1) *Profit*, (2) *Investment*, and (3) *R&D Expenditure*, together with (4) *Added Value*. We use here the term 'Added Value' in a different way from its common usage. We define it as follows:

$$\text{Added Value (AV)} = \text{Sales} - \text{Cost of Sales}$$

where 'Cost of Sales' means the total cost of the products except for the depreciation of investment and R&D expenditure, and

$$\text{Profit (P)} = \text{Added Value (AV)} - \text{Depreciation of Investment (DE)}$$
$$- \text{R\&D Expenditure (R\&DE)}$$

---

[2] Private communication between a senior researcher of the Hitachi Research Institute (Hitachi Soken) and an analyst of Stanley Morgan Company.

(1) Basic Idea

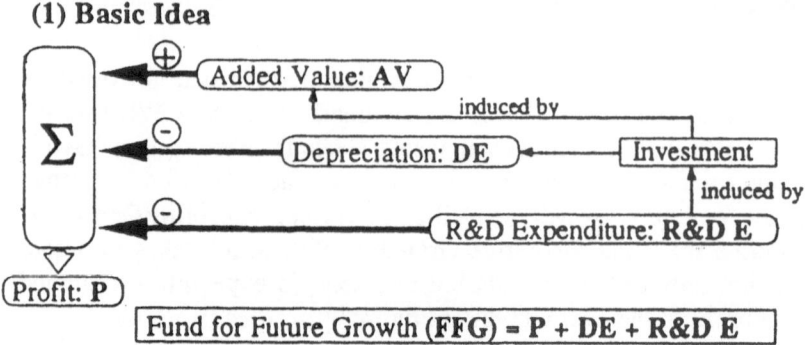

Fund for Future Growth (FFG) = P + DE + R&D E

(2) How to Manage These Indices
- Enlarge FFG = P + DE + R&D E
- Control Ratio of "P : DE : R&D E"
- Ensure Life Cycle Return = $\int P \, dt$ (total life of the product)

Fig. 4.4. Key management indices for the Company of the Future.

(a) *Profit* (P) is equivalent to *Operating Income*, which is a matter of major concern for the company's stockholders and managers. As stockholders expect profits as a return on their investment, managers are assessed *via* the financial statements of the company. Profits are also used to increase cash flow

(b) *Investment in production*[3] is also a concern for stockholders and managers of the company because it affects the *short* term business prospects. Investment should begin to generate a return on profits after a certain period, the length of which will depend on the character of the business. A quick return can be expected on a progressive business opportunity bearing some risk, but only a small return on more conservative businesses. Investment is followed by *depreciation* (DE). The profit from and depreciation of the investmentcontributes to the cash flow, and generally helps to determine the next round of investment, including R&D expenditure.

(c) *R&D expenditure* (R&DE) should be another concern of stockholders and managers of a company because it affects medium and long-term business prospects. It is usually spent on a continuous basis. The pe-

---

[3] Investment in production has a wide range of meanings, including investment in real estate, equipment, utilities, manufacturing lines, logistics and sales channels.

riod of R&D in the life cycle for a high-tech product in a progressive business is usually 5 - 10 years, but for R&D in a conservative business 15 - 20 years may be necessary. These are the periods required for the results from R&D to justify investment in the production equipment that is essential prior to earning profit. We go into greater detail on these aspects in the following sections of this chapter.

The sum of (1) Profit, (2) Depreciation of Investment and (3) R&D Expenditure is called the *Fund for Future Growth (FFG)*. We can evaluate the effect of R&D Expenditure from investment and profit, which are processes that follow on from the R&D effort. One of the major concerns of stockholders and company managers has been how to increase the FFG (which is equal to the added value). Consequently, it was thought that the larger the FFG the better. To pursue continuous prosperity in the Company of the Future, we would like to propose that the combination of P, DE, and R&DE over a year should be kept in suitable balance for the company. This implies that we should also consider the balance between profit, cash flow and the fund for future growth.

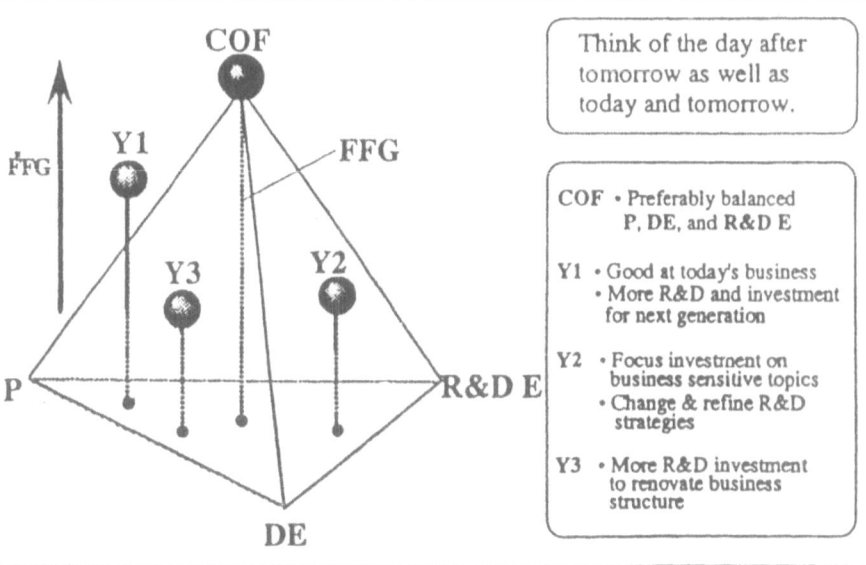

Fig. 4.5. Technology management in the Company of the Future.

Figure 4.5 gives a pictorial representation of technology management in the Company of the Future. Four cases are indicated: In Case Y1 the company is good at today's business and this depends on existing production technology, but more R&DE and investment may be necessary for future growth of the company and success with the next generation of products. Case Y2 is typical of a business which consists of many different kinds of products, each made in small quantities; it may be necessary to change and refine R&D strategies and invest more in production engineering to produce more profit and larger FFG for the company. Case Y3 is the so-called mature business having low profit for individual products; a specially selected R&D effort is recommended to rejuvenate the product spectrum.

In the ideal Company of the Future, the value of FFG is high, and P, DE, and R&DE are maintained in healthy proportions. We stress again that a high level of funds for future growth, FFG, and a good balance between P, DE and R&DE are essential. The actual ratios between these elements will depend on the nature of the company's business.

This concept is implicitly recognised by today's managers, but whilst managers can control profit and depreciation, R&D expenditures are sometimes seen as part of fixed costs since they amount to expenditure on a continuous basis. We must therefore improve the mechanism for determining an R&D expenditure which will fit the company's strategy.

4   Resource Allocation for R&D Activities

Since R&D expenditure induces investment which turns into depreciation, and investment leads to profit, decisions on R&D Expenditure should take into account how and when it can contribute to the investment which eventually leads to profit. Thus, we can categorise R&D activities and their resource allocations in terms of the factors indicated below:

(a) 'Development' is an activity aimed at developing prototype products or at significantly improving manufacturing technology, and it leads to the type of investment which contributes to the fastest profit generation. Manufacturing companies in electronics normally assign greater than 70% of their R&D resources to these kinds of activities.

(b) 'Applied Research' is an activity for producing the key technologies required for the next generation of a series of products and it induces investment contributing to medium-term profits. The allocation of R&D resources to 'Applied Research' activities is normally around 20% in manufacturing companies in electronics.

(c) 'Objective Research' is an activity aimed at creating new types of products or business and takes certain risks, but it leads to investment which will contribute to medium- or long-term and large profits if successful. The allocation of R&D resources to research of this kind is normally supported by corporate funding, and is less than 10% of the R&D resources for manufacturing companies in electronics.

In addition to the three kinds of R&D activity indicated above, there can also be some fundamental or basic research. This kind of research starts at a very early stage of exploration, and normally aims to create seeds for breakthrough ideas for new business in the future; this is far beyond the time span of 'Objective Research', but still has some strategic directions. This type of activity has been called 'North Star Research' (NSR) [5] to indicate that it is long range but has a clear vision of industrial application. This can be contrasted with 'Blue Sky Research' which is open-ended and has no clear directions or goals in view.

NSR need not be a big burden for managers, but very few of them maintain this kind of activity. NSR is very important for the company for the following reasons:

1. Big industrial innovations are sometimes introduced which are based on fundamental research. This is best pursued only by committed bright researchers with a keen sense of what is required. They need to be deep thinkers and have great persistence, and include some 'product champions' who will ensure that the idea is progressed within the company [4].In other words, real NSR can be done only when there are gifted researchers available to the company.
2. Seeds for innovation do not always exist within the company itself. In order to identify seeds and ideas for industrial innovation it is advisable to maintain contacts with organisations outside the company, especially in academic spheres. The company should retain some selected top-level researchers whose activities are highly regarded in the world in general. Such researchers can communicate well with members of universities and research institutes throughout the world, and can sometimes generate and participate in international collaboration or form corporate alliances. In other words, they can exchange knowledge or wisdom external partners with the aim of benefiting future business activities.

In its early stages, NSR rarely induces large-scale investment or generates much profit, and the visible output for NSR is mainly intellectual property. Consequently, research of this type is usually generated by means of a corporate fund collected as a tax' from the business divisions. It is not a large proportion of the R&D and can be as little as 1% or so of the total expenditure in this sector.

5 Strategies for Technology Management (1): Phase Management of a Product Life Cycle

The establishment of new business is clearly the biggest driving force in the growth of industry. To determine the level of R&D expenditure appropriate for identifying and developing new businesses, senior managers should consider the expected returns from these activities, using management data. Successful R&D greatly depends on management's ability to increase the probability of success *via* use of suitable strategies and tactics, and the ability to control the time span for product development by focusing their resources in the most efficient manner. In this sense, managing a high-tech company has some similarity with 'Go'.[4]

In Figure 4.6, we illustrate how a product innovation life cycle can progress, including passage from one stage to the next. It shows only the R&D related to a new business area (see later); and the other R&D, *ie* 'objective research and NSR, sponsored by the corporate fund is not included. Applied research starts at point A. The switch from research to development starts at point B. At point C, it is decided to make some investment for production, and the depreciation begins. Product shipment and the recovery of R&D expenditure starts at point D. This is when the business enters the 'High-Activity Phase'. At point E, added value for a particular financial period equals the sum of R&D expenditure and depreciation. If the added value for that product continues to grow, all of the expenditure for product innovation is recovered at point F.

Gross profits reach a peak at point G, then begin to decrease at point H; and the business enters the 'Defensive Phase'. Finally, the business ends at point I. If a large positive return is obtained over the life cycle of the product, the innovation is recognised as having been very successful.

In a company, it is normal for several product innovation projects to be proceeding simultaneously, as indicated in Figure 4.7. The life cycle for each project is different, and at any particular time each project will be at a different check point. Consequently it is essential that effective company managers should be sensitive to the life-cycle pattern and status of each project. The span of each project (Points A to I in Figure 4.6) depends on

---

[4] 'Go', the strategic game with 362 black and white stones, came from China to Japan in the 8th century, is increasingly popular because of its chess-style mental demands.

the type of business. For instance, the life cycle span for information systems and electronic devices is 5 - 15 years, and that for heavy industries, such as power plants, is sometimes as long as 20 - 50 years.

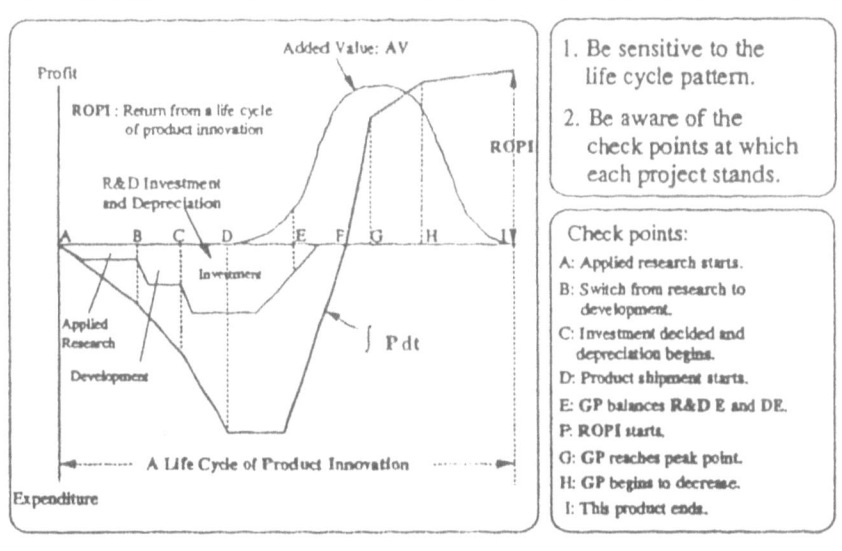

Fig. 4.6. A life cycle for product innovation, with check points.

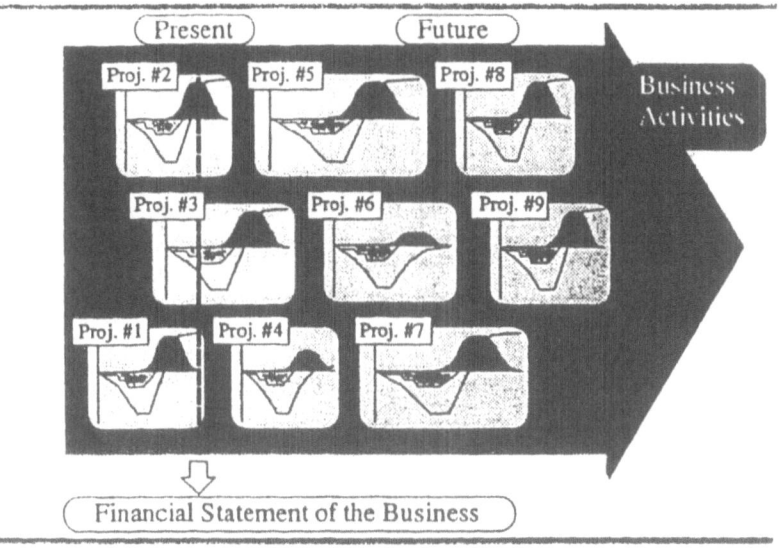

Fig. 4.7. Business activities depicted in terms of summation of product innovations.

6 Strategies for Technology Management (2): Determination of Project Priorities

It is important for company managers to increase the size of FFG, and also to balance P, DE and R&DE to ensure continuous progress for the company. In addition to controlling FFG, managers should make efforts to determine the priority of projects and resource allocation for R&D. Putting it more precisely, they should run ambitious projects successively, not only in parallel.

There are a number of methods for allocating resources to R&D activities. One is a 'portfolio method' which classifies business situations in terms of both attractiveness and competitiveness in the market. Figure 4.8 shows a classification of priorities for allocating R&D resources to a range of different business situations. The combinations marked I, II, and III indicate the priorities with which R&D priorities should be allocated. It is recommended that this method should be used at each transition point (A,B,C, D....) in the life cycles of the products, in order to avoid confusion between priority and phase of product innovation.

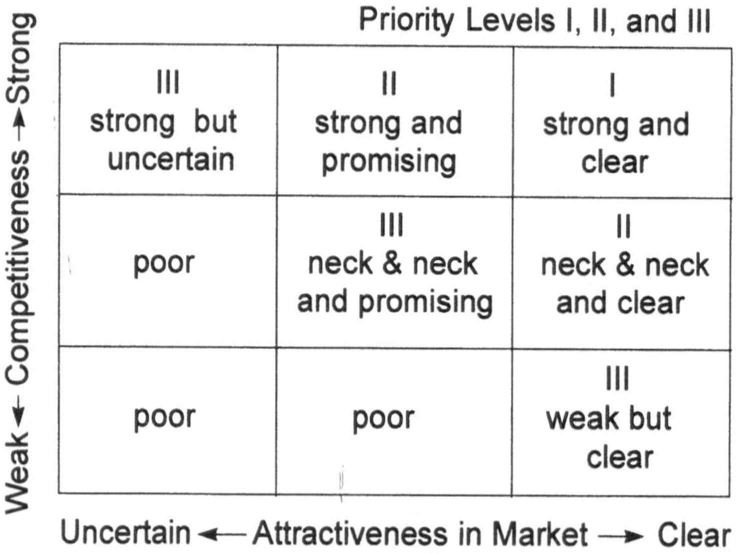

Fig. 4.8. R&D resource allocation strategy for the Company of the Future.

When managers can recognise the status in the life cycle for each of their company's projects, and can properly allocate R&D resources to projects based on the priorities, they can predict the financial status for the company in the future. This can be done on a short-, medium-, and long term basis because R&D resources will be decided by looking at FFG and the balance of Profit, DE, and R&DE.

7 Management of a Global Company

In order to explain the idea of technology management based on practical experience, we will consider the operation of a fictitious high-tech company called 'Company X'. An autonomously decentralised style of management [6] has recently appeared in many large companies engaged in a range of business fields. In these companies there are several divisions, each of which deals with a particular market sector and has strategies for this market, and is sensitive to competition in their market. Such divisions must be able to establish their action plans quickly and make their own decisions. Such self-contained divisions within a company function like individual companies.

The motto for Company X is 'contributing to global society through technological competence'. The business area for Company X is scientific instruments; and its major products are instruments for physics, chemistry, medical applications, *etc.* The company has particularly strong competitiveness based on technological competence in the field of measuring and testing instruments and has some excellent products. These first-rate products satisfy customers by providing added value to them. The market is moderately progressive, and the product life cycle is 5 - 15 years. Annual sales of the company are set at 120 billion yen.

Now a good example can be given for the restrictions imposed physically by the life cycle (Fig. 4.6) and financially by the FFG for the R&D resource allocation (Fig. 4.8). The company's FFG/Sales ratio is 13%, consisting of 3% for profit, 4% for DE, and 6% for R&DE. The CEO of Company X, Mr Y, tells his FEO colleague in the board that he expects sales for the company to increase by 20% over the next three years with a FFG/Sales ratio of 14.2%. Profit/Sales will increase to 3.8%, DE/Sales to 4.6%, and R&DE/Sales will change to 5.8%. The arguments are as follows:

Referring to Fig. 4.8, the 20% increase in sales will be achieved by the products in the box Strong & Clear (I), and either in the Strong & Promising or in the Neck and Neck & Clear boxes (II). These products should be already close to the market. Connecting with Figure 4.6, they should be beyond R&D in the phase between points E and G of the life cycle. Top priority is to increase their market share, which means to invest in production. Given the FFG, there is now less money for R&D, and sales will increase, so that the R&D to sales ratio will decrease. It is of course not the intention of Mr. Y to decrease R&DE, because promoting new products of category III in Fig. 4.8, ranging in the R&DE phase between points C and D in Fig. 4.6, is also a top priority. But he promised the sales increase. Therefore, a moderate growth of R&DE compared with sales growth will result in the value of R&DE/Sales decreasing slightly, and this resolves the allocation problem to the benefit of the company.

Looking at the steady growth of the related business market, a tentative goal for the FFG for Company X is close to 15% (P : DE : R&DE = 1 : 0.8 : 1.2). Target values for three years in the future are just milestones on the way to the final goal. A basic policy for the company is to keep and continuously strengthen the vital ability to create first-rate products. Mr Y will give high priority to investing in R&DE, even if today's profits cannot reach the predicted value. He feels that there is not enough R&D activity to catalyse investment in the near future. He will review the current R&D resource allocation in order to strengthen R&D activities in the 'development' and 'applied research' categories whilst sustaining 'objective research'.

Company X has two excellent products. One of these is in the measurement and testing business and is based on its own technological competence; and the other is in the medical electronics business, successfully aligned with a foreign company that has complementary expertise. Mr Y's assessment shows that both products are in the phase between E and G in the life cycle of product innovation shown in Figure 4.6. He is therefore very eager to accelerate progress in several development projects in the phase between C and D with products having position (I) and (II) in Figure 4.8, in order to create new first-rate, profitable businesses within a few years. The allocation for this purpose is 70% of the total R&D budget. This new high grade business will be based on the technological competence available within the company, and it is aimed to foster new and attractive markets. It should be stressed that the technological competence is actually centred on a certain group of high quality people. Mr Y thinks that the most important asset for the CoF is the people rather than the facilities or equipment. He believes that it is important to recognise their capabilities, and give them encouragement and opportunities to meet other challenges for the new business based upon their competences. He is eager to assess the value of human resources and to reflect this in the company assets.

He also spends some R&D resources in the areas of applied and objective research to foster growth in some seedlings for new businesses, where there are also certain risks. The allocation for this is 29% of the total R&D budget, with a 75/25 split between applied and objective research. The choice of subjects for objective research is influenced by co-operation amongst members of the marketing, sales, procurement, production and R&D operations of the company, in accord with corporate strategy. The remaining 1% of the R&D budget is assigned to encourage growth of technological seeds created both within and outside the company. Basic research, North Star Research, and communicating with academics can all be very effective means for identifying these seeds.

Applied research is performed in the corporate laboratory under the sponsorship of business sections. Both objective and basic research are also carried out in the corporate laboratory, but supported by corporate funding. It is desirable that this corporate funding is recovered in the short term *via* technology licensing. It is therefore necessary for researchers who are involved in objective and basic research to generate intellectual property as a result of their research activities. Mr Y is now trying to find a way to evaluate this intellectual property as a company asset. Research of this kind and the intellectual property generated is a means of putting knowledge barriers between Company X and its competitors - see above [4].

For the future growth of the company, Mr Y has defined his vision of Company X as one which encompasses the creation of excellent products in such business areas as environmental monitoring systems, health care systems, and advanced medical systems. These types of systems are likely to be widely required in society by the beginning of the 21st century. Mr Y is striving to enhance his vision by communicating with directors of the board and managers of the divisions and laboratories all over the world in order to improve his company's strategy, whilst also taking into account proposals from within the company. He has called this style of company management 'Symphonic Management'.

Numerical data for Company X are given in the Appendix to this chapter.

8   Conclusions and Recommendations

* The important mission for the 'Company of the Future' is to contribute to global society *via* value-added innovation derived from its own strategy and resources, drawn from both inside and outside the company. The most important resource for a Company of the Future is knowledge and wisdom. The mission of the intellectuals employed within the company is to integrate such knowledge and wisdom into the company strategy and also to

generate new strategy for the company. A global information infrastructure can support this integration.

* The Company of the Future should have its own core competence in both technological and managerial aspects. Most of the people in R&D work towards creating the technological competence. The managerial competence includes setting business goals, determining business strategies and priorities for projects and realising the concurrent engineering. Establishment of such managerial competence is the responsibility of top and middle managers in the Company of the Future.

* R&D investment is necessary in order to sustain a company's core competence and to realise the generation of excellent products based on this core competence. For the Company of the Future it is important to watch the balance between profit, investment, and R&D expenditure within the Fund for Future Growth and use them as management indices. Although cutting the R&D budget is an easy way to increase profit in the short term, both managers and investors need to maintain a medium to long range view in their style of company management.

* It is important to clarify resource allocation and to set project priorities so that the R&D budget is used effectively. A portfolio of projects must be used for this purpose, and the R&D must be categorised with respect to the life cycle phase of the products. There is no rule for determining the amount of basic (North Star and Blue Sky) research pursued inside a company. The principal reasons for it are to create intellectual property for a future business barrier towards competition, and to introduce fresh technology and concepts to act as seeds for future products.

• Global partnerships are becoming important. Management must clarify the company's strategy with respect to the mix of leadership in technology, production, and marketing.

References

1. G. Hamel and C.K. Prahalad, 'Competing for the Future', Harvard Business School Press, Boston, USA
2. W. Robb, 'How Good is our Research?', *Research Technology Management,* 1991, March - April, pp. 16 - 21
3. Y. Takeda, 'Co-operation of Government, Industry and Academia in Research and Development Activities in Japan, Looking Towards the 21st Century', *Int. J. Technology Management,* 1991, 6, 450 - 458
4. E. Konecny, C.P. Quinn, K. Sachs and D.T. Thompson, 'Universities and Industrial Research', Royal Society of Chemistry, Cambridge, UK, 1995
5. Y. Takeda, 'Synergetic Management of Technology for the 21st Century', Technology Management in Japan, Joint Symposium AAAS Annual Meeting, 1993, pp.153 - 159
6. Y. Takeda, 'Autonomous Decentralisation of Society Structures and Information Systems', *Proc. 20th Int. Computer Software and Applications Conference,* Seoul, Korea, 1996, pp.228 - 232

Appendix

Numerical Details for Company X

As can be seen from Table 4.1, the business of 'Company X' is in instruments; its major products are instruments for physics, chemistry, and medical applications.

At present, the sales for Company X are 120 billion yen per year. There are 2,000 employees and 1,000 in its subsidiary companies. Monthly income before tax is 300 million yen, depreciation for investment in plants, equipment, and computer infrastructure 400 million yen, and R&D expenditure 600 million yen, including corporate R&D of 100 million yen. The world wide market size of Company X's business is increasing by 6% per year.

The cost of sales is 8.7 billion yen per month. As a percentage of cost, selling costs are 4%, finance, administration and advertisement costs are 6%, purchasing costs of sales are 60%, and labour is 30%.

The company's capital is 100 million shares with a face value of 50 yen. The market price is currently 1,000 yen per share. The total aggregate market value of its shares is therefore 100 billion yen, total assets are 120 billion yen. The company pays an annual dividend of 15 yen per share, so the stock yield is 1.5%. The overall income tax rate is 50%. Income after tax is therefore 150 million yen per month, so the dividend pay out ratio is 83%.. In order to improve these indices and to raise the market value of its stock, the company plans to increase sales and income as shown in Table 4.1.

Table 4.1. Management of Company X

Business Area: Instruments.
Products: Physics and Chemistry Instruments, Test and Measurement Instruments,
Medical Electronics Instruments, etc.

	Now	3 years later
Number of Employees		
Inside X	2,000	1,950
Subsidiaries	1,000	1,150
Sales (MV/Month)	10,000	12,000
Income (MV/Month)	300	450
Income Taxes (50%)	150	225
Depreciation (MV/Month)	400	550
R&D Expenditures (MV/Month)	600	700
(Corporate R&D)	(100)	(120)
Income through Trading of Patents and Technological Know-How	+30	+45
Capital (MV)	5,000 (face value of 50V)	5,000 (face value of 50V)
Stock Price (V)	1,000	Uncertain (1,200?)
Stock Dividend (V)	15	15
Dividend Payout (%)	83	56
Total Assets (MV)	120,000	135,000

The directors intend to decrease the dividend pay out ratio from 83% to 56%, and the company's CEO (Mr Y) will set targets for three years ahead. Monthly sales should increase to 12 billion yen per month, which would match the market growth for this business. Income before tax should be 450 million yen per month, which means that if the stock dividend is still 15 yen per share, the dividend pay out ratio would drop to 56%. Mr Y intends to achieve these targets mostly through depreciation from investment in plant and equipment; and he sets depreciation at 550 million yen per month. He sets total R&D expenditure at 700 million yen per month, which includes corporate R&D of 120 million yen.

Company X currently has a net income of 30 million yen/month *via* the trading of patents and technological know-how, which is 25% of the corporate R&D expenditure. Company X reasonably expects to increase this income to 45 million yen per month, or 38% of corporate R&D.

The number of employees in Company X is expected to drop from 2,000 to 1,950, whilst it is planned to increase employment in its subsidiaries to 1,150. Labour costs are projected to increase by 11% over the three years. Monthly sales per employee are currently 3.3 million yen, and are expected to increase to 3.9 million yen over the three years. The cost of sales will increase to 10.3 billion yen per month over three years, so gross profits are expected to be 1.7 billion yen per month. Mr Y plans to decrease managerial and administration costs and to increase investment on computer networks to promote better communication within the company and to help intellectuals make quick decisions and construct action plans.

Table 4.2 shows the changes which are planned to take place in the management indices. The fund for future growth, FFG, should increase from 1.3 billion yen per month to 1.7 billion. FFG as a percentage of sales should increase from 13 to 14.2%, and the ratio of P, DE, and R&DE should change from (1 : 1.3 : 2.0) to (1 : 1.2 : 1.6)

Table 4.2. Changes in the key management indices for Company X

	Now	3 years later	Near future
Profit:P (M¥/Month)	300	450	5% of sales
Depreciation:DE (M¥/Month)	400	550	4% of sales
R&D Expenditures:R&D E (M¥/Month)	600	700	6% of sales
Fund for Future Growth:FFG (M¥/Month)	1,300	1,700	15% of sales
Sales (M¥/Month)	10,000	12,000	
FFG/Sales (%)	13	14.2	15
P : DE : R&D E	1 : 1.3 : 2.0	1 : 1.2 : 1.6	1 : 0.8 : 1.2
Income through technology licensing / Corporate R&D (%)	30	38	100

In the near future, *eg* five years from now, Mr Y hopes to achieve a profit of 5% of sales, a DE of 4% of sales, and an R&DE of 6% of sales, *ie* an FFG of 15% of sales and a (P:DE:R&DE) ratio of (1:0.8:1.2). Furthermore, corporate R&D activities could be entirely supported by income from technology licensing.

Company X is currently exporting 20% of its products, manufacturing 10% of its products and components overseas, and importing 15% of its purchased components. It is strongly recommended that the managers buy standard components or software and some application-specific components or software from all over the world. Mr Y also hopes to be able to protect the company from changes in currency exchange rates, so he is planning to decrease the export ratio to 15%, and to increase the overseas manufacturing ratio to 15% and the component importing ratio to 20%. This will balance the company's trading.

To obtain a 50% increase in overseas manufacturing, Mr Y has to make 25% of his total investment overseas. The money for this investment is intended to be recovered through technology licensing and dividends from overseas subsidiaries. In the near future, the overseas manufacturing will be supported by the local research and development activities. As mentioned above, the total sales are expected to increase by 2 billion yen per month within three years, with 800 million of this coming from overseas manufacturing. This increase in overseas manufacturing, plus the increase in overseas component purchasing, will result in new employment overseas but will have only a small effect on domestic employment. In order to sustain domestic employment, Mr Y has to create new business by paying attention to opportunities created by global partnership.

For his R&D allocation, Mr Y decides that about 70% of total R&D resources will go into development, 22% to applied research, 7% to objective research, and 1% into North Star Research.

Chapter 5
Global Strategies and the Role of Research

Tsuneo Nakahara

The Company of the Future must pursue different strategies depending on the industrial development levels of the countries in which it operates. Governments also compete with each other in attracting business and in securing employment. The example of Sumitomo Electric Industries Ltd highlights the differences between the management styles used in the US and Japan. Cultural merger is neither simple nor recommended. The role of R&D for growth and diversification is stressed. A capitalisation method for R&D is proposed which would improve performance, shareholder value, and future benefits to society. Intellectual property and tax laws would need to be homogenised.

---

1 Global Strategies

1.1 Competitive Position

The industrial consolidation, derived from first principles in Chapter I, which occurred simultaneously with the end of the cold war, has forced industries in advanced countries to reconstruct and re-engineer their business approaches. Consequently, R&D investments have been reduced. The world economy has been moving toward a borderless one. Now the advanced industrial countries meet the developing countries in a fairly competitive and open world market.

Table 5.1 indicates the differences in the two types of countries. Companies must operate in line with their position in this table or fail. In advanced countries, labour and welfare costs are higher because of their well developed, expensive infrastructure and life style (see Chapter I). In labour intensive industries competition with emerging industrial countries cannot be maintained. The time that it takes to reach a competitive position is of the order of two generations (see Chapters I and IV).

Table 5.1. Differences between industries in advanced and industrialising countries

type of country	advanced	industrialising
GDP per capita	high	low
labour and welfare cost	high	low
infrastructure	well developed	developing
demand	saturated	increasing
competitive key points	innovation	production
type of industry	highly automated	labour intensive
	aerospace	rail and road
examples	pharmacueticals	construction materials
	ICT technology	consumer electronics

Figure 5.1. indicates the three options open to the Company of the Future, *ie* to transfer its technology to industrialising countries, to generate new technology in and for advanced countries, or to do both in parallel.

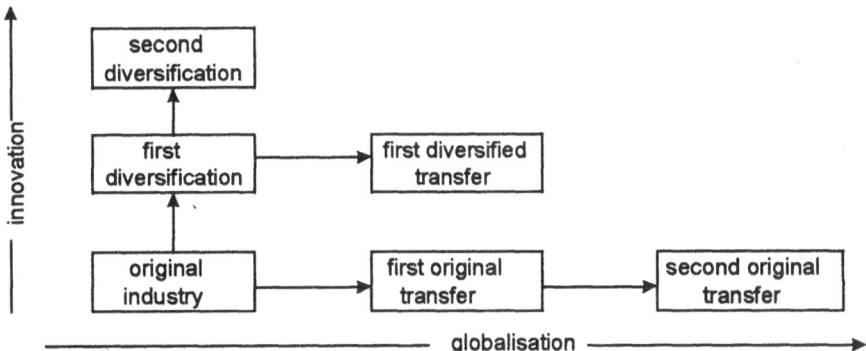

Fig. 5.1. Strategic options for the future.

If companies simply transfer their technology, the advanced countries' industry will be hollowed out. Unemployment will result, and the social standard will not be maintainable. The developing countries will essentially carry the burden of environmental problems in addition to their social and educational problems. This first option is clearly undesirable for all concerned. It is essential therefore that the Company of the Future maintains a powerful base in advanced countries; develops new technologies, products, and services with high value-added; and for volume and market development, transfers its competence to developing countries until there is a better global balance of wealth. This dual strategy should to be pursued not only in the interest of survival, volume, and shareholder value. It is a social imperative for the Company of the Future.

In fact, overseas production by Japanese manufacturers of consumer goods such as TVs, recorders, refrigerators *etc* has increased considerably. Table 5.2 shows the ratio of production transferred overseas in 1985 and 1993 for a number of products:

Table 5.2. Ratio of production transferred out of Japan in 1985 and 1993 (In per cent). (Source: Japan Home Electronic Products Society)

products	1985	1993
colour TVs	38.8	71.9
VTRs	6.3	41.6
tape rcorders	26.1	55.2
microwave ovens	22.7	63.3
refrigerators	18.1	40.5

In contrast to other leading countries, where diversification proceeded mainly by starting new companies, Japanese industry diversified through existing companies. For instance, the Nippon Steel Corporation remained a leading steel manufacturer and diversified into non-ferrous metals, ceramics, chemicals, engineering, electronics, and communications. For Sumitomo Electric Industries Ltd (see Section 5.3) the ratio of its original products, *ie* wire and cable, is now less than 50% of its total sales. Itsproducts now include electronic and fibre optics components, communication systems, powder metallurgical products, and new materials.

Consequently, research, development, and the management of intellectual property has become more and more important. Clearly, as has already been generally recognised, 'big science', *eg* R&D performed in connection with nuclear fusion energy or outer space, as well as that done with the objective of solving population and environmental problems, needs international co-operation and industrial consortia. But the need for international and intercorporate co-operation will need to go much further, as the example of soaring development costs of mass components such as D-RAMs shows. The Company of the Future will therefore develop a worldwide, dynamically changing web of competition and co-operation. Co-operative projects in such areas as intelligent manufacturing systems[1] will be of considerable importance in such webs.

1.2 The Role of Governments

In the open world, governments both co-operate and compete with each other at the same time. They know that favourable conditions in terms of infrastructure, regulations, taxes, labour cost and benefits, environmental protection, and education are important for the location of factories, research and development, and ultimately also of headquarters. Countries whose governments are not enthusiastic about business development policies will have problems with employment, revenues, and budget deficits.

In the advanced countries, governments fight saturation and employment problems by encouraging and supporting new businesses. The US is known for its low threshold towards start-ups. Although venture capital is

---

[1] Intelligent Manufacturing Systems International is an incorporated consortium of companies now collaborating at a level of $200 million in 12 global research projects on manufacturing. It was initiated by Japan. Canada, the EU with Norway, Korea, Switzerland and the US have now officially joined. The present international office address is 'Engineering House, 11 National Circuit, Barton, ACT 2600, Australia' Two of this book's authors serve as members of its international steering committee.

readily available in all G7 countries, most of them seem to prefer to support research and development efforts, specifically for high technology.

In Japan, consideration is being given as to whether venture businesses should be brought up within large companies as diversification, or as independent companies. The Japanese Government is preparing, through the Ministry of International Trade and Industry (MITI), various measures to foster venture businesses in co-operation with regional governments and investment banks.

Some major governmental incentives introduced since 1995 include:

1. A law for the promotion of creative activities by small and medium companies
2. The opening of a second over-the-counter market
3. The modification of New Business Law through a Stock Option Plan
4. The creation of a Venture Support Foundation
5. The creation of the Industrial Infrastructure Fund for the registration and introduction of venture specialists to evaluate the technology behind new ventures
6. A study on the evaluation of intellectual property (IP) by the Institute of IP
7. The deregulation of the Pension Fund to allow its use for venture businesses
8. Support for the Association of Investment Business

1.3 Growth through Innovation vs Acquisition: Japan's Case

The history of modern manufacturing industry in Japan is comparatively short. Nevertheless, a leading industry has been built up by changing from manufacture of textiles and steel to the manufacturing of appliances, home electronics, automobiles and semiconductors. This rapid development may explain why in Japan company trading (start, dissolve, merge, acquire, divest) has never been very popular, but there is of course a strong cultural inhibition to gamble with institutions. Most companies have successfully overcome saturation problems entirely by endogenous innovation. Key factors in this success story were the introduction of automation, top class production engineering, and total quality control.

This may be the time to reconsider the Japanese choice, even though cultural inhibitions are the most difficult to overcome. Table 5.3 compares the two basic policies:

Table 5.3. Effects of growth through innovation vs. merger and acquisition

type of growth	innovation	merger&acquisition
initial investment	small	substantial
social confusion	small	serious
time of action	medium	short
initial risk	small	large
operating risk	medium	medium
flexibility	large	small
technical resources	open	limited
business scope	open	limited

Growth through merger and acquisition may have the advantage of fast completion if the problem of overcoming the different cultures can be managed effectively. In most cases the difficulties are underestimated, and most failures occur for this reason. It would be very helpful to have an internationally accepted set of objective indices for acquisitions drawn up along the lines of the pilot's mandatory check list before takeoff. But such a checklist does not yet exist. It may not even be possible to construct an all embracing list of this type. The US culture is still quite adaptable to fast changes, but we do not recommend copying US methods in the Company of the Future. The Japanese culture appreciates the merits of good preparation and smooth implementation of changes perhaps to a greater extent than in any other culture. The message to be drawn from Table 5.3 is clear: Choose endogeneous growth through innovation.

2 Capitalisation of Intellectual Property, Research, and Development

2.1 Historical and Legal Differences

While the tax laws for profits and fixed assets are straightforward and converging throughout the world, the taxation of soft assets seems to vary considerably. Admittedly it is difficult to assess the value of goods which escape market forces, such as tacit knowledge, or the results achieved from innovative work such as research and design. Thus, the global confusion on taxes and tax benefits from research to start-up is understandable.

Nevertheless, it appears strange that depreciating assets like plant and equipment are currently capitalised whilst appreciating assets such as people and their know-how are written off immediately. The opposite would make more sense. This is particularly true in R&D where there is exceptionally high investment in staff, and this applies to all functions, including R&D in marketing, services, and production (see Chapter I, Section 10).

We can understand this fundamental attitude only if we take account of its historical origin. In Adam Smith's 1776 plot of the industrial society the division of labour and capital was installed as the main operating principle [2]. Capital was precious at that time, and labour was comparatively cheap. Only in a short note in Smith's publication was it stated that every shop floor needs a 'clerk' since neither the worker nor the capitalist would understand the machines and technologies. As an aside, he coins the term 'tacit knowledge' in order to justify the clerk's right to exist. However, in the meantime labour has become precious, and capital more abundant, and the 'clerks' are called scientists and engineers. They often generate the largest value added and constitute the largest in-house work force in their core company. They need their laboratories and their global network. Whoever tries to organise a company without giving due respect to continuity in R&D will regret this bitterly five years later, because it takes longer and requires more skill to rebuild institutional tacit knowledge in non-repetitive work than anything else in a company. A good example is the generation of software, where the reproduction cost and wear are negligible compared with that for hardware.

It is obvious that the adjustment of tax and depreciation rules to more closely fit the changes in business and society which have occurred since the beginning of industrialisation is long overdue. It is also essential that the Company of the Future is able to work within the global standards which will be created in order to cope with these changes. The European Union, for example, is well aware of this.

In accordance with the provisions of the Corporate Law and the tax laws in Japan, research and development costs are allowed to be listed in the balance sheet as deferred assets. They can be written off within a maximum of five years. On the one hand it is still advantageous in most countries to write them off immediately for tax reasons. Alternatively, there are numerous financial incentives, derived from publicly funded research and development, to start up technology companies and new joint ventures - this kind of finance is available at both central and regional government level. For the Company of the Future it would be highly desirable if the whole set of positive and negative incentives had a simple, homogeneous, global logic.

Quite recently, investors in Japan have been considering the use of patents and software as collateral for financing venture businesses. This is an unprecedented event in the conservative world of banking, and Japan's Institute of Intellectual Property is studying the use of suitable evaluation methods. In the US, intellectual property became a commercial item, and partial capitalisation is mandatory. It is unfortunate in this regard that there are fundamental differences in the patent laws and procedures between the US and the rest of the world. These must be resolved as soon as possible through renewed negotiations between Asia, the EU and the US.

2.2 Capitalisation and the Shareholder's Value of Research and Development

One crucial point when considering the capitalisation of soft assets is the fact that their value cannot be established via the market because they are not openly traded. To trade tacit knowledge is a contradiction in terms. For the Company of the Future we would claim that tacit knowledge is intangible in every respect and should not be subject to tax; but it will certainly be an important part of the goodwill involved when making acquisitions.

The methods which should be used for determining the goodwill, and specifically the value of R&D, are described in Chapter I (Sections 9.3 and Section 5.1). Accordingly, it would be straightforward to capitalise R&D, provided that this process is beneficial or at least neutral with respect to taxation. But this condition boils down to a very simple mathematical exercise involving a transition period from the present chaotic treatment (see Section 2.1 above) to a simple, future oriented system.

Again, it is easy to see how this approach would work in a software company or department, since the assets of its business are essentially embodied in its R&D staff. Let us assume that the effective lifetime of the relevant knowledge possessed by the company or unit is three years (knowledge becomes quickly outdated in this type of business). Then the capitalisation value of this asset should be set at three times the total annual cost of the staff, including fringe benefits, pensions, and continued training. In contrast to the often imaginary and temporary value of a company's stock, this product of annual cost and effective lifetime of relevant knowledge is a real value for shareholders . Let us call it 'Competence Product' (CP) for short.

The condition of initial tax neutrality for both sides would be assured to first order if the write-off period of the CP is set to cover the same three years, because this would make the annual amount written off equal to the untaxed annual cost of production. Fine tuning with respect to interest on the CP can be included, or better left to further experience. Generally, if the write off period is larger than the lifetime of relevant knowledge, R&D will be taxed; if it is smaller, R&D will be supported.

This is one of the best examples of how the legal system can install substantial progress towards the knowledge society. If implemented, government and industry would have an excellent tool to stimulate innovation. The relevant knowledge, which according to Chapter I makes all the difference to the Company of the Future and to society, would get due recognition. For the whole spectrum of businesses this tool would correct the shareholder value in line with the substantial changes which have occurred between Adam Smith's time and the Company of the Future's time.

In most businesses the effective lifetime of knowledge will be longer, *eg* in electric power engineering it may be 15 years (see Chapter IV). Eventually there will have to be some tax categories as in current tax laws.

There then remains the question of who gets the interest and/or the dividends on the additional CP capital in the transition period, which must at least be equal to the effective lifetime of the businesses' knowledge. For a first class company this question is irrelevant because its stock value and dividends are already large just as a result of the effectiveness of its R&D. The shareholder just sees that part of his speculative stock value is now a real value in the balance sheet, and therefore in his pocket. He may congratulate the legal system for its contribution to rationalise and hereby stabilise the stock markets. The same can be said for start-up companies, since the start-up capital includes the initial cost of running the company. The only critical cases may be with poorly rated companies maintaining substantial R&D departments such as the former RCA Inc., where the book value would significantly increase if their R&D were suddenly capitalised. However, in such cases the effectiveness of their R&D is obviously very low. The discrepancy between book and stock values would become more visible to the shareholder, and hopefully lead to correct or end the status quo earlier.

These examples demonstrate that the CP method proposed here possesses the additional appeal of self-adjustment. The social and commercial advantages of the proposal to introduce this tool are obvious.

3 The Example of Sumitomo Electric Industries Ltd

3.1 On the Management of R&D

Sumitomo Electric was established over a century ago as part of a large metal mining and refining group which itself has a 400-year history. Its development to the present size with $ 23 billion annual sales proceeded within the context indicated by Figure 1.2 of Chapter I, but on a compressed time scale (see Figure 5.2).

Growth proceeded entirely by innovation through in-house R&D. At present, the R&D budget amounts to 3.5% of sales, ranging between 1 and 10% depending on the operating group. It is divided into four categories:

The R&D for the formation of new businesses (1) and the R&D for new products and/or processes (2) are both funded by headquarters. The policy and resource allocation are determined by the head office's Top Management Committee, which is composed of corporate top management, heads of corporate staff, and leaders of the related development organisation. Nine of the present twenty-six operating groups have been established through this procedure. In order to expand business further, the company is developing a venture support system for employees who have the desire and capability to start a new venture business on their own.

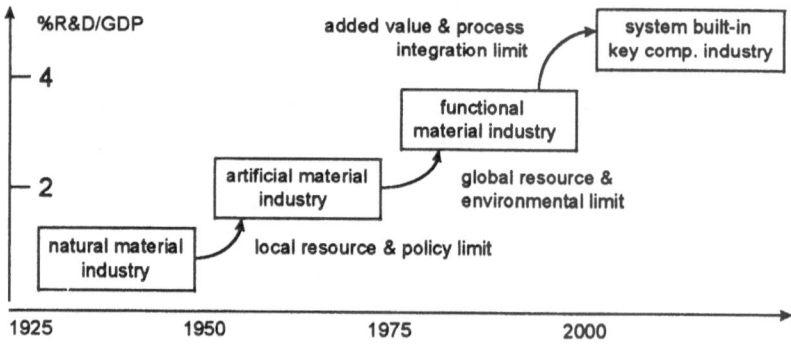

Fig. 5.2. Sumitomo Electric's development.

R&D support for developing new products and/or processes (3) and R&D support for modification and improvement of existing products and/or processes (4) are both funded by the operating groups. The subjects and extent of support are agreed upon *via* regular meetings between the operating groups and the relevant R&D Department.

Globalisation (see Figure 5.3) started after the second world war, but has gathered momentum only within the last 15 years.

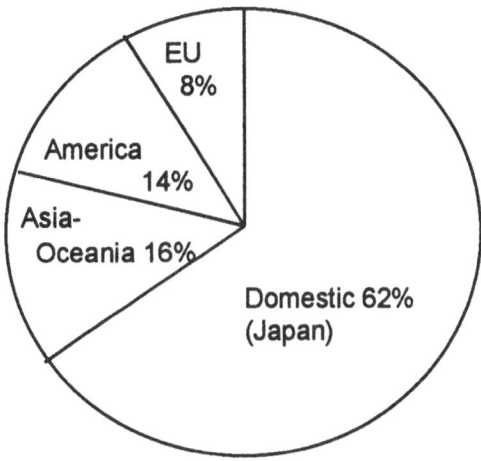

Fig. 5.3. Sales composition of Sumitomo Electric's 114 companies in 1996.

3.2 The Future of Sumitomo Electric

The company will develop two types of businesses: New materials and key components, and services and system operations. A synergistic interaction between the two types will promote R&D intensive businesses such as multimedia and fibre optic communication systems, storage and control systems, and the necessary key components and materials required in these systems. Ultimately some miniature key components will be integrated into other components such as optical fibres containing amplifiers, modulators, filters and detectors (see the fourth level in Figure 5.1).

The company will not only manufacture products for sale. It will provide full solutions for its customers, ultimately to the extent that it does not matter where the hardware originates. In order to survive, Sumitomo Electric will have to increase its international business from 10 to 40 per cent within the next 15 years, and this may require strategic alliances in addition to strong efforts in R&D. Still more challenges are listed in Table 5.4:

Table 5.4. Challenges of the future for Sumitomo Electric

subject	past	future
global business framework	GATT	WTO
products	hardware	hardware to services
market	domestic	global
priority function	mass production	innovation
management concern	refining technology	leading technology
diversification	internal ventures	global partnerships
investment	reengineering	strategic
R&D concern	design to cost	originality
ICT goals	elementary functions	social systems

4   Conclusions and Recommendations

* It will be imperative for companies operating in advanced countries to devise new management strategies to cope effectively with the new integrated world economy which is emerging since the end of the east-west cold war. These strategies should take into account the differences in requirements from the advanced and developing countries in the world. A comparison between the approaches which have been used to date in the US and Japan is instructive and leads to the conclusion that both international and intercorporate co-operation will become increasingly important in the Company of the Future.

* New initiatives by government agencies in Japan have been designed to encourage new business initiatives. Japanese companies have traditionally grown endogenously but it is now realised that there is also a case for starting new companies. This will be examined alongside cases for mergers and acquisitions *etc* which have to date been rare in Japan compared with the current practices in other G7 countries.

* A new approach to the capitalisation of R&D is proposed, and the Competence Product is recommended as taxation base. Its implementation would lead to benefits for business, shareholders without any negative side effects.

* Sumitomo Electric has radically changed the emphasis of its business activities over the years. Sumitomo will introduce new products and services which can be integrated into a common business strategy.

Reference

1. A. Smith, 'An Inquiry into the Nature and Causes of the Wealth of Nations', 1776, Reprinted by Oxford University Press, 1993, ISBN 0-19- 281796-5

Chapter 6
Accountability of Technology

Manfred Perlitz

The accounting methods developed to date for use in R&D budget alloca-tion are described in order to identify their strengths and weaknesses. It is concluded that the requirements for accounting in a technology-intensive Company of the Future will be quite different from those used in classical manufacturing. A new Flexible Innovation Accounting System (FIAS) has therefore been developed and exemplified by its recent use in a large chemical company. The potential for advantageous use of this and two other new methods - Goal Oriented Performance Evaluation (GOPE) and Process-oriented Cost Accounting (ProCoRD) in R&D is considered. GOPE has been exemplified by use in a pharmaceutical company and ProCoRD in the automotive manufacturing division of a large company.

1   The Need for New Accounting Systems

Accounting[1] is a key component of business information systems, and this function assists management to achieve its organizational goals. It includes such aspects as identification, measurement, accumulation, analysis, preparation, interpretation and communication [1]. This comprehensive approach to accounting has traditionally been applied to manufacturing. Now that other business functions, including marketing and R&D have gained in importance for the generation of value-added as well as cost centres, modern accounting techniques have attempted to take care of long term problems and general overhead management, but the focus still lies mainly on manufacturing, and procedures which take a longer term view will be required in the Company of the Future.

Although differing approaches to accounting have been developed by various nations, one aspect has been common to them all - they focused primarily on *manufacturing,* and within manufacturing on *direct labour and materials costs* [2].Kaplan's evaluation of current accounting systems was useful in developing methods such as activity-based accounting, but it did not address the evidence that more and more technology-intensive production processes are shifting their value-added from manufacturing to R&D, or more generally to technology development in all stages of the business process. Since knowledge-intensive technology-based processes will dominate the operations in the Company of the Future, they will require new accounting tools for their management. Many of these processes will be complex and non-repetitive in nature and require sophisticated control systems.

Process costing should be part of the internal accounting system which should focus on cost management in order to secure the company's long term cost competitiveness in the market place. To achieve this, process costing requires an efficient overhead management. As the tasks performed in the Company of the Future will concentrate on activities currently labelled as 'overhead', it will be of paramount importance to include this cost component directly into the cost procedure.

The 'operational control' function should be enhanced and not limited simply to the operational level implicit in this term. Technology development is an activity having a strong strategic component, and accounting systems designed to support management in this area should be capable of including long term, strategic perspectives and goals. The term 'perform-

---

[1] For the purposes of this chapter, accounting is regarded as an information system and covers both 'management accounting' and 'internal accounting'.

ance measurement system' gives a much more accurate representation of what is required to provide management support in technology development. By measuring the performance of a technology development process from a long- as well as a short-term perspective it should be possible for *all* the members of the organization to become aware of developments in the 'competitiveness' of a process. Both financial and non-financial data will be required and the process involved will include the factors given in Figure 6.1:

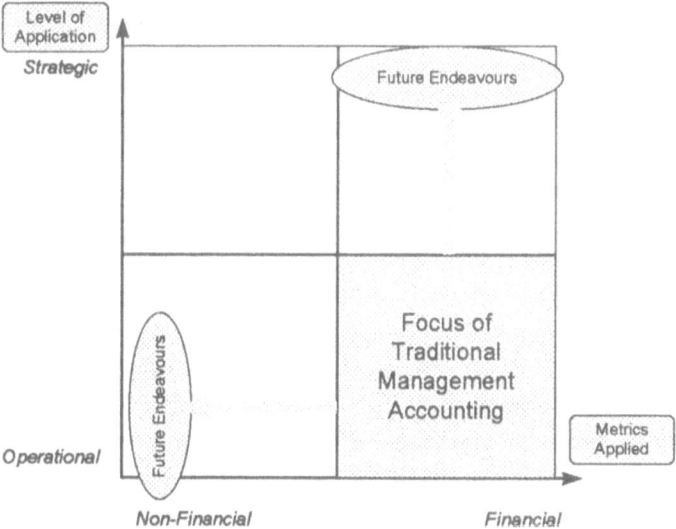

Fig. 6.1. Concept of management accounting for the future.

It is critical that an accounting system which is really capable of supporting technology management decisions should adopt a multi-level approach, and endeavour to cope with issues of an operational as well as a strategic nature. Current accounting systems usually focus on operational control using financial information and tools such as variance analysis and standard costing. This narrow view should be enhanced in two directions.It is crucial that the processes performed work efficiently; but an accounting system should also give information on the achievement of long term goals and the fulfilment of the basic purpose of the company, *ie* the generation of value. This information has to be derived from the final source of value generation, *ie* the market, and can also be used to allocate resources in the budgeting process.

Thus, the higher levels of organizational accountability should be included in the considerations. Secondly, the use of purely financial measures within performance measurement focuses the operation to an unnecessary degree on the monetary dimension of economic performance. The inclusion of non-financial information of performance will enable the attainment of a broader perspective.

Before the new FIAS approach is presented, a summary of traditional accounting methods will now be given, in order to describe the traditional features into which new ideas must be introduced for use in the Company of the Future.

2 Current Accounting Practices for R&D

In planning R&D budgets, managers also have to take into account the uncertainties and time lags and consequently performance measurement. There is uncertainty because money must be invested now in order to generate uncertain cash flows in the future. It is not known when these projected cash flows will actually take place. Furthermore, R&D managers have to make decisions on the size and structure of R&D budgets, taking into account strategic aspects. An analytical optimization model could help to deal with these problems.

In contrast, practical experience has led managers to prefer heuristic budgeting rules, which can either be based on past-orientated (*retrospective*) or experience expected in the future (*prospective*) [3]. A complementary characterization is to distinguish between goal oriented, financial resource oriented, competition orientated, project orientated, and R&D capacity-oriented budgeting rules [4]. Empirical research shows that in most cases R&D budgeting decisions are based on more than one criterion [5].

2.1 Status of R&D Budgeting in the West

The principal traditional methods used for R&D budgeting can be summarized as follows:

'Sales Dependent' Budgeting

Here, management decides on the size of the R&D intensity r, with $0 \leq r \leq 1$, which in turn fixes the amount of the R&D budget $R_T = r \cdot S_T$ to invest in period T. The management also has to decide how to determine the sales of period T S_T, eg expected sales in period T, and sales in period T-1, or to use a linear regression of past sales. The big advantage of this rule is that it can easily be applied and controlled through one single variable, the R&D intensity.

'All You Can Afford' Budgeting

Since most companies wish to pay a dividend to their shareholders equal to a projected return on sales D, they will not be able to invest the whole gross profit on R&D. Just an excess of the actual return on sales Y of the planning period over the projected return on sales D will be spent on R&D. It is at the discretion of the management to quantify and vary the return on sales objective D and to control the R&D budget from a strategic viewpoint. Brockhoff uses the following budgeting rules [6]:

$R = 0$ for $(S-C) < 0$
$R = 0.5 \cdot (S-C)$ for $(S-C) \geq 0$ and $Y \leq D$
$R = \max \{0.5 \cdot (S-C); S-C-D \cdot S\}$ for $(S-C) \geq 0$ and $Y > D$

with $(S-C)$ = Gross profit

'Planning Gap' Oriented Budgeting

In contrast with the first two, this budgeting approach is based not on past values, but on expectations about future sales developments. A planning gap is the difference between the strategically planned future sales and the expected future sales based on the existing product and development programme. A possible positive gap has to be closed by extending R&D expenditures in proportion to this gap in order to generate increased sales. In the case of a negative gap, the R&D-Budget will be frozen on its current level [7]. Parameters which can be influenced by the management are the planning horizon and the methods used to forecast the future sales.

Budgeting Tied to a Target Rate of Innovation

A second future-oriented budgeting approach is the budgeting tied to a target rate of product innovation, where a planned rate of innovation is compared with the rate of innovation in the past and attempts are made to remove the difference by changing R&D expenditure. The rate of innovation is expressed as the relationship between the sales of newly launched products and the total sales for the period. Thus there exist two parameters, the planned rate of innovation and the pace or intensity of adoption. If the difference between the two rates of innovation is negative (planned rate < past rate) the R&D budget has to be increased [7].

'Zero Base' Budgeting

The main objective of Zero Base Budgeting (ZBB) is to distribute financial resources amongst tasks in close relationship to their relative importance [8]. In order to achieve all these activities in the corporation we start from a zero activity base and then assess how those activities can be entered into with the lowest costs. The ZBB-process runs in nine steps, as indicated in Table 6.1:

Table 6.1. Zero Base Budgeting (ZBB) procedure

1	Fixing of strategic and operative corporate goals and the ZBB-areas.
2	Division of activities to be analysed into decision units and derivation of partial goals.
3	Determination of performance levels, based on the size and quality of the results.
4	Search for the least expensive process for each performance level.
5	Creation of decision boxes for each decision unit. A decision box is a description of the extent of the performance, the least expensive process, and the associated costs. There is a decision box for each performance level.
6	Establishment of a hierarchy to classify the decision boxes according to cost/benefit-relationship of each decision box compared with the others in relationship with the corporate goals.
7	Budget is fixed. Management determines the size of future financial resources. Some decision boxes will not be financed.
8	Fixing of the actions necessary to achieve the objectives represented by the boxes which are financed.
9	Determination of the newly created unit budgets and control.

ZBB allows R&D staff to be involved in the budgeting process and saves financial resources by concentrating on the most important activities. It does not use past data to quantify the size of the investment required. Due to the complexity of its implementation, ZBB is better directed towards fulfilling strategic goals rather than saving on costs in the short run. Furthermore, ZBB is a method used to restructure the existing cost structure of the corporation, but the logic behind it can be used for continuous R&D budgeting.

'Scratch Line' Budgeting

Scratch-Line-Budgeting (SLB) is a special form of Zero Base Budgeting, where the management tries to split repetitive activities from the ZBB process by determining a *scratch-line (SL)*. A high SL means that few activities are included in the ZBB process. The activities not included are then budgeted by traditional budgeting rules, as in sales-dependent budgeting, which is less complicated. In SLB R&D unit budgets are tied to the R&D programme, and therefore project-oriented (For further details of SLB see Lücke [9])

Scratch Line Budgeting and *Zero Base Budgeting* take into account both the size and structure of R&D Budgeting. They also include R&D staff requirements and market necessities in the budgeting process. By so-doing they help to prevent the phenomena of budget-slacking and budget-wasting.

Having explained some selected concepts of R&D budgeting, we summarize in Table 6.2 some of the main criticisms of the single methods.

Table 6.2. Weaknesses of traditional methods

Method	Weaknesses
Sales Dependent Budgeting	Purely past oriented (*ie* no link between past sales and next year's R&D budget), no consideration of corporate strategy and market necessities
'All You Can Afford' Budgeting	Maximum R&D budget is not necessarily equal to the optimal R&D Budget, no consideration of corporate strategy and market necessities, high volatility of R&D budget
Planning Gap oriented Budgeting	No rules to determine the optimal planning horizon
Budgeting tied to a target rate of innovation	No consideration of external influences, *eg* technological shift paradigms, since target rate of innovation is a relation, no precise assessment of the changing effects is possible
Zero Base Budgeting	High complexity. No rules to determine optimal hierarchical structure and the budget cut
Scratch Line Budgeting	No rules to determine optimal hierarchical structure and the scratch line

As a result, none of the above concepts has the potential to derive an appropriate generally applicable concept for R&D Budgeting. Procedures based on financial criteria alone have tended to be too rigid and to deter technological innovation.

2.2 Current Budgeting Techniques Used in Japan

In general, it can be said that all the Japanese companies interviewed (see Chapters II and III) agree that the R&D budget is a function of the overall economic situation. Accordingly, the central R&D budget is increased when the economy is booming, but directors of R&D reduce their budget when the economy is moving towards a recession. Most of the companies also stressed that in the business units, where concrete projects are pursued, market and product considerations dominate, whereas the strategy pursued by central R&D focuses more holistically on the core technologies that are promoted by each project. This makes sense, as only the central R&D managers are in a position to assess the technology orientation of each project in relation to the general corporate strategies.

A first distinction can be made based on the data available as information. The majority of the companies are past-oriented and, consequently, develop their budget based on past experience, *ie* percentages of actual sales and profits from past periods; but the remainder work in a future-oriented fashion basing their R&D budgets on expected sales and profit figures provided by the corporate planning group. Moreover, companies can be classified by looking at the procedure of decision making. It may either be based on a top down approach which means that a general budget is developed in central R&D, then it is shared out among the different business units according to the importance of the single product development projects planned. The top management of a big manufacturer of electronic equipment, for example, develops a general budget according to sales forecasts. Then, half of the budget goes to the corporate laboratories that belong to the central R&D group and the rest is allocated by the heads of the five business groups.

Alternatively, some companies prefer a 'bottom-up' approach starting from a project level and aggregating the single budgets for all business units. Business unit managers propose projects and calculate the budget according to requirements for people and equipment. Finally, the manager responsible for the central R&D budget discusses each project and takes the final decision. Some companies use a mixture of both techniques as they believe that this fosters communication and thus produces better results. However, in some cases the director of the business unit decides upon his own R&D budget. This means that business units independently develop the size of their R&D budget, but this procedure is used only when managers have at least five years experience.

A further way to analyse the companies interviewed is looking at the complexity of the methods used in practice to calculate R&D budgets. Again, an overwhelming majority of companies still use traditional methods, such as sales-dependent or all you can afford methods. A big chemical company, for example, uses sales figures exclusively as a basis for the R&D budget and sets an upper limit of 6% of sales. Only very progressive companies invest more effort in developing the necessary R&D budget to maintain their competitive position as well as their technological advantages. A leading electronics company, for example, makes substantial use of ZBB every six months although they are well aware of its increased cost. The upper limit is based on the general profit planning carried out by the corporate planning office. Naturally, there always has to be a cost-benefit balance between the increased cost of applying a complex method and the increased quality and reliability of the results obtained thereby.

A final consideration in budgeting is the issue of the relationship between the central R&D group and the business units as far as the treatment of the research results is concerned. The reason is that this may directly affect the amount of the R&D budget with which each R&D laboratory and business unit will eventually use.

Given that central R&D focuses on basic research whereas business units concentrate on applied research for product development, research results can be assigned a monetary value. Thus, some companies organize themselves as an internal market with business units buying research results from central R&D laboratories. Using this approach, central laboratories can increase their budget with the help of additional sources of income, but at the same time business units have to cover these expenses from their R&D budget. In this way an organization fosters motivation and internal competition.

Sometimes research results are sold to external contractors and/or bought from external research institutes or other companies' R&D laboratories. In one particular case, a car manufacturer has outsourced its R&D activities into an independent company that fully participates in the market and may sell its R&D findings to any customer it likes.

In this context, it is not always easy to evaluate the research results. Consequently, two of the companies interviewed make the business units participate in the evaluation of the R&D results provided by central R&D. If the central R&D laboratories sell them to the market, the market itself will help to allocate the appropriate price.

2.3 Accounting-Based Performance Evaluation and Financial Ratio Systems

It is an often cited fact that the performance information that is needed for management decisions is not included in the classical information systems used by companies, and this particularly applies to accounting- and finance-based decision criteria [10]. Though the evaluation of performance is a generic objective of accounting in general and management accounting in particular, its periodical structure, past orientation, and its close focus on financial data have given rise to doubts regarding its reliability. All three pitfalls are posing a major threat to the use of such data for performance evaluation in R&D and innovation processes.

Consequently, modern accounting research is including long-term and more strategic data into its systems. The development of these *'Perform-ance Measurement Systems'* has been strongly influenced by Kaplan and Norton who developed the *'Balanced Scorecard'* approach, which remains the most favoured method for performance measurement [11]. The concept of performance is divided into four aspects, *ie* the financial, innovation and learning, customer, and internal business perspectives. These categories are in turn broken down into several relatively broad sub-categories or sub-goals.

Moser's [12] survey on performance measurement in R&D identified the frequency of the use of performance measures in 124 companies. The outcome illustrates once again a core problem of technology and R&D accounting. This is that the most accepted measures in practical R&D management were the ones that are difficult to quantify, *ie* quality, goal attainment and amount of work done in time. Quality, time and efficiency are the factors receiving top ranking from R&D, and these are close to the ones often used for manufacturing, *eg* by Fischer [13]

Gentner [14] presents one of the very few broad, systematic approaches to measuring R&D efficiency and effectiveness focused on the example of the automotive industry. He builds on the success factors of time, effi-ciency, and output - these are categories that are quite comparable to the factors stressed by contemporary manufacturing performance measure-ment systems.

Schumann *et al* [15] have derived a quality focused system for R&D performance measurement. The approach used is along the lines of the Kaplan/Norton framework [11], but was especially designed for the R&D function. In the general concept derived from performance measurement systems the focus on quality would indicate quite a narrow perspective. Schumann's definition of quality as a concept ".. produced and maintained by aligning the values of the organization with the market.." is, however, so broad that it can serve as a framework for generally measuring R&D effectiveness. Efficiency is not seen as a relevant factor. Szakonyi's [16] approach also exclusively focuses on effectiveness.

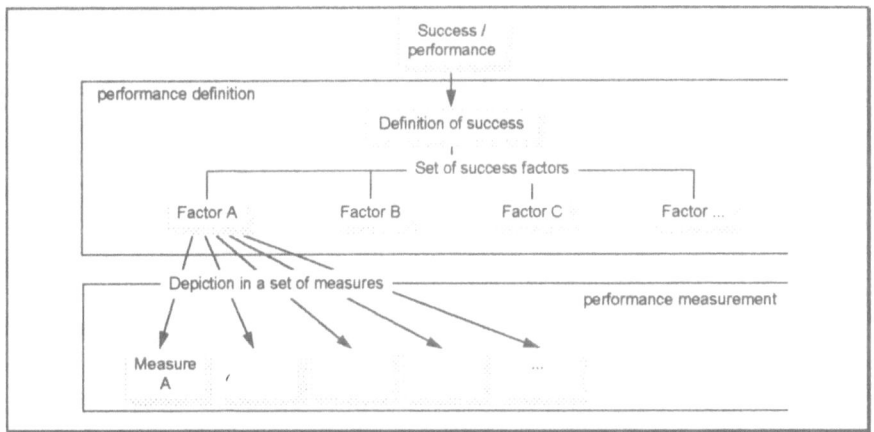

Fig. 6.2. Basic structure of contemporary performance measurement systems.

Basically, all of the systems mentioned follow the approach depicted in Figure 6.2. A major underlying assumption is that success is not defined by a financial measure. Moreover, often qualitative, hard to quantify non-financial determinants of financial success are evaluated. This approach is in general much more appropriate for R&D settings than the traditional accounting rationale of measuring performance based on profit, ROI or comparable measures. The time lag between the creation of the determinants of success and the actual financial payback is explicitly taken into account, and their nature is very close to Rockart's concept of critical success factors [17]. The approach contemporary performance measurement systems take is to select a set of factors that serves as a basis for the system.

After success factors are chosen, they are depicted by a set of measures. Though the measures are often not defined in detail, the factors do set a certain framework that always provides some subjectivity and is influenced by the specific intention of the respective author.

A major shortcoming of this approach is however its lack of *flexibility*, a factor that is essential for R&D environments. In the sense it is used here, the term 'flexibility' stands principally for the contingent nature of performance measurement systems. As R&D environments differ a lot depending on the nature of the underlying technologies, a fixed set of success factors that have to be measured is not appropriate. Moreover, it is necessary to relate to the specific strategic and technological environment within which the company operates. The different nature of the fit for the technological strategic backgrounds in a particular case may be illustrated by one of the examples from Japan. The company, which is a subsidiary of a large multinational, was operating in a high-tech market for medical equipment, a market in which the mother company was quality leader. The close focus on high technical performance as a dimension of quality in the market was dominated by the strategic focus of the subsidiary which was to develop low cost versions of these systems in short periods of time. This changed the relative importance of the success factors cost and time in relation to quality.

At this stage, the relative importance of different factors on the same level must be taken into account. The performance evaluation will provide an information base for managerial decision making. As these decisions have to focus on the key parameters of the business activities, they should be supported by information that is also focused on such key parameters. There are also different levels in a hierarchy of measures that have to be related to each other in a quantitative way in order to achieve information on different operational and strategic levels. The problem that has to be solved here is comparable with consolidation procedures in standard accounting and will be called 'the vertical problem'.

Finally, based on a literature review and case study findings, it can be stated that an appropriate *performance measurement system for R&D* has to meet the following requirements:

— Adaptable to changing, technology-specific environments
— Related to the strategy of the company, and linked to the strategic planning process
— Solution to the 'vertical' problem must be offered to cope with linking lower level measurement factors to upper level factors
— Solution for the 'horizontal' problem should be included, *ie* the relative importance of factors on one level has to be considered

3 A New Approach to Technology-Oriented Accounting: The Flexible Innovation Accounting System (FIAS)

We have during the course of this project devised a Target Budgeting approach to R&D accounting and its characteristics and use are described below.

Background and Roots of the New Concept

The determination of the correct level for the R&D budget is achieved in various ways in different cultures and industries. The new budgeting method described here has been developed along the lines of Target-Costing. This new method involves deducting the maximum R&D budget from market realization and in so-doing evaluates the situation from the customer's point of view. In developing this special budgeting technique the requirements of day to day work have been taken into account, thus increasing the likelihood of its acceptance.

Since classical management theories have been strongly influenced by the need to optimize them for mass production, they have only a limited relevance to the R&D of high-tech companies. Only classical data such as profitability and depreciation have been used, and many promising innovations have been terminated in the past, even before they could be put into economic use. Supporters of innovation have to employ both qualitative and strategic considerations, and to combat vague forecasts. This has led to low priority ratings when competing with investments in new machinery and installations which are easily calculated and show a certain Return on Investment (ROI). We have therefore derived a new improved budgeting system for R&D, which is innovation friendly and is oriented towards the needs of the Company of the Future.

A process that runs over some years, creating mainly costs at the beginning and a return only later, cannot be described and evaluated with a one-period calculation. Traditional concepts which make evaluations based on the ROI and are limited to one period can produce cash-cows and the traditionally successful products; but if we adhere only to these short time scales this will lead to investment in today's products, when emphasis would be better placed on products that bring greater profits in the longer term.

Some companies loose 50 % of their turnover if they come into the market 6 months after their competitor. Practice shows, that even if outstanding marketing techniques are employed it is not possible to get back that 50%. If a strategy focuses only on the cash-cows this effect will not be taken into account. Consequently, this lost profit must be treated as an additional cost for supporting the cash-cows. This may lead to them being seen as less desirable ventures, and will strengthen the case for investment in innovation.

An Innovation Oriented Budgeting Concept

Innovation oriented budgeting is needed that transcends the old boundaries and changes the procedure from a budgeting to an information tool which produces the important data at the right time, place and in the correct form. The model is developed for calculating the future value of R&D activities for the company which avoids backward- and competition-oriented budgeting. A central principle of the new 'Target-Budgeting' system is having to look at the R&D budget not as an input, but as a result or better output, which is calculated from the expected revenues in the future. Strategic turnovers for current and future product generations are forecast, using a statistical simulation model. An IT-based Delphi-method is used to arrive at relevant internal and external information for the company. As a possible setting for the analysis, Porter's [18] concept of five competitive forces can be used, as this allows a systematic testing of feasible parameters on the micro-level. An overview of the product and project classifications used on the different technology S-curves for calculating the Target-Budget is illustrated in the Figure 6.3 (see also Chapter I):

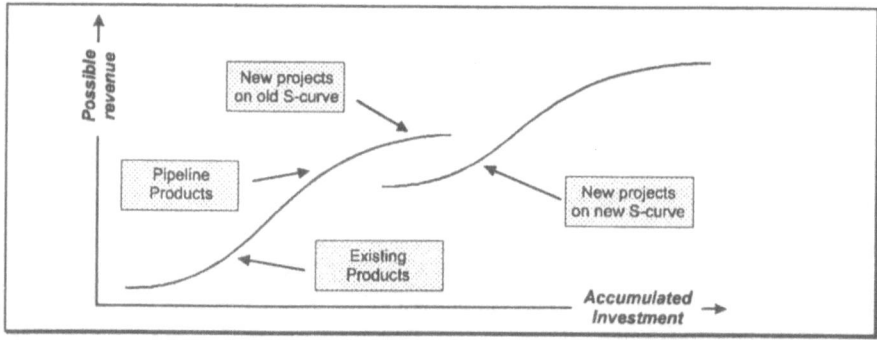

Fig. 6.3. Technological roots of the single project and product categories.

'Innovation-Target' and 'Innovation-Gap' as Central Reference Figures

The data compiled with the EDP-based Delphi-method are managed in a data-base. The data is offered to the other software-modules in the necessary edited form. Figures are derived from the data-base-system which includes operational figures for the innovation-target and innovation-gap, which try to describe the future technological situation of the company during a given time period.

The *innovation target* is calculated as the inverted value for the product life cycle of certain product groups. If, for example, a product group has an average product life cycle of four years, the resulting innovation-target is 25% per annum. This means, in a very static sense, with a fixed product life cycle and turnover distribution in this product segment, a company has to generate 25% of their turnover with innovations. This is necessary because 25% of turnover in this segment is eroded every year.

If the innovation target is met, the company is as fast as the average competitor. If the company wants to take over the technological leadership, this implies among other things that a shortening of the duration of the product life cycle is essential, and a higher proportion of the total expenditure will be on R&D. The innovation-target and the innovation-gap are the central reference points.

If the life cycle in the segment described is shortened from 4 to 3 years, the company must generate 33% of its turnover in this product segment with the help of innovation. Consequently, the duration of the product life cycle becomes a central strategic variable within the budgeting model (compare Chapter I, section 6.3). The duration of the life cycle and related variables can thus be used to install a modern control system which is focused on financial as well as non-financial measures. A healthy company will need to develop a project portfolio containing overlapping time profiles for its various members, in order to deploy its resources with maximum efficiency and produce a steady series of innovations.

The *innovation gap*, is the second important variable of the model, and results from the difference between the feasible future turnovers and the targeted turnovers, which are given by strategic decisions from top-management. An idealized situation for the turnover in relation to the innovation gap and products and projects is shown in Figure 6.4.

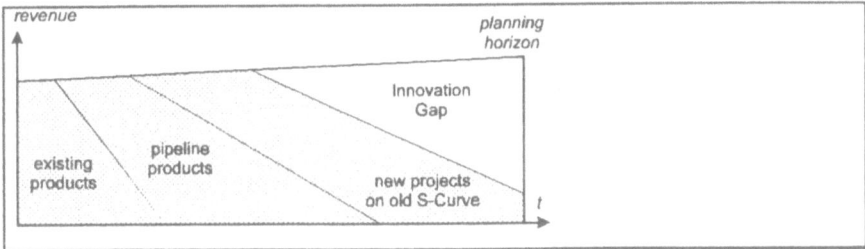

Fig. 6.4. Revenue in relation to selected products and types of projects.

Future turnovers are calculated on the basis of forecasts for the existing products, the pipeline products and the potential turnovers for new projects based on an old technology. For the time being the existing products are still able to generate the necessary turnovers. In line with their life-cycle, the turnover will decrease over the following years until no turnover can be generated. There are of course likely to be sales after that particular year, but static market behaviour has been used to demonstrate the idea. If planning is carried out correctly, the present pipeline products will be able to close the turnover gap in future years. Assuming a steady product life cycle these turnovers will also decrease to zero in due course. The aim of the model is to foster the preparation of an R&D budget which will allow the closing of the resulting turnover gap with new products in the future. For this reason the R&D Target Budget for the pipeline products and the new projects has to be determined in relation to the old S-curve (see Figure 6.3 and Chapter 1).

Determination of the Target Budget

After the determination of the core ratios of the budgeting model the maximum R&D Target Budget is derived from the figures for the innovation target and innovation gap and the discounted expected turnover with the help of a financial mathematical model. The fundamental procedure for determining the R&D budget is indicated in Figure 6.5. The first step is to forecast the future sales from each R&D project. Several implementations of FIAS have proven that the better the ability to forecast increases, the more accurate are the forecasts of market share, market size, market dynamic and product prices. After the sales have been forecast, the Present Value is calculated using a typical formula from NPV (Net Present Value) models. This amount is then weighted with the ROS (Return on Sales) demanded from the product to be developed. Once the Budget has been derived it must be allocated to each year of development, using for example ProCoRD (see below).

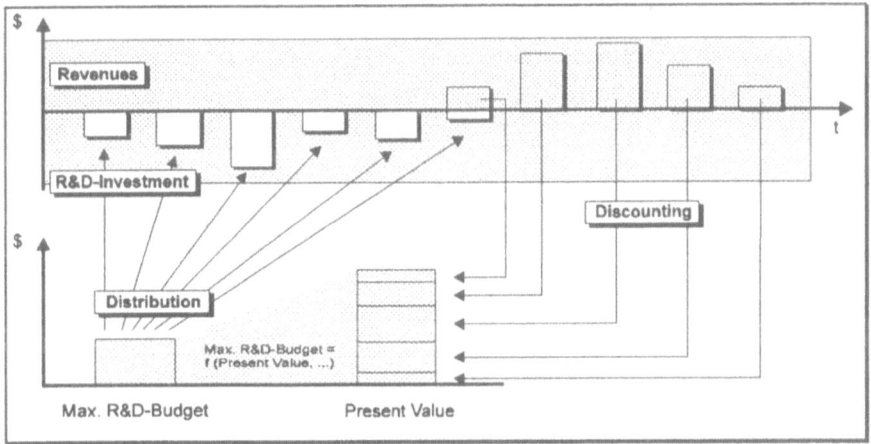

Fig. 6.5. Procedure for determining the Target R&D Budget.

The *current value* of the different technology categories can be derived from the future revenues; and this value represents the maximum total budget to be allocated. For the four product/project categories the maximum **R&D** Target Budget is calculated as follows:

$$V_i^{R\&D} = \sum_{j=1}^{s} \text{ROS}_j \sum_{l=1}^{4} \sum_{t=i+k}^{k+n} \frac{R_{jlt}}{(1+a_j)^t} \tag{6.1}$$

- • I = reference year
- • a = discounting rate
- • j = business units index
- • l = product/project categories
       index
- • R = Revenue forecast
- • ROS = Return on Sales

- • k = development cycle
- • n = product cycle
- • s = number of business units
- • t = index for time

- • V = Value

The determination of the Target Budget is based on the ideas which under the name of Target Costing found their way into production and manufacturing. While in the Target Costing concept the target costs are derived from the highest possible price, the Target Budgeting concept calculates the Target Budget from the highest feasible turnovers. A simplified comparison of both principles is indicated in Figure 6.6.

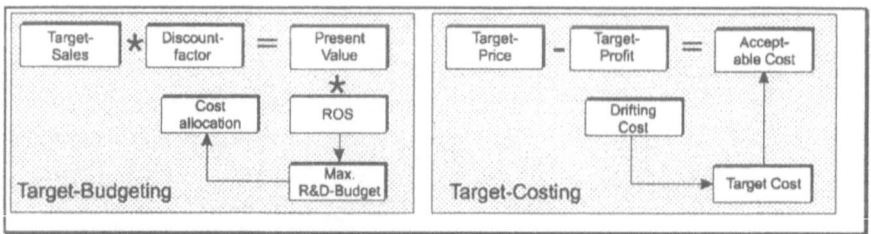

Fig. 6.6. Target Budgeting vs. Target Costing.

The Target Budget is allocated to internal and external projects bearing in mind the financial and capacity constraints. The information required for the distribution can be gained using a process-oriented cost system. This process cost system is necessary because the classical systems of cost accounting cannot provide sufficiently accurate information about project development related costs. Provided that the overheads are allocated on the basis of the cost of material, the materials-handling overheads increase or decrease, if the value of the material changes. An overview of the basic idea for the application of the process-oriented cost accounting in R&D will be given later.

The determination of the R&D budget does not end with the calculation of the maximum budget. The total budget must be allocated to the different product and project classifications of the respective business product areas. After the calculation of the individual R&D-Budgets per category the different budgets for each R&D activities are allocated using an activity analysis to which the above mentioned process-oriented cost accounting belongs.

Procedure for Deriving the Target Budget

The Target-Budget for research and development is determined within a multistage process. The sub-processes themselves are conducted sequentially or in parallel if possible. Figure 6.7 summarizes the necessary steps.

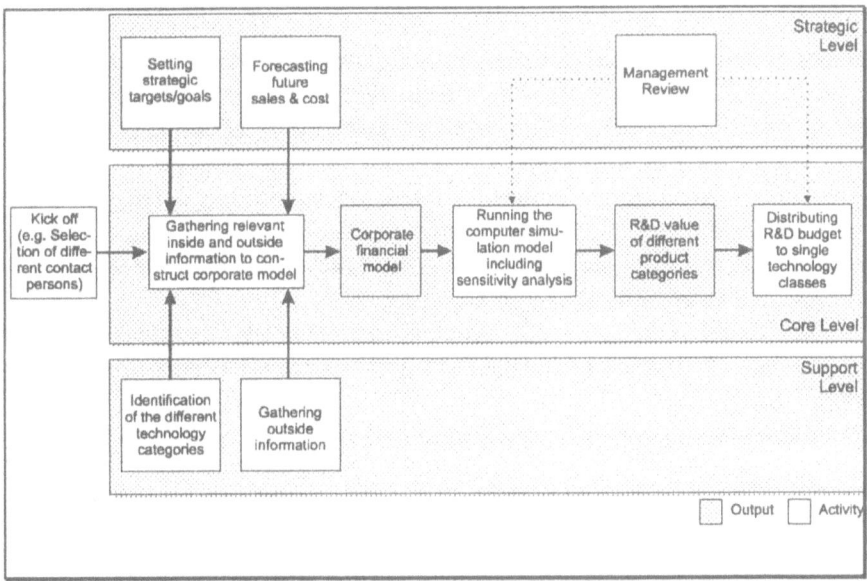

Fig. 6.7. Procedure for defining the Target Budget for R&D activities.

Determination of Data

The starting point for the definition of the budget is an initial planning meeting, where both the process-owner for the budgeting process and the contact persons for the following modules are selected. It is intended that the process owner is responsible from the beginning for the whole process to the point where the R&D Budget is calculated and distributed.

The different input variables for the budgeting model have to be determined. This implies among other things the setting of strategic targets. As mentioned above, the targets are determined by the corporate management using a structured way of finding the strategy with the help of an hierarchically organized decision model. It has to be checked if the information is available from a data base or is newly generated or updated.

Thus the corporate management determines whether the company should strive to become the leader in a selected product segment or if it is more appropriate to select the strategy of being the first-follower. With this information and the defined products and projects of the product segment the contact persons are then interviewed. This will be done using a printed or an EDP-based questionnaire, depending on the information required.

Experts drawn from both inside and outside the company are interviewed about individual subjects. The information required will include future development on the macro-level, and such factors as national and international rates of inflation and growth, trends in technology *etc.*

A typical person will provide information on the products and projects in one product segment and will be questioned only about selected activities within their special segment. The central R&D department can only give information about projects but not about products, whereas sales managers are better qualified to give product information. Identification of who has the relevant know-how on a particular product or project must be determined at the initial planning meeting.

The Delphi interview itself must be conducted very carefully, because any further calculation of the R&D-Budget strongly depends of the quality of the data derived.

Figure 6.8. illustrates the procedure used.

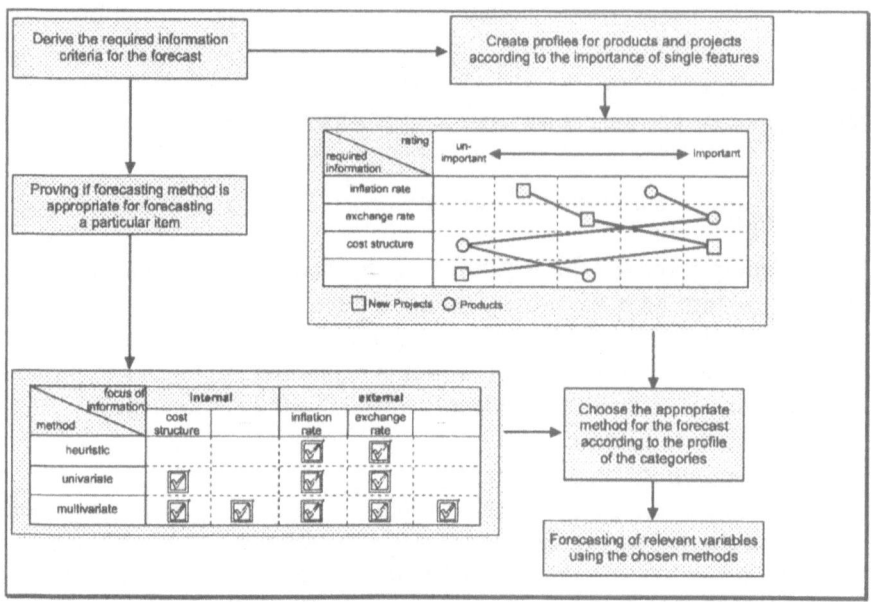

Fig. 6.8. Process to find the appropriate forecasting method.

Forecasting procedures must be devised to obtain all the different variables and as a first step suitable methods of interviewing must be devised for the individual groups of variables. Trial and error (heuristic) methods are used if the gathering of data is expensive or time consuming - these include the Scenario Technique [19] or conclusions by analogy. Univariate forecasting methods derive future values from existing data, where *time* is the only independent variable, but exponential smoothing and autoregressive methods have both been used. Multivariate analysis methods try to forecast the value of the dependent variable based on changes of the independent variable. They implicitly consider causal relations and this is a major advantage of methods such as multiple-regression analysis.

The determination of the optimal forecasting procedure starts by identifying the necessary variables for which the information is needed. A distinction between internal and external variables must be made. The latter includes inflation, exchange rate, economic rates of growth etc. The variables describing the company situation could include information about cost structures. When these variables have been selected the best forecasting procedure for each must be chosen and the relative importance of each variable assessed. The best method for a particular R&D activity will be chosen in line with the profile obtained.

Data Processing

The analysis of the necessary information is carried out within the framework of the total system. The basis for this evaluation will be an EDP-based risk analysis and a sensitivity analysis. These methods supplement the capital budgeting. These supplements attempt to integrate the permanent uncertainty of R&D activities in the decision making process and help to demonstrate the effects of uncertainty on the relevant decision variables.

The *Delphi-Method* was developed in the fifties by the Rand Corporation in the United States [19] and was originally a method for identifying ideas, creating opinions and forecasting, based on a questionnaire. The target group are selected experts. The survey is carried out in various steps. The main point is that the single questions are presented to the participating experts once or several times successively in order to identify deviations or changes. The results from the preliminary round are then presented in the second round so that an individual interviewee can compare his/her decision with the opinions of the other experts and may then wish to modify his statement. This results in stabilization by the second round, and only in exceptional cases is a third round necessary.

Data Evaluation

The variables to be included in the financial model of the company are selected *via* Sensitivity Analysis - this determines the overall influence that a change in a single independent variable produces in the result of a particular dependent forecast variable. Thus the *Sensitivity Analysis* helps to identify external variables which have a large impact on internal variables. It also separates important from less important variables.

Before running the analysis the results of a *Risk Analysis*, or another capital budgeting method, should be available for reference. Taking into consideration the analysis for different variables the overall picture will be of the kind depicted in Figure 6.9.

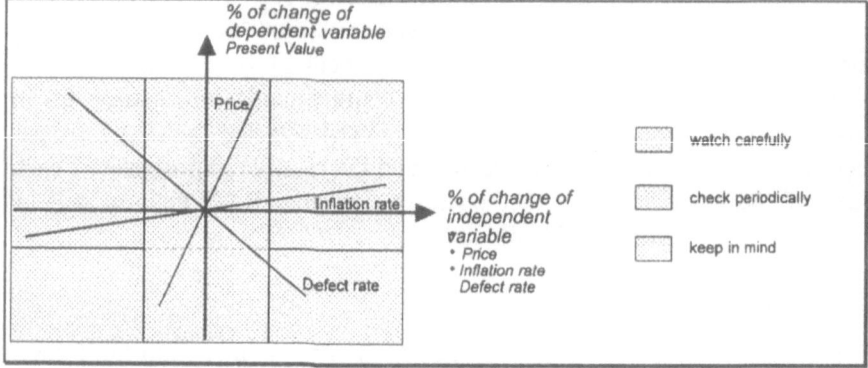

Fig. 6.9. Sensitivity-Analysis.

The steeper the slope of the line the higher the impact of the independent on the dependent variable. The figure shows that the variables of the first category (*watch carefully*) must be included in the model, while the variables of the second category (*check periodically*) increase the information provided by the model; but the variables in the third category (*keep in mind*) are not of significant importance and can be neglected for a first descriptive model. Variables with a high slope can be interpreted as value drivers, *ie* it is very important to have a closer look at these since a small change has an enormous impact on the target variable. Thus, the different independent variables can be ranked in order of importance by the degree to which their line slopes. The data generated is then edited statistically.

For the Risk Analysis to be carried out later a probability distribution has to be defined. A so-called three-point-estimation can be used, where participants are asked to estimate three values for each single variable - a pessimistic, a realistic and an optimistic value. Risk analysis for a capital investment aims to derive a probability distribution (*risk profile*) of the project's evaluation criterion (*Present Value, ROI, etc*) from subjective probability distributions of the uncertain key input factors. One investment is clearly better than another if it offers a greater probability of achieving any given level of return on investment.

Data Administration

The IT-based capital budgeting model uses three software programs. Microsoft Access[2] provides the data base, which is used to administer the diverse external and internal data. Moreover it is used to generate data by means of the Delphi-Method. An interactive graphical user interface (*GUI*) has been developed to facilitate the input of the interviewees for their various estimations. Figure 6.10 depicts the starting menu for the program.

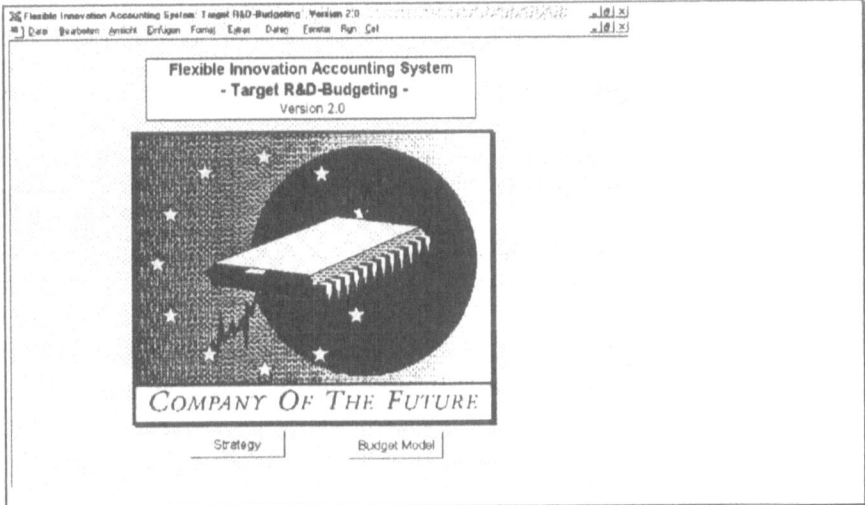

Fig. 6.10. Starting menu for the program.

After having chosen the strategy part of the program one gets the next menu which allows the calculation of the innovation gap and the use of scenarios (Figure 6.11.).

---

[2] 'Microsoft Access' is a registered trademark of Microsoft Corporation

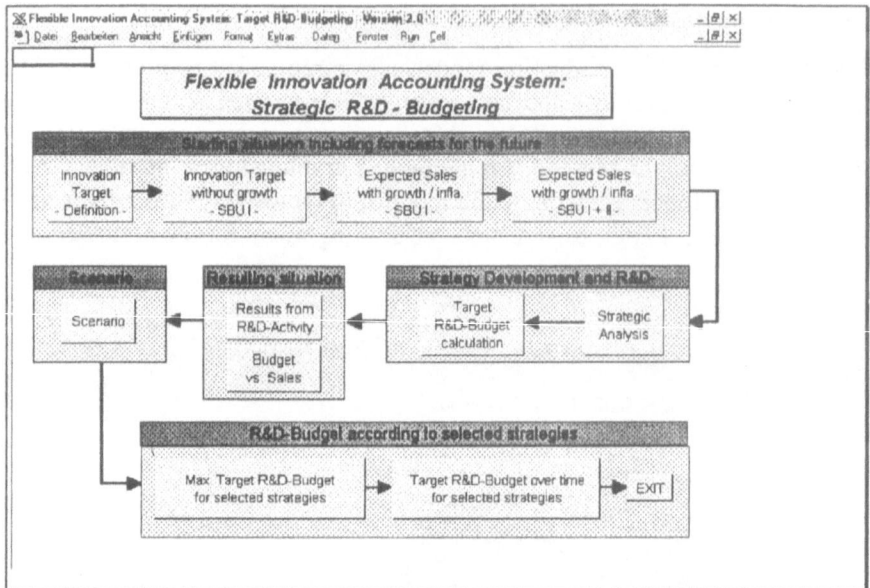

Fig. 6.11. Main menu for FIAS.

After having identified the innovation gap for each single SBU, the Target Budget for R&D is calculated using the following menu (Figure 6.12):

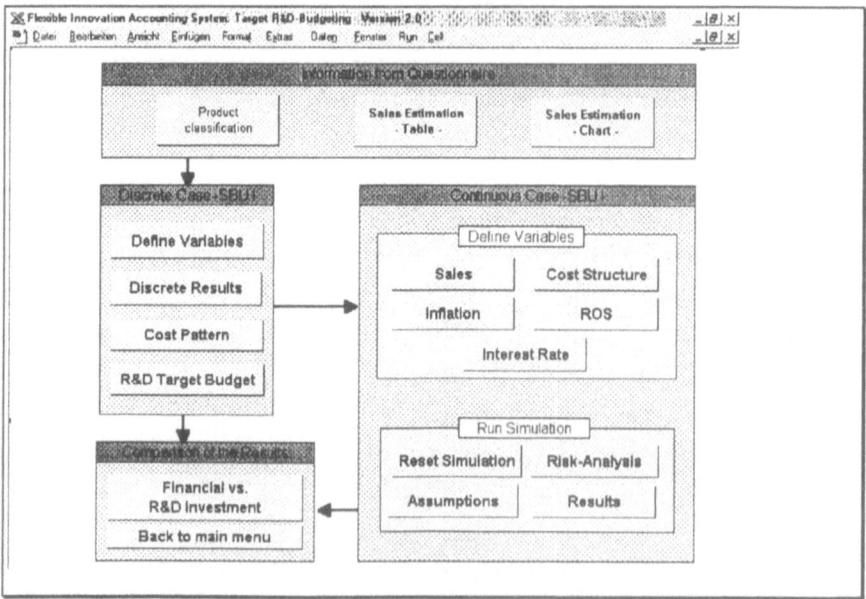

Fig. 6.12. Menu used to calculate the R&D Budget.

At the end of the calculation of the Target Budget for R&D one can compare a typical financial investment with an investment in R&D.

The main module of the capital budgeting model is based on Microsoft Excel[3] which enables all the necessary calculations for the determination of the Target Budget. The module also includes the relevant data base in an edited form. For simulation of a range of scenarios and for risk- and sensitivity-analysis Excel uses Crystal Ball[4] software which is a forecasting and Risk-Analysis tool. In contrast to classical calculation programs, Crystal Ball allows the allocation of probability distributions to specific cells. Deriving the probability distribution of the dependent variable uses the well-known Monte-Carlo-Simulation.

The results from a typical calculation of an R&D Budget are given in Figure 6.13:

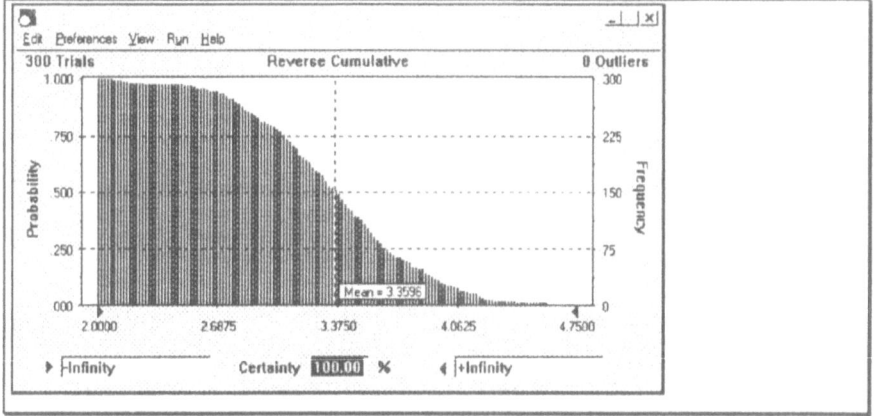

Fig. 6.13. Target Budget for R&D for a 1996 example.

The chart in Figure 6.13 should be read as follows:

1. With a likelihood of 100%, the R&D budget must exceed $ 2.00 Mio.
2. The budget must not exceed $ 4.75 Mio.
3. An acceptable but unadventurous budget would be $ 3.36 Mio

---

[3] 'Microsoft Excel' is a registered trademark of Microsoft Corporation
[4] 'Crystal Ball' is a registered trademark of Decisioneering Inc

Integrated Procedure for Deriving the Maximum R&D Target Budget

Having described the single activities within the R&D budgeting process it is necessary to understand the connections between the single modules. The main sub-processes are arranged around the core of the concept as depicted in Figure 6.14:

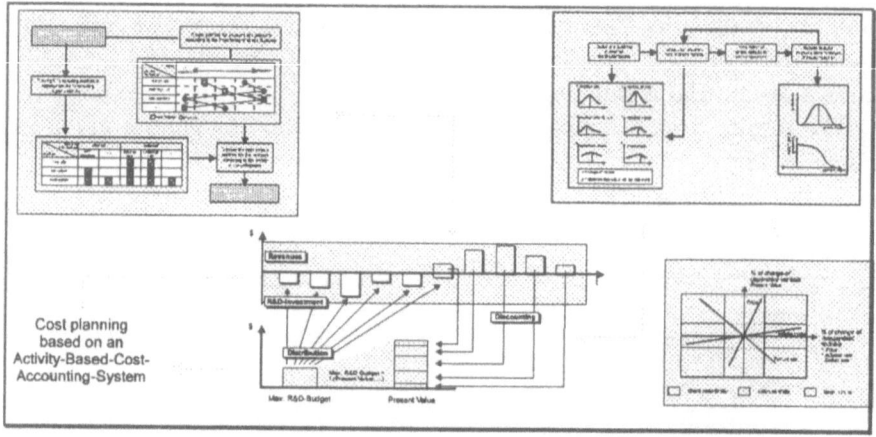

Fig. 6.14. Integrated procedure to derive the maximum R&D Target Budget.

The sales forecast should be calculated at the beginning of the whole process and be the basis for all the other calculations. The results can then be used as input into the *Risk and Sensitivity Analyses*. A main purpose of this module is to separate important from less important variables and to evaluate the data from the sales forecast. The aggregated information from this procedure is the input for the calculation of the component individual R&D budgets. Based on these budgets, a process oriented R&D cost accounting system helps to allocate the budget to each research and development activity.

Example of the Use of FIAS in a Chemical Company

The target budgeting tool FIAS was originally used in the central research laboratory of a major German chemicals company in collaboration with m²c consulting, a management consulting firm which employs personnel who were involved in the Company of the Future project. The aim of this project was to prove the applicability of the target budgeting tool within an R&D environment. As a result, the tool was used successfully in the R&D lab and will now be used, after appropriate adjustment, in several other laboratories. From the first meeting to the final presentation covered a period of eight months, and a key ingredient for success was the early involvement of representatives from Marketing, Strategic Planning, Production and Control. From the very first initiation meeting a cross-functional team could be set up. At the beginning, there were several concerns about the approach, and these came mainly from the marketing side. After a pilot project had been selected, the team started to build a model to describe all the different aspects of this selected pilot case. The market with variables such as market size, market share and their respective dynamics had to be modelled. As a next step, existing and new products were integrated in this model, thereby taking into account market as well as production oriented factors.

After finalizing the model the team started to work towards future developments. At that time, the tool also reached full acceptance from the marketing side. The software tool with the graphical use interface (GUI) approach helped management to think about different activities like changing the price policy, entering new markets *etc* and to obtain the results in terms of economic profit immediately. In collaboration with the other team members the team was then able to create strategies for the future. In addition to Marketing and Control, R&D staff also derived a major benefit from the target budgeting project. Having put the data for a new product idea into the system it then becomes easy to make a case for a specific size for the R&D budgets. Using the risk analysis part of the software a quantitative value can be given for the risk of incorporating their idea into the financial project plan.

4 Other New Approaches to Technology-Oriented Accounting

We have recently developed two additional new accounting procedures, *ie* Goal Oriented Performance Evaluation (GOPE) and Process-oriented Cost accounting in R&D (ProCoRD). The approaches are summarized briefly here and further information will be published elsewhere in due course when these methods have been more thoroughly evaluated in practical use by companies.

4.1 Goal Oriented Performance Evaluation (GOPE)

The target budget sets a major frame for the implementation of R&D strategies. However, the important factors which have to be controlled are of an operative and non-financial nature and need to be measured. There should be a switch to an R&D performance measurement system which includes significant non-financial indicators, such as the overall objectives and goals for the company. The system we have devised is designed to work in a similar way to the well known DuPont system of financial success [20]. Like financial success, innovation success can be traced down to its roots (see Figure 6.15).

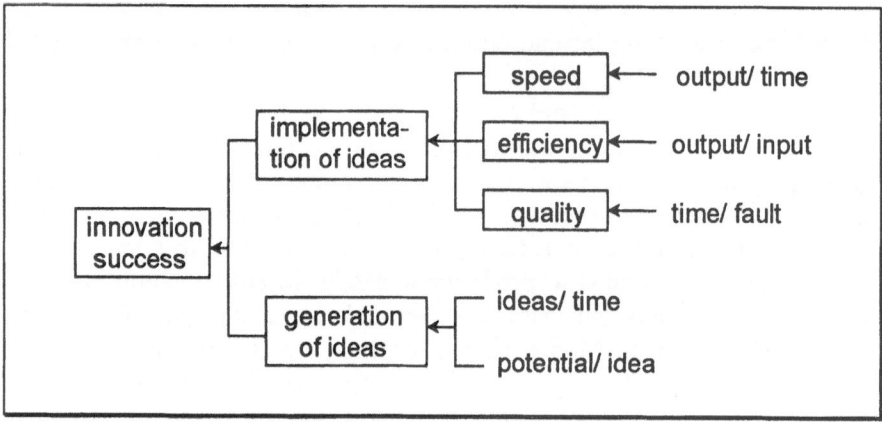

Fig. 6.15. Example for the roots of innovation success.

As indicated in our description of the FIAS scheme (see Section 3 above), the starting point for the development of an appropriate performance measurement system for R&D is not a fixed structure as in the Kaplan/Norton- [11] or Gentner- [14] style set of success factors but a new approach suitable for a technology- and company-specific system. The nature of this procedure should leave space for adjustments to a wide range of applications and also provide a structure to be followed in order to obtain consistent results. The knowledge that is required for performance evaluation is inherent in the organization and the derivation of the basic structure of the system is a group decision. Consequently, a modern process-oriented approach was chosen which is being used more frequently in performance measurement research [21].

The GOPE process has to consider similar requirements to those used for the FIAS approach (Section 3 above) and can be divided into the following steps:

- the generation of a structure for the R&D organization that identifies its goals and strategies
- the evaluation of that organisational structure in order to identify its most important areas
- the design of a measurement concept to depict the critical factors as indicators
- collection of performance data
- consolidation of that data on all the different levels and
- the graphical analysis of performance to provide a basis for management decisions

Research, development and innovation are structured into processes. The interrelated nature of innovation processes makes this perspective of prime importance. The three dimensions for GOPE are represented in Figure 6.16:

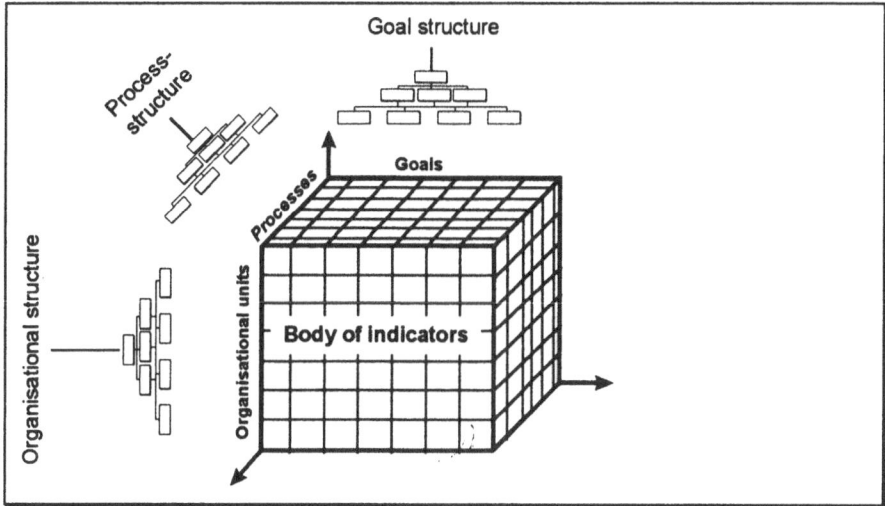

Fig. 6.16. The three dimensions for GOPE.

While performance data are collected and entered into the information system for each success factor, later analyses can consolidate the data according to different goals, units or processes on different hierarchical levels. The same structure can be used as a guideline to identify and allocate performance indicators 'step by step'.

The strategic hierarchies should be derived by a unit specialized in strategic planning, a design for an appropriate evaluation procedure has to be found and it is best if these are as simple as possible. When the goal hierarchy has been evaluated, a hierarchy of weights for the whole set of relevant attributes is then created. This outcome is helpful to tackle the vertical problem associated to Performance Measurement Systems. By assessing the importance of different factors for the overall strategy, a critical path of activities can be identified that should provide the focus for measurements. Measurement intensity can be defined by the number of measures used and the resources allocated to account for key areas to be controlled. Using the hierarchical structure of the AHP, the vertical problem outlined earlier is also addressed because each indicator on each layer is calculated in relation to its importance for the next higher level and can be calculated for all other higher levels right up to the overall goal. For details of the evaluation procedures the reader is referred to a number of useful publications [22 - 27]. A simple indexing system has been described by Lee [28] and shown to be useful for measuring performance.

Based on the consolidation procedure, a strategic feedback should take place which is based on the data generated in the period where R&D strategy implementation actually took place. To provide a basis for a strategy audit, actual performance has to be compared with the desired performance and the areas of under- or over-performance categorized according to their strategic importance. The use of the performance measurement system is comparable to the use of the DuPont scheme in analysing financial success. If top level performance shows a deviation from the target, the information content of this number is relatively low. Consequently high level numbers should be split down to trace the roots of performance changes and to decide on actions to be taken. A graphical representation separating the dimensions as in Figure 6.17 is recommended. This performance feedback matrix presents the results of a performance/strategic importance trade off for use by management.

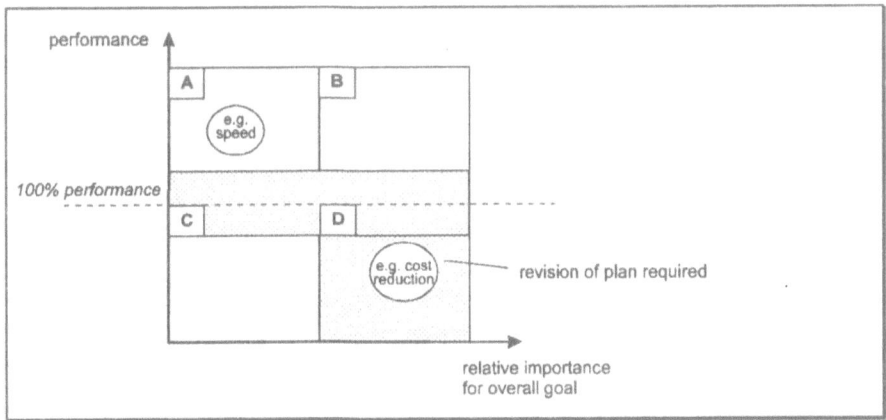

Fig. 6.17. The performance feedback matrix.

The performance is defined in terms of a percentage of achievement and an 'acceptable range' is defined within which performance deviations can be tolerated. The second dimension represents the importance as defined by the AHP evaluation procedure. Factors relating to different laboratories, business units or success factors can be placed in the strategic matrix. A performance portfolio can be derived for each level of the strategic matrix. The sample matrix in Figure 6.17 indicates the success factors cost and speed. In this case, the crucial factor cost needs correction and the relatively unimportant speed factor is performing well. An analysis of the roots for under- performance should be traced back and this must show which departments and indicators influenced the outcome most. On the basis of this analysis, which may again be done using the performance matrices of lower levels, it has to be decided whether counter measures should be taken or even if the strategic focus might be changed. Due to the uncertainty inherent in R&D decision making it might turn out that the strategy originally chosen is not optimal any more because the performance achieved has other strengths and weaknesses. Factors placed in quadrant D provide an early warning that revisions of the general plan and budgeting forecasts are required. Based on this feedback, the next planning and budgeting procedure can take place. It is of vital importance that the R&D performance measurement system is revised at regular intervals.

Use of GOPE in a Multinational Pharmaceutical Company

A multinational, Germany-based pharmaceuticals firm (Sales [1997] 6 billion DM) began the implementation of a performance measurement system based on GOPE principles in 1997. The strategy structuring sessions where held in key affiliates in Europe and the US, whereas the output was integrated into a performance evaluation system depicting several success factors. During this exercise, the necessity of integrating the more qualitative parts from the performance evaluation perspective with the financial data from FIAS target budgeting became obvious. This resulted in the development of strategic checklists used in the assessment of single projects that supplement the target budgeting data and serve as a link to the performance measurement system.

The performance measurement system approach was also applied to other institutions in the fields of commissioned research, fine chemicals, and the food industry. The process of linking target budgeting to perform-ance evaluation in a company-wide model is still being improved in the pharmaceuticals firm, and a major achievement for the whole project was that people from marketing and R&D, from both top management and operational levels had to think about company and technology strategy in a joint process rather than keeping their own position in their respective 'ivory towers'. The transparency created by the different tools encourages communication and goes beyond the usual benefits of pure 'number crunching'.

4.2 Process-oriented Cost Accounting in R&D (ProCoRD)

Process orientation becomes relevant for R&D in cases where different areas of responsibility are affected. On the highest level, for the whole R&D department, there are the links to both customers and production. On a lower, but no less important level there are connections between single, parallel-run R&D projects. Furthermore, process orientation helps us to visualise the creation of values. For accounting purposes, one aspect to bear in mind at the outset is the efficiency of the cost accounting. A high degree of correctness in cost determination usually implies a large effort in the registration of costs.

Strecker [29] was one of the first advocates of process costing in R&D. From the basis of experience gained in a medium-sized engineering com-pany, he strongly focuses on development projects, which are considered more easily accessible for accounting than research projects. He empha-sises the crucial role of experience data bases that must be updated regu-larly. The R&D-specific part of his contribution is the attempt to structure the work in the development department into different phases which are characterised by milestones, and the definition of milestones is indeed widely practised in industry for R&D projects.

After the overall R&D budget has been derived from sales forecasts, it has to be allocated to individual R&D projects. To allocate resources to the most useful projects, a clear understanding of what can be performed with a finite budget is necessary *ie* a clear idea of the 'efficiency' of in-house R&D; but efficiency in this context does not strictly mean the ratio between input and output, because in R&D it is difficult to measure both of these using the same tool. The output of R&D activities consists of technical knowledge, the value of which cannot easily be quantified. However, it can be described by its technical characteristics and – to a certain extent – be compared among different activities or projects. In any case, it is necessary to determine the correct input into R&D activities. This input can be measured to some extent in financial terms, *ie* according to the costs of the R&D projects. So the goal is to determine the costs of a particular R&D project as precisely as possible.

Only when the input necessary to reach a certain result is known can R&D budgeting decisions be successful. From a basis of technically similar projects, cost comparisons can be carried out between single research units within one company. These might take place between central R&D and an R&D department in the divisions or between departments in various divisions. A cost comparison is also absolutely indispensable when decisions are required as to whether R&D should be outsourced. The price that would have to be paid to an external research organization must be compared with the total internal cost of an R&D project. For this reason the aim is to develop a project cost planning system, which will allow the taking of make-or-buy decisions based on the knowledge of internal project costs.

From a consideration of the organizational levels of R&D activities in a company at least three different levels can be identified where overheads emerge. These levels are illustrated in Figure 6.18.

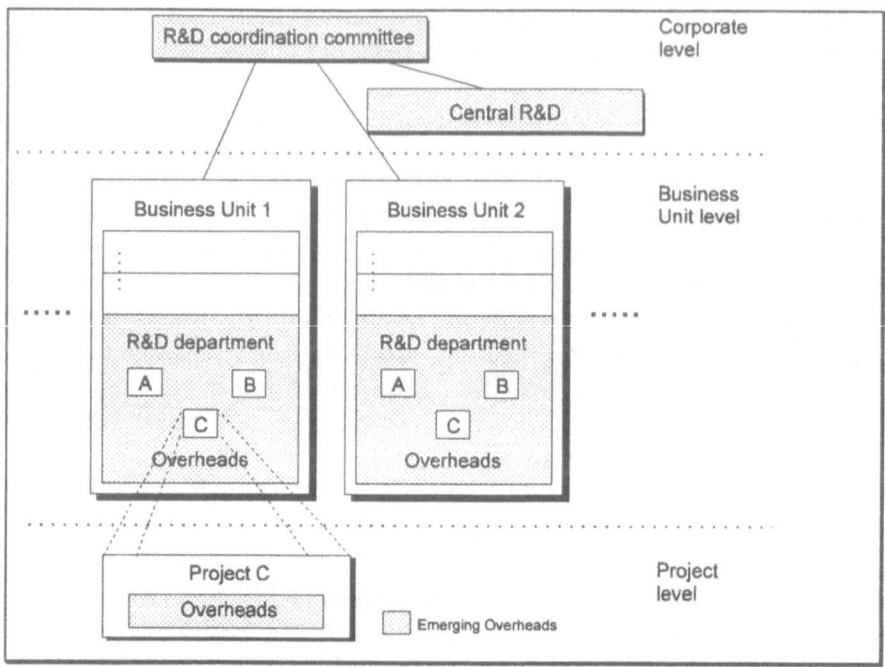

Fig. 6.18. Levels of overhead in R&D.

The first level is the level of coordination between central R&D and R&D departments in the business units. Many companies have an R&D steering committee, which decides on the distribution of research objectives between the various parts of the organization. Overhead costs on this level mainly consist of top managers' salaries. The second level is the level within one research unit referring to overhead costs that emerge department-wide. In general, these are costs of activities that ensure the ability of this institute to work on the project. Examples of these costs are the department head's salary and the costs of training activities. The third level is the project level and its overheads can only be determined if products are regarded as cost objectives. It is necessary to differentiate between two kinds of projects: specific projects which influence only a single product and general projects which influence more than one product. Only for the second type of projects is the allocation of overheads to products a problem because in the first case all costs can be allocated as direct costs to the product that the project was initiated to produce. It becomes clear that simply speaking of overheads in R&D is not specific enough.

ProCoRD Project Cost Planning for R&D

The system we are using is based on some aspects of conventional process costing systems and its composition can be represented as in Figure 6.19.

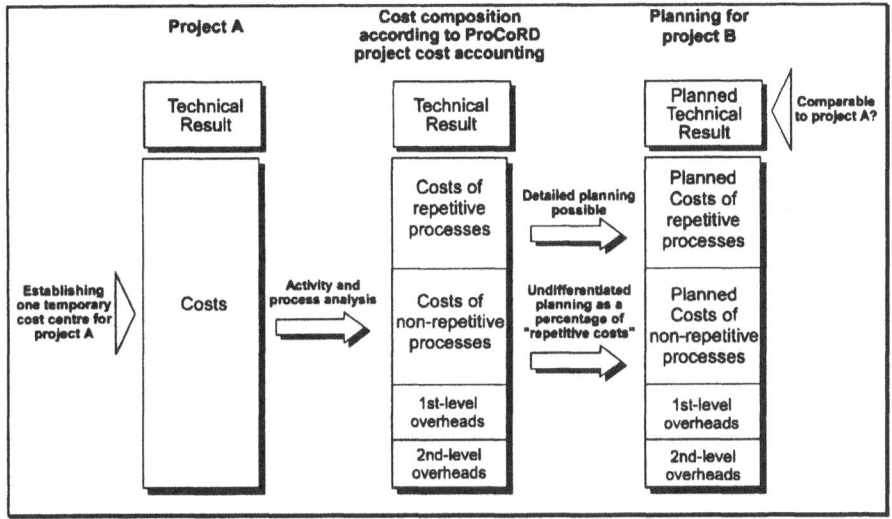

Fig. 6.19. ProCoRD project cost planning scheme.

The system described covers the full costing involved. For a make-or-buy decision full costs are the relevant decision bases. The planning procedure itself can be described as follows: At first, a temporary cost centre has to be established for every project. In this cost centre the costs of all activities within a first reference project are listed in detail, as well as the resources used. This collection of costs follows the rules used in traditional accounting systems, and a percentage of overheads is included. After the project is completed a detailed activity and process analysis takes place. Unique processes which are not likely to be repeated (non-repetitive processes, *eg* knowledge generation) must be separated from repetitive processes (*eg* testing procedures). In the next step, the costs of all repetitive processes and of all non-repetitive processes will be added up in order to determine the ratio between them. This procedure is then used for several projects to find out if this ratio is entirely stable in a particular R&D division. To increase transparency, overheads must be indicated according to the different levels at which they emerge. To use the data collected for the planning of a subsequent project it is necessary that the technical output is, at least to some extent, comparable to the technical output of the reference project.

For the new project, all the processes needed must be planned. Again there will be repetitive and non-repetitive processes. For the processes viewed as innovative in the new project it is necessary to check whether there will be comparable processes in the reference project. If this is so, cost planning for these processes can take place based on experience data. For the repetitive processes in the new project it is necesssary to check whether cost data on these processes is available in the experience data base of the reference project (Changes in prices, inflation, and the handling of learning curve effects must be considered). If this is not the case, these processes must be viewed as non-repetitive for the new project. If the new system has been installed for a certain time all the projects performed and surveyed in the way described can act as reference projects.

Costs of non-repetitive processes cannot be planned in detail because experience is not available. They have to be planned *en bloc* – maybe as a percentage of the costs of repetitive processes. Overheads can be viewed as independent of a single project at first and must be derived from reference projects. For the purpose of financial solvency it must be established in which stage of a project will the largest part of the costs occur. In this context it is usually best to quote costs on a monthly rather than an annual basis. Time can also be used as an indicator for defining the stage that a project has reached and this can also help in locating the causes of the largest costs.

Unlike the process costing system designed by Strecker, ProCoRD project cost accounting works not only for development projects but also for research projects. This is because non-repetitive processes, which are typical for the R&D area, are no longer excluded from the cost analysis and planning procedure. The effort of structuring volume-independent activities to processes is reduced because volume-independent costs will be handled as overheads emerging on different levels, and avoid the use of overheads which are not linked to causes.

The ProCoRD project cost planning system can be used to determine how many different R&D projects can be carried out with the budget determined by the FIAS budgeting system.

Process Improvements Based on ProCoRD

The preparatory work that has to be conducted to make ProCoRD project cost planning work should be used for identifying potentials for process improvement, which lead to a cost reduction. Process improvements can be thought of in four different respects: improvements as regards contents, reduction in personnel, reduction in time, and reduction in employing resources such as material and space. Since defining success in R&D is extremely difficult use of this method at least guarantees that the way the processes are run is checked [30]. However, the identification of cost cutting potentials should not be the main function of accounting in the R&D area because too rigid a control is very likely to hinder the production of innovative ideas.

ProCoRD should now be developed to devise methods for allocating the costs of unsuccessful R&D projects, and the benefits of the knowledge gained from them. A knowledge transfer between different projects certainly takes place, especially if the same employees work successively on a number of projects.

Use of ProCoRD in an Automotive Manufacturing Division

ProCoRD project cost planning was successfully tested in the R&D part of an automotive division of a medium-sized industrial enterprise in Germany. This enterprise reached an annual turnover of more than 6 billion DM in 1997 and employed some 26,000 people. The use of ProCoRD project cost planning took place from September 1997 until May 1998. At the beginning of the evaluation period two similar projects were chosen. The first, which had already been finished, served as a reference project (Project A); and the second was the object of planning exercise (Project B). The evaluation concentrated on two selected work packages (mechanical engineering and electronic engineering). From about 40 interviews the most important processes in Project A were identified. Many of these processes could then be used for planning in Project B. By aggregating the costs of all the planned processes, the total costs for the two packages of work could be calculated. After Project B had been finished, the planned cost figures were compared with the actual figures: The costs of all the repetitive processes in the planning differed by only one per cent from the actual costs of the repetitive processes. The total costs of the two work packages (costs of repetitive and non-repetitive processes) differed by only ten per cent from the costs planned with ProCoRD project cost planning. These costs were closer to the actual result than those planned by the people in charge of project management in this enterprise, who had used a traditional method of experience-based cost estimation. In the case selected it was therefore demonstrated that ProCoRD project cost planning could be used as a reliable tool for planning project costs in an R&D division.

5 Conclusions and Recommendations

* The requirements for accounting in a technology-intensive Company of the Future will be quite different from those used in classical manufacturing companies.

* We have reviewed the accounting methods used to date and then developed more appropriate flexible methods for the future which overcome the deficiencies of the traditional systems and take account of the variables needed in R&D budgeting.

* Three new accounting methods, FIAS, GOPE, and ProCoRD, have been devised and evaluated *via* their use in large companies. Valuable lessons were learned in each of these three trials which will help in the development of the methods for their implementation and wider use in the future.

* FIAS is a flexible cost accounting system oriented towards promotion of innovation. It can be used to determine the R&D budget and make appropriate allocations of it to each R&D activity.

* The use of GOPE, based around the objectives for the company and the quality of performance of its operations, leads participants to think about the overall strategy for their company and the contribution of each of its units.

* ProCoRD allows detailed cost planning for R&D projects based on process orientation, including relationships with other operations within the business. In this way ProCoRD promotes the most appropriate project selection in an R&D environment.

* GOPE and ProCoRD can be regarded as embracing the same general principles as FIAS, and they provide the user with additional viewpoints relevant to their accounting activities.

References

1 C.T. Horngren and G. Foster, 'Cost Accounting - A Managerial Emphasis', 7th Edition, Prentice Hall, Englewood Cliffs, NJ, USA, 1990

2 R.S. Kaplan, 'Accounting Lag - The Obsolescence of Cost Accounting Systems', *California Management Review*, 1986, **28** (2), 174 - 199

3 G. Schanz, 'Kriterien zur Bestimmung des Forschungsbudgets in Unternehmungen der Industriegruppe Elektronik', *Zeitschrift für betriebswirtschaftliche Forschung*, 1972, **24** (2), 81-90

4 W. Kern and H.H. Schröder, 'Forschung und Entwicklung in der Unternehmung', Hamburg, 1977

5 K. Brockhoff, 'Forschung und Entwicklung in der Unternehmung', Reinnbeck bei Hamburg, 1992

6 K. Brockhoff, 'A Simulation Model of R&D Budgeting', *R&D Management*, 1989, **19** (3), 265-275

7 K. Brockhoff, 'Budgetierrungsstrategien für Forschung und Entwicklung', *Zeitschrift für betriebswirtschaftliche Forschung*, 1987, **57** (9), 846-869

8 P. Horváth, M. Kieninger, R. Mayer and C. Schimank, 'Prozeßkostenrechnung - oder: Wie die Praxis die Theorie überholt', in: DBW 53, 1993, Vol. 5, pp. 609-628

9 W. Lücke, 'Scratch-Line Budgeting', in 'Bankpolitik, finanzielle Unternehmensführung und die Theorie der Finanzmärkte: Festschrift für Hans-Jacob Krümmel zur Vollendung des 60, Lebensjahres, Berlin, 1988, S 263-308

10 P.F. Drucker, 'The Information Executives Truly Need', *Harvard Business Review*, 1995, **73**, 54-62

11 R.S. Kaplan and D.P. Norton, 'Putting the Balanced Scorecard to Work', *Harvard Business Review*, 1993, **71** (10), 134-147

12 M. Moser, 'Measuring Performance in R&D Settings', *Research - Technology Management*, September/October 1985, pp. 31-33

13 T.M.Fischer, 'Kostenmanagement strategischer Erfolgsfaktoren', Vahlen, München, 1993

14 A. Gentner, 'Entwurf eines Kennzahlensystems zur Effektivitäts- und Effizienzsteigerung von Entwicklungsprojekten: Dargestellt am Beispiel der Entwicklungs- und Anlaufphasen in der Automobilindustrie', Vahlen, München, 1994

15 P. Schumann, B.L.Ransley and D.Prestwood, 'Measuring R&D Performance', *Research and Technology Management*, 1995, **38**, 43-54

16 R. Szakonyi, 'Measuring R&D Effectiveness - I', *Research and Technology Management*, 1994, **37**, 27-55

17 J.F. Rockart, 'Chief Executives Define Their Own Data Needs', *Harvard Business Review*, 1979, **57** (3-4), 81-92

18 M.E. Porter, 'Competitive Advantage', The Free Press, New York, 1985

19 P. Kotler, 'Marketing Management: Analysis, Planning, Implementation, and Control', 8th Edition, Prentice Hall, Englewood Cliffs, New York, 1985

20 'Executive Committee Control Charts: A Description of the Dupont Chart System for Appraising Operation Performance', American Management Association Bulletin, 1960, No 6, pp 1-7

21 A.D. Neely, J. Mills, K. Platts, M. Gregory and H. Richards, 'Performance Measurement System Design: Should Process Based Approaches be Adopted?, *International Journal of Production Economics*, 1996, **46-47**, 423-431

22 E.N. Weiss and R. Vithala, 'AHP Design Issues For Large Scale Systems', *Decision Science*, 1987, **18**, 43-61

23 W.W. Cooper and A.S. Zeff, 'Critical Commentaries: Kinney's Design for Accounting Research', in 'Critical Perspectives on Accounting', 1992, **7** (3), 87-92

24 T. Tomczak, 'Forschungsmethoden in der Marketingwissenschaft - Ein Plädoyer für den qualitativen Forschungsansatz (1993)', *Marketing ZFP*, 1995, **12** (2), 77-87

25 K.M. Eisenhardt, 'Building Theories from Case Study Research', *Academy of Management Review*, 1989, **14** (4), 532-550

26 G. Morgan, and L. Smircich, 'The Case for Qualitative Research', *Academy of Management Review*, 1980, **5** (4) 491-500

27 R.Yin, 'Case Study Research: Design and Methods', Sage Publications, Newbury Park, London, New Delhi, 1988

28 J.Y. Lee, 'How to Make Financial and Non-financial Data Add Up', *Journal of Accountancy*, September 1992, pp. 62-66
29 A. Strecker, 'Prozeßkostenrechnung in Forschung und Entwicklung' München, Vahlen, 1991
30 H.-D.Striening, 'Prozeß-Management, Lang, Frankfurt/Main, Bern, New York, 1988

List of Recommended Tools for the Company of the Future *

---

* These two tools are not new.

Some Abbreviations and Acronyms

AHP	Analytic Hierarchy Process
AT&T	American Telephone and Telegraph Company
AV	Added Value
B/S	Balance Sheet
BCG	Boston Consulting Group
BG plc	Formerly British Gas plc
CEO	Chief Executive Officer
CFO	Chief Financial and Control Officer
CMO	Chief Marketing and Sales Officer
CoF	Company of the Future
CP	Component Producer or Competence Product
CTO	Chief Technology (and sometimes including Production) Officer
CTP	Company Technology Pattern
DGIIIF	Directorate IIIF of European Commission (now ICT Directorate General XIII)
EDP	Electronic Data Processing
EDSCA	Endogenously Determined Sustainable Competitive Advantage
EIRMA	European Industrial Research Management Association
EQ	Economic Quality
ESPRIT	European Strategic Programme for Research and Development in Information Technology
EU	European Union
FFG	Fund for Future Growth
FIAS	Flexible Innovation Accounting System
FM	Finmeccanica
GaAs	Gallium Arsenide
GDP	Gross Domestic Product
GEC	General Electric Company
GOPE	Goal Oriented Performance Evaluation
GTE	General Telephone and Electronics Company
GUI	Graphical Use Interface
IAS	International Accounting Standard
JATES	Japanese Techno-Economics Society
M&A	Mergers and Acquisitions
MITI	Ministry of International Trade and Industry (Japan)
NEC	Nippon Electric Company
NPV	Net Present Value
NRCB	Nokia Research Center Board
NSR	North Star Research

OECD	Organization for Economic Co-operation and Development
P	Profit
P/L	Statement of Profit and Loss
PARC	Palo Alto Research Center
PICMET	Portland International Conference on Management of Engineering and Technology
ProCoRD	Process-oriented Cost accounting in R&D
R&D	Research and Development
R&DE	Research and Development Expenditure
ROI	Return on Investment
ROS	Return on Sales
Route 128	A highway belt of high technology companies 40 miles around Boston, MA, USA
SC	System Company, Steering Committee
SIRM	Shell Internationale Research Maatschapij
SL	Scratch Line
SLB	Scratch Line Budgeting
TB	Technical Board
TGV	Train Grand Vitesse
TQC	Total Quality Control
ZBB	Zero Base Budgeting
ZVEI	Zentralverband der Elektrotechnischen und Electronischen Industrie

Authors

Angelo Airaghi

Dr. Airaghi is Senior Vice President Business Development at Finmeccanica. He is Chairman of a number of high-tech companies and a board member of others. He serves on many Italian and International Committees in various sectors (*eg* energy, space, information technologies). His academic background includes applied mathematics and informatics. He is professor of Industrial Policies at the Tor Vegata University in Rome.

Justus Bardenhewer

Dr. Bardenhewer joined ZF Friedrichshafen, Germany in 1997 after his doctorate in economics at the University of Kiel where he was a scientist at the Institute for Research in Innovation Management. Before this he worked at Siemens Medical in Toronto, Canada, and Strasbourg, France.

Klaus Brockhoff

Dr. Brockhoff is Dean of the Wissenschaftliche Hochschule für Unternehmensführung. Before this he was professor of technology and innovation management at Christian Albrechts University of Kiel, Germany. He has initiated innovation management programmes at this university at the masters level and at the doctoral level. He consults with companies and government agencies. He has published more than 200 articles and 17 books, most of them dealing with new product management and technology management.

Hans G. Danielmeyer

Dr. Danielmeyer is the Vice President of the Japanese-German Center in Berlin. Until retirement in 1996 he was a board member of Siemens AG in

Munich, responsible for Corporate R&D. From 1978 until 1986 he was the founding president of the Technische Universität Hamburg-Harburg and Professor of Experimental Physics at the University of Hamburg. He developed lasers for optical communications at AT&T Bell Laboratories and worked in the Max Planck Institute of Solid State Physics in Stuttgart. He has served on many educational, industrial, and scientific boards, has been President of the German Physical Society, and Chairman of the German Electrical and Electronics Industry Commission for R&D. He has obtained numerous patents in communications and lasers, and published over 200 papers in physics, management, and economics.

Tsuneo Nakahara

Dr. Nakahara is Executive Advisor to the CEO of Sumitomo Electric Industries, Ltd, Japan. He also serves on various industrial strategy and government policy committees, such as the Industrial Technology Council of the Ministry of International Trade and Industry (MITI), and the Panel on General Planning of the Prime Minister's Council for Science and Technology. He is Special Adviser to the Minister of Science and Technology Agency, and Vice President of the Engineering Academy of Japan. He joined Sumitomo Electric Industries, Ltd, and has been engaged in research and business activities in a wide range of areas, including fibre optics, wire and cable, electronics, and communication systems. He has received many awards, including the Blue Ribbon Medal from the Emperor of Japan in 1994 for his contribution to the developments of optical fibre and superconductor systems.

Manfred Perlitz

Dr. Perlitz is professor of international management at University of Mannheim, Germany, a consultant to numerous American, Asian, and European companies, and chairman of a consulting company developing also software packages for the management of innovation. He has taught at universities in Brazil, China, France, Japan, the Philippines, South Africa, the UK, and the USA. His main research area is the comparison of innovation management in Europe, Japan, and the USA. He has published over 100 papers and five books.

Yasutsugu Takeda

Dr. Takeda is President of Hitachi Koki after completing his career as Senior Executive Managing Director of Hitachi Ltd. He was responsible for Research and Development, Intellectual Property, the Scientific Instrument Business Division, and the Automotive Products Division. He began his career with Hitachi in 1958 at its Central Research Laboratory. In 1970 he was appointed senior researcher and unit leader of the Electro-Optics Research group. After numerous other appointments, including general Manager of the Central Research Laboratory, he became Executive Managing Director of Hitachi in 1989. As a Fellow of the IEEE he served as Vice Chairman of the IEEE's Tokyo Section in 1993 and 1994. He was President of Japan Society for Industrial and Applied Mathematics in 1991 and 1992, President of Japan Television Society in 1994 and 1995, and Director of the Engineering Academy of Japan from 1989 until 1995. Since 1994 he is Chairman of Keidanren's Policy Affairs Committee of Science and Technology.

David T. Thompson

Dr. Thompson has participated in and managed upstream, basic and applied research activities in universities (Imperial College, London and University of California, Los Angeles, USA), at ICI, and at Johnson Matthey in the UK. His published papers are concerned with catalysis and materials topics as well as organic and inorganic chemistry. He is currently a consulting chemist, advising international industrial organizations on the management and content of research programmes, with emphasis on the generation of original ideas for new products and processes. He has a special interest in work involving precious metals and their derivatives and is Technical Editor of the multidisciplinary international journal 'Gold Bulletin'. Some of this work is carried out in collaboration with universities, and he advises commercial enterprises on how to optimize their contacts with university research. In addition to writing chapters for a number of books, he has made coordinating contributions to the writing and editing of three other books in addition to this one - two on chemistry and one on research collaboration between university and industry.

Authors' Addresses

Angelo Airaghi
Finmeccanica, Piazza Monte Grappa 4, I-00195, Roma, Italy
Fax: +39 06 32 473 611

Justus Bardenhewer
ZF Friedrichshafen AG, SV-BWC, D-88038 Friedrichshafen, Germany
Fax +49 7541 77 6649

Klaus Brockhoff
Wissenschaftliche Hochschule für Unternehmensführung, Burgplatz 2, D-56179 Vallendar
Fax +49 261 6509159

Hans G. Danielmeyer
Meisenstr. 4, D-85521 Ottobrunn, Germany
Fax: +49 89 6083658

Tsuneo Nakahara
1-3-12 Motoakasaka, Minato-ku, Tokyo 107-8468, Japan
Fax: +81 3 3423 5008

Luigi Paganetto
Universita di Roma-CEIS, Via di Tor Vergata, snc,I-00133 Roma, Italy
Fax: +39 06 725 95504

Manfred Perlitz
Universität Mannheim, Schloss, D-68131 Mannheim, Germany
Fax: +49 621 292 5750

Tasutsuga Takeda
Hitachi Koki, 2-15-1 Kounan, Minato-ku, Tokyo 108-6020, Japan

David T. Thompson
'Newlands', The Village, Whitchurch Hill, Reading RG8 7PN United Kingdom
Fax: +44 118 984 5717

Index